Coding

All New Edition

by Paul McFedries

Coding For Dummies®, All New Edition

Published by: **John Wiley & Sons, Inc.,** 111 River Street, Hoboken, NJ 07030-5774, www.wiley.com

For general information on our other products and services, please contact our Customer Care Department within the U.S. at 877-762-2974, outside the U.S. at 317-572-3993, or fax 317-572-4002. For technical support, please visit https://hub.wiley.com/community/support/dummies.

Wiley publishes in a variety of print and electronic formats and by print-on-demand. Some material included with standard print versions of this book may not be included in e-books or in print-on-demand. If this book refers to media that is not included in the version you purchased, you may download this material at http://booksupport.wiley.com. For more information about Wiley products, visit www.wiley.com.

Library of Congress Control Number: 2025946286

ISBN 978-1-394-36556-2 (pbk); ISBN 978-1-394-36558-6 (ebk); ISBN 978-1-394-36557-9 (ebk)

C9781394365562_160925

Printed and bound by CPI Group (UK) Ltd, Croydon CR0 4YY

Table of Contents

Introduction

O
kay, whoa, wait a minute: a book about coding!? Now!? With our new artificial intelligence (AI) overlords about to take over everything, especially
programming jobs? Are your eyes deceiving you? Is the author deluded,
possibly even insane? Will these questions never end?

Fortunately for you, I can answer all these queries by paraphrasing the eminently
paraphrasable Mark Twain:

The reports of the death of coding are greatly exaggerated.

Sure, AI tools such as ChatGPT and Microsoft Copilot are very good at generating
and fixing programming code, but we've learned over the past year or two that the
human element in coding is still very much needed. Coding is a craft just as much
as it is a science, and coding well requires the kind of creativity that is noticeably
lacking in current AI models.

And I'll let you in on a little secret that no one seems to talk about very much:
Coding generates joy. It's true! When you get to the point where you know enough
about coding that you can think of an idea, write the code for it, and then get your
computer to run that code, well to my mind there's no better feeling. It's pure
coding joy.

Oh, and I might as well let you in on yet another secret: Getting to the point where
you can code whatever idea comes to mind is not that hard and does not take very
much time! Even if you've never coded before, I promise that you are *this* close to
getting there.

So, yes, a book about coding!

About This Book

Welcome, then, to *Coding For Dummies, All New Edition.* This book teaches you
everything you need to know about coding, from what it is, to how to get started,
to writing and running your first programs. My goal is to show you that going

from being clueless about coding to being comfortable with not one but *two* different programming languages is a lot easier than you probably think. This book shows that even the greenest rookie coder can learn how to build programs that will amaze their family and friends (and themselves).

Notice that I didn't say that this book teaches you everything there is to know about coding. If you're looking for lots of programming history, computer science theory, and long-winded explanations of coding concepts, I'm sorry, but you won't find any of those things here. My philosophy throughout this book comes from Linus Torvalds, the creator of the Linux operating system: "Talk is cheap. Show me the code." I explain what needs to be explained and then I move on without further ado (or, most of the time, without any ado at all) to examples and scripts that do more to illuminate a concept that any verbose explanations I could muster. (And believe me, I can muster verbosity with the best of them.)

Why does this book's title have *All New Edition* tacked on to the end? Because this version of the book has been reimagined, reorganized, and rewritten from the ground up. What you get inside these pages is a fresh and modern take on learning how to code.

How you approach this book depends on your current level of web coding expertise (or lack thereof):

>> If you're just starting out, begin at the beginning with the three chapters in Part 1. This will give you all the knowledge you need to pick and choose what you want to learn throughout the rest of the book.

>> If you want to learn how to code for its own sake or you want a solid foundation for learning other programming languages, the Python language is your best bet, and it's the subject of the chapters in Part 2.

>> If you want to learn how to build dynamic web pages, that's the province of JavaScript, so head straight to Part 3.

Foolish Assumptions

This book is not a primer on using a computer or editing text. This is a book on learning to code, pure and simple. This means I assume the following:

>> You know how to operate a basic text editor and how to get around the operating system and file system on your computer.

>> You have an internet connection.

>> You know how to use your web browser.

Yep, that's it.

Okay, well, not quite. For the JavaScript portions of the book, I assume you're already familiar with HTML and CSS. If you're not, you can check out Chapter 17 to learn a few basics. However, if you really want to get into web coding, may I not-even-remotely-humbly suggest my book *HTML, CSS, and JavaScript All-in-One For Dummies* (Wiley), which will tell you everything you need to know.

Icons Used in This Book

REMEMBER

This icon points out juicy tidbits that are likely to be repeatedly useful to you — so please don't forget them.

TIP

Think of this icon as containing the fodder of an advice column. It offers what I hope is wise advice or a bit more information about a topic under discussion.

WARNING

Look out! In this book, you see this icon when I'm trying to help you avoid mistakes that can cost you time, money, or embarrassment.

TECHNICAL
STUFF

When you see this icon, you've come across material that isn't critical to understand but will satisfy the curious. Think "inquiring minds want to know" when you see this icon.

Beyond the Book

Some extra content for this book is available on the web. Go online to find the following:

>> **The examples used in the book:** You can find these in the following places:

   ● **My website:** https://paulmcfedries.com/books/coding-fd

   ● **GitHub:** https://github.com/paulmcfe/coding-fd

The examples are organized by chapter. For each example, you can view the code, copy it to your computer's clipboard, and run the code at the command line or in the browser. If possible, please resist the temptation to just copy and paste the code. The best way to learn any programming language is to get what I call a "fingertip feeling" for it by typing the code yourself. Sure, it takes more effort, but the code will seep into your brain faster this way.

» **The Web Dev Workbench:** To try your own HTML, CSS, and JavaScript code and see instant results, fire up the following site:

```
https://webdevworkshop.io/wb
```

You won't break anything, so feel free to use the site to run some experiments and play around with HTML, CSS, and JavaScript.

1
Coding Basics

IN THIS CHAPTER

» **Understanding how programming works**

» **Perusing a few programming languages**

» **Taking a peek under the coding hood**

» **Figuring out why you'd want to learn to code**

» **Learning how code is used in the real world**

Chapter **1**

What Is Coding?

Everybody should learn to program a computer because it teaches you how to think.

—STEVE JOBS

O kay, I'll admit it: I'm not one of those look-before-you-leap types. I'm a dedicated leaper. With almost every new thing I learn, my philosophy is that I learn best when I *do* the thing. I usually just jump in, get my hands dirty, make mistakes, fix them, and before long I develop a feel for this new hobby or skill.

Notice, though, that I said I do that with *almost* every new thing I learn. I don't do it when I'm learning something related to coding. Why not? "Just jumping in" is a lousy strategy for learning to code because the mistakes you make are dumb ones that teach you nothing (as opposed to smart mistakes that you can learn from). When it comes to learning anything related to code, it's always best to start with the basics and work your way slowly and steadily to competency, then proficiency, then mastery.

This chapter is your look-before-you-leap introduction to coding. Here you explore what coding is and how it works. You discover the myriad reasons why it's good to learn to code, and you investigate quite a few real-world uses for coding.

Programming: Making a Computer Do Your Bidding

A computer is a machine that follows instructions. Or, to put a finer point on it, a computer is a machine that does nothing until someone or something tells it what to do. That might sound surprising. After all, computers cost many hundreds, sometimes even thousands, of dollars, and are positively bristling on the inside with electronic gadgetry. Surely something so expensive and so complex must be capable of doing some useful tasks on its own.

Nope.

Sure, when you turn on a new computer for the first time, some hieroglyphics appear on the screen and you eventually end up in Windows or macOS or some other desktop. Doesn't that so-called boot process mean that the computer is doing something on its own?

Again, nope.

When you turn on a computer, it automatically loads a set of instructions that tell the computer what it must do to get the hardware (keyboard, mouse, screen, and so on) up and running and to get the operating system (Windows or macCS or whatever) loaded. That set of instructions is known as the computer's *firmware,* which is a special type of program embedded in the computer hardware. When the firmware has completed its job, it calls the *bootloader,* which loads the operating system.

Okay, that's all fine, but where did the firmware and bootloader come from? I'm glad you asked because at long last I can get to the point of all this: Someone coded them.

Some very smart person versed in the esoterica of computer hardware and system software programmed the firmware, and some other just as smart person coded the bootloader. So, let me repeat myself: Computers can't do anything unless someone or something tells them what to do. And the way you tell a computer what to do is via code.

Coding firmware or a bootloader is hideously complex and requires years of study. Happily, you won't be going anywhere near that level of complexity in this book. Whew! But everything you do learn here will be a variation on the overall theme of this section: telling a computer what you want it to do using code.

Am I talking about making a computer do anything you want? Alas, no, although that would be very useful! When you code, you're given a set of tools for the job; the tools you work with vary depending on the language you're using. As I discuss later in this book, the tools you get with Python (refer to Part 2) are much different than the tools you get with JavaScript (check out Part 3). As an analogy, the types of home projects you'd take on would be very different depending on whether you had a carpenter's toolbox or a sewing kit.

REMEMBER

But no matter how you code — no matter what programming tools you have at your disposal — you're almost always doing one (or sometimes both) of the following:

>> **Solving a problem:** One of the most common reasons that a piece of code gets written is because the coder had a pain point or an inefficiency in their life and saw a way to use code to make their life easier or more streamlined.

>> **Creating something new:** Another common reason to start coding is when you get a great idea and want more than anything to bring that idea to life.

No matter what you work on in your coding career, you're almost always doing one (or both) of these things — solving problems, creating new stuff, or combining the two to make something that's both new *and* improved.

What Is a Programming Language?

Python and JavaScript are programming languages. Okay, fine, but what does it mean to call something a *programming language?* To understand this term, you need look no further than the language you use to speak and write. At its most fundamental level, human language is composed of two things — words and rules:

>> The words are collections of letters that have a common meaning among all the people who speak the same language. For example, the word *book* denotes a type of object; the word *heavy* denotes a quality; and the word *read* denotes an action.

>> The rules are the ways in which words can be combined to create coherent and understandable concepts. If you want to be understood by other speakers of the language, you have only a limited number of ways to throw two or more words together. "I read a heavy book" is an instantly comprehensible sentence, but "book a I read heavy" is gibberish.

The key goal of human language is being understood by someone else who is listening to you or reading something you wrote. If you use the proper words to refer to things and actions and if you combine those words according to the rules, the other person will understand you.

A programming language works in more or less the same way. That is, it, too, has words and rules:

>> The words are a set of terms that refer to the specific things that your program works with or the specific ways in which those things can be manipulated. These words are known as *reserved words* or *keywords.*

>> The rules are the ways in which the words can be combined to produce the desired effect. In the programming world, these rules are known as the language's *syntax.*

The crucial concept here is that just as the fundamental purpose of human language is to be understood by another person, the fundamental purpose of a programming language is to be understood by whatever machine is processing the language. The key, however, is that being "understood" by the machine really means being able to *control* the machine. That is, your code "sentences" are commands that you want the machine to carry out.

The Role of Programming Languages

Let's say you travel to Igboland in Nigeria and want to ask a local for directions to the nearest bathroom. If that person speaks only Igbo (the native language of Igboland), one solution would be to find someone who speaks both English and Igbo and ask that person to translate your request as well as the response. Problem solved!

The person who can translate your English into Igbo is called an *interpreter,* and that task is essentially how we're able to program a computer. The problem is that a computer understands only its native language, which is called *machine language* and consists of 1s and 0s. (I won't get into this topic here, but if you're curious to know more, check out the sidebar "How computers work: A crash course for would-be coders.") A very simple machine language instruction to a computer might look something like this:

```
10111000 00000001 00000000 00000000 00000000
10111111 00000001 00000000 00000000 00000000
01001000 10111110 00000000 01100000 01100000
00000000 00000000 00000000 00000000 00000000
10111010 00001101 00000000 00000000 00000000
```

```
00001111 00000101 10111000 00111100 00000000
00000000 00000000 00110001 11111111 00001111
00000101
```

Yikes! No sane human wants to deal with something as weird as machine language, so one of the first things that engineers did after computers were invented was come up with two remarkable inventions:

>> A way of representing machine-language instructions as human-understandable English words

>> A way of converting those English words back into the machine language that the computer understands

The first invention is called a *programming language* and consists of, in part, English (or, sometimes, English-like) words such as `if`, `while`, and `return`. You use these generally comprehensible terms to construct *statements,* which are commands that you want the computer to carry out on your behalf.

For example, the preceding machine language code began life, in part, as the following statement:

```
printf("Hello, World!");
```

This statement, which is written in the C programming language, outputs the text *Hello, World!* C is an example of a *high-level language*, which describes any programming language that abstracts away the mind-numbing complexity of the computer's native machine language.

HOW COMPUTERS WORK: A CRASH COURSE FOR WOULD-BE CODERS

You might have heard someone say, with great authority, that "computers operate by processing 1s and 0s." If, upon hearing that, you were flummoxed, let me tell you that your reaction is utterly normal. It really *is* incomprehensible to us mere mortals that computers, which can do all these incredible things, perform those wonders by slinging around just two values: 1 and 0. What's behind this mystery?

At the lowest level, a computer is basically a collection of billions of unimaginably teensy components called *transistors,* which operate essentially as on/off switches for electrical

(continued)

(continued)

current. When a transistor allows electrical current to pass through, by convention that state is represented by a 1. When a transistor blocks electrical current from passing through, by convention that state is represented by a 0. Each 1 or 0 is called a *binary digit,* or *bit.* One bit offers only two options: 1 or 0. Combining two bits offers four options: 00, 01, 10, or 11. Skipping ahead, I can tell you that combining eight bits offers 256 options, from 00000000 to 11111111 and every combo in between. A string of eight bits is called a *byte* and the 256 possible byte values is enough to code every letter, every number, every punctuation mark, plus a few other standard symbols that make up the American Standard Code for Information Interchange (ASCII) table. The upper-case letter *H,* for example, is 01001000 in binary. So, combine eight transistors, set them so that they form the byte 01001000, and you've got the letter *H* stored on your circuit board (which might be a memory module).

Do you need to memorize the byte values for every letter, number, and symbol to code a computer? No, not even close! In fact, the history of coding can be seen as the moving farther and farther away from how information is physically stored using transistors to being able to make the computer do your bidding using relatively simple English words.

C is a notoriously difficult language to learn, so aside from a brief mention in Chapter 3, I steer clear of it in this book. Instead, you learn two languages that reside at an even higher (read: easier) level than C: Python (covered in Part 2) and JavaScript (tackled in Part 3).

The second of the inventions I mentioned is called either an *interpreter* or a *compiler*, depending on the programming language. (I explain the difference between interpreters and compilers in Chapter 3.) Either way, the purpose of this invention is to take the English-like code of a programming language and convert it to something (such as machine language) that the computer can read and run. All of this happens behind the scenes, so, as a coder, you never have to lay your eyes on a single 1 or 0 (unless it's part of your Python or JavaScript code, of course).

Understanding How Code Is Written and Executed

At this very early stage of your programming career, the process of coding might seem more than a little mysterious, possibly even downright puzzling. After all, from the outside a computer is a mystifying machine, so the idea that you can somehow *control* this inscrutable hunk of electronica might seem the stuff of fantasy. Or even if you've already convinced yourself that you can make a computer do your bidding, *how* you do that might still have you scratching your head.

Perhaps the secret to being able to code a computer is having the right equipment, something like needing a loom for weaving or a lathe for woodworking.

Nope, you're way off. Maybe the most surprising thing about code is that it's nothing but text. (To keep things simple, for now I'm ignoring non-text files such as images and videos that you might incorporate in, say, a web page.) Ever used Notepad in Windows or TextEdit on a Mac? Those bare-bones text files are essentially what you use to write your code.

REMEMBER

To describe the programming process in its most generic terms, I like to use what I call the "three-and-a-half Rs" of coding — write, run, revise, and repeat:

>> **Write:** In a text file, you write your code as a series of statements, each of which is essentially an instruction to the interpreter or compiler for whatever programming language you're using.

>> **Run:** You invoke the programming language's interpreter or compiler and tell it to process the code in the text file you wrote. The interpreter or compiler then executes the code, and the results appear, which could be the program's output or one or more error messages.

>> **Revise:** Based on the results of the run, you edit your code to fix any errors that crop up or to improve your code.

>> **Repeat:** You write more code (to, say, add new functionality), run it, revise it as needed, and then repeat the cycle until your program or app or web page or whatever is complete.

That's the bird's-eye view. The next two sections bring things slightly closer to the ground by looking at the coding processes specifically for Python and JavaScript.

How Python code works

I go into a pleasing amount of detail about Python in the chapters that make up Part 2, so here I just provide you with a quick overview of the Python coding process:

1. **Using a text editor or code editor, write your Python language statements in a plain text file.**

   When you save your text file for the first time, be sure to name the file with the .py file extension, which identifies it as a Python file.

2. **At the command line, type** python, **a space, and the name of the Python file, and then press Enter or Return.**

For example, the following runs a file named hello.py:

```
python hello.py
```

The python part of the command invokes the Python interpreter, which processes the content in the Python file one statement at a time. Note that the Python interpreter is available on your computer only if you have installed Python, as I describe in Chapter 4.

The interpreter then displays the results of the code, which might be some output you defined or one or more error messages.

TECHNICAL STUFF

As I discuss in Chapter 4, there are other ways to execute Python code, including an interactive Python shell that enables you to run one Python statement at a time and code editors that enable you to run Python code from the editor's development environment.

3. **Return to your code editor and modify the code as needed based on the results of the most recent run, especially to troubleshoot any errors that cropped up.**

4. **Repeat Steps 1 through 3 as required until your Python program is complete.**

How JavaScript code works

JavaScript is the subject of the chapters in Part 3, so I'll just whet your appetite here with a short-and-sweet review of the JavaScript coding process:

1. **Using a text editor or code editor, write your JavaScript language statements in a plain text file.**

I assume for simplicity that you want to run your JavaScript statements in a web page (that is, an HTML file, which usually uses the .html file extension), so there are two ways to go:

- *Create an external JavaScript file:* Save your text file using the .js file extension, which identifies it as a JavaScript file, and then modify your web page code to tell the browser about the file. For example, the following tags reference a file named hello.js:

```
<script src="hello.js"></script>
```

- *Embed the JavaScript code inside the HTML file:* Your JavaScript statements reside within a <script></script> block:

```
<script>
    JavaScript statements go here
</script>
```

REMEMBER

If this rapid-fire overview is confusing, don't sweat it for now. I discuss all this in more careful detail in Chapter 10.

2. **Open the HTML file in a web browser or, if the HTML file is already open in the browser, refresh the page.**

   The web browser contains a built-in JavaScript interpreter, so as soon as the browser loads the HTML file, it begins processing the JavaScript code one statement at a time. The browser then displays the results of the code, which might be some output you defined, a web page modification, or one or more error messages.

3. **Switch back to your code editor and edit the code as required given what happened when you opened or refreshed the HTML file. In particular, be sure to tackle any errors that cropped up.**

4. **Repeat Steps 1 through 3 as required until your JavaScript code is running the way you want it.**

Why Learn to Code? Let Me Count the Ways

Since you're reading this book, I think it's safe to assume that you want to learn how to code. If that's true, feel free to skip merrily over the rest of this section. However, if you're still on the fence, trying to decide whether you want to spend the time and effort to learn to code, have I got a section for you!

If you're short on time, my immediate answer to the question, "Should I learn to code?" is a real timesaver: Yes, absolutely! If you still need to be convinced, let the next few sections serve as my long answer.

Coding isn't just for nerds

You might have an image of a stereotypical coder in your head, one that no doubt envisages some not-recently-washed nerd sitting in a dank, dimly lit basement surrounded by empty pizza boxes and crushed energy drink cans. Ah, so you *have* seen photos of my office!

I'm sure many coders fit that stereotype, but most don't and you certainly don't have to stop bathing and ruin your diet to code.

Lots of nerds code, but not all coders self-identify as nerds, so if the geeky reputation of coding is holding you back, forget about it. You can code just as you are.

Coding teaches you how to think

While it's true that the essence of coding is writing instructions for a computer to follow, it's not like writing a list of items for your spouse to pick up when they go to the grocery store. That is, you can't just pick up the coding equivalent of a pen and start writing things down as they pop into your head. Coding requires multiple kinds of thought, so in a sense coding teaches you how to think.

For example, when you're considering how to tackle a coding project, it always helps if you can break down the project into smaller, more manageable chunks. Similarly, computers are relentlessly logical beasts, so successful coding requires that you use your logical reasoning skills to "think" like the computer. Every program ever written contains errors, so a big part of coding is troubleshooting problems, which requires understanding how your code works. Converting an idea in your head into code that brings the idea to life is a task that requires large doses of imagination.

REMEMBER

All these skills — breaking down problems, logical reasoning, troubleshooting problems, critical thinking, and imagination — not only make you a good coder but are also tremendously useful outside programming. Whether it's business, finance, science, or trying to assemble some piece of IKEA furniture with its inscrutable instructions, the thinking skills you hone via coding will help with whatever you're doing.

Coding is fun and creative

In the preceding section, I mentioned that getting code to run requires a logical, channel-the-computer approach. I stand by that, but I'll also admit that "think like the computer" isn't a clarion call for fun. That's okay, though, because thinking logically is only part of what it takes to get a program running. Most of us associate creativity with artistic endeavors, but I'm here to tell you that coding is one of the most creative skills you can learn.

For starters, every non-trivial coding project you work on will present you with hurdles that at first seem insurmountable but will soon yield to some creative problem-solving.

But coding creativity really begins with designing and implementing whatever idea has fired your imagination. Want to make a game? Design a website? Create an app? Craft some digital artwork? Whatever it is, coding enables you to take almost any idea, no matter how pie-in-the-sky it might seem to you now, and turn it into an actual, working project that you and others can play, run, or view. Believe me when I tell you that building things from scratch and watching them come to life not only gives your creativity circuits a workout but is also the very definition of fun.

You can build (almost) anything you can imagine

Being able to code is like having a superpower: If you can imagine something, you can build it. Want to create a website for your side hustle? Code it. Have an idea for an awesome game? Make it. Need an app to remind you to drink water? Build it. (Then send it to me. I could really use that app!)

When you learn to code, you give yourself the near-magical ability to create something out of nothing. This ability is incredibly rewarding because now you're not just *using* apps — you're *making* them.

Scoot over to the "Real-World Uses of Coding" section for a few practical and useful project ideas.

Coding is a universal language

When people with different native languages want to communicate, they can sometimes use another language that they have in common. That common language is called a *lingua franca.*

In today's technical world, code often acts as a kind of lingua franca because programming is one of the few skills that works the same across every industry and country. A JavaScript developer in Japan writes the same kind of code as one in Canada. A Python script written in the U.S. can be used by someone in Germany.

This means coding opens up opportunities around the world. If you ever dream of working internationally (or remotely for a global company), coding can help you get there.

Coding opens the door to high-paying jobs

Speaking of working, coding is one of the best ways to land yourself a great job. Let's start with a big one: money. Tech jobs consistently rank among the highest paying careers. What about opportunities? Even in the age of AI, the demand for programmers continues to grow. Companies in nearly every industry — finance, healthcare, entertainment, even agriculture — need developers. And many programming jobs offer remote work opportunities, flexible hours, and great benefits.

Here are just a few example careers:

>> Software developer

>> Web developer

>> Data scientist

>> Cybersecurity analyst

>> AI/machine-learning engineer

But you need a computer science degree, right? Not necessarily. Plenty of people who become professional programmers are self-taught using books just like this one!

You don't have to be a pro to benefit from learning to code

Yep, I get it: Being a professional programmer isn't for everyone. It might be the hours, the constant sitting, all that screentime, or whatever. Turning pro is one coding path, but it's not the only one. Whatever field you work in (or want to work in), having even basic coding know-how can give you an edge over your peers.

For example, if you work in marketing, knowing how to code can enable you to automate reports and analyze customer data. If you work in finance, coding can help you write scripts to track stock prices and investments. If healthcare is your field, knowing how to code can help you manage patient data efficiently. If you're an educator, you can use code to create fun and interactive learning tools for students.

Whatever your career, knowing how to code is a bonus skill that makes you more valuable, more productive, and more creative.

Coding is easier to learn than ever before

Back in the dim mists of time otherwise known as the twentieth century, learning to code was hard. A few dedicated hobbyists taught themselves to program, mostly using a relatively simple language called BASIC, but the vast majority of programmers learned to code by obtaining expensive college degrees that required reading enormous textbooks filled with abstruse technical jargon and recondite computer science theory.

Today? Ah, today we have beginner-friendly languages like Python and JavaScript that enable *anyone* to learn to code, no fancy-schmancy college degree required. Forget the jargon and the theory. If you can think reasonably logically and you can break down a problem in smaller challenges, you can learn to code.

Coding is the future

Back in 2011, the venture capitalist Marc Andreesen wrote an op-ed piece titled "Why software is eating the world." He meant that software was and is transforming entire industries and disrupting traditional ways of doing business. He predicted that software would become a crucial and more deeply baked-in component of company operations, products, and services.

However, before software can eat anything, it has to be coded. Before software can be embedded into every facet of business, someone has to program it. Software is all around us now and will soon be ubiquitous. Learning to code now future-proofs your skills, ensuring that you stay relevant in this rapidly evolving, being-eaten-by-software world.

Real-World Uses of Coding

The overall theme of this chapter has been that coding, at its most basic, is just cajoling a computer into performing some task. As the early chapters in Part 2 (Python) and Part 3 (JavaScript) show, it's not that hard to write code that makes a computer do something trivial, such as display text on the screen. Simple and straightforward examples are a great learning tool and an easy way to build your coding confidence, but they lack, well, substance.

After writing and running a few such examples, you might start to wonder whether that's all there is to coding. Is programming all bun and no hamburger? All sizzle and no steak? Are any vegetarians still reading this?

Fortunately, even beginner-welcoming languages such as Python and JavaScript can be used to build useful and fun projects. You build some in this book a bit later, but for now I want to give you a taste of what's possible. Here, broken down into five development categories, are a few things that folks in the real world are building using Python:

>> **Automation:** Python can automate boring, repetitive tasks like renaming files, sending emails, and scraping data from websites. For example, a marketer can write a Python script to automatically send out weekly email reports instead of doing it manually.

>> **Data science:** Big-time firms such as Google, Netflix, and Facebook use Python to analyze the massive amounts of data they generate. Many business users take advantage of Python libraries such as Pandas and NumPy to help them make sense of customer behavior, market trends, and sales predictions.

>> **Machine learning:** This branch of AI enables computers to learn from data and make decisions or predictions without being programmed. Python-based machine-learning tools such as TensorFlow and scikit-learn enable companies to develop AI-powered systems, such as recommendation engines (I'm looking at *you*, Netflix suggestions).

>> **Scientific computing and engineering:** NASA and other scientific institutions take advantage of Python to create complex simulations and calculations. Python also helps engineers analyze large datasets in fields such as genetics, physics, and climate modeling.

>> **Web development:** Python is used to build web applications using tools such as Django and Flask, and companies such as Instagram and Spotify rely on Python-based web services. However, in web development, Python is most often called upon for building server systems for handling chores such as data storage, user authentication, and security.

REMEMBER

Once you're comfortable with Python, be sure to read Chapter 9, where I take you step-by-step through a few useful Python projects.

Here are some projects that coders in the real world are building using JavaScript, arranged into five development categories:

>> **Web page development:** A sprinkling of JavaScript turns a boring web page into something interactive and dynamic. Browser-based JavaScript can request data from a server, display that data on the page, and handle user input. For example, when you type some text in a web page search box and a list of matching items appears lickety-split, that tells you that JavaScript is working feverishly in the background to fetch and display those search results.

>> **Web server development:** A JavaScript tool called Node.js runs on many web servers and is used for *back-end* tasks, such as dealing with data, authenticating users, and providing cloud services. Behemoth companies such as LinkedIn and PayPal use Node.js to power their web apps.

>> **Mobile apps:** JavaScript tools are available that enable developers to build mobile apps. Using the framework React Native, Facebook and Instagram (and many others) use JavaScript to offer apps that work on both iOS and Android devices.

>> **Games:** JavaScript tools such as Phaser.js enable developers to use JavaScript to build games that run either in the browser or on mobile devices.

>> **Smart devices:** JavaScript is used to program smart home devices, such as lights, security cameras, and thermostats. And with Node.js, developers can connect JavaScript applications to Internet of Things (IoT) systems.

REMEMBER

After you have the JavaScript basics down, head over to Chapter 15 to learn how to code several practical JavaScript projects.

Chapter **2**

Coding Concepts You Need to Know

Well begun is half done.

—ARISTOTLE

A certain class of programmer self-identifies as a kind of "high priest" of software, versed, unlike us laypeople, in the esoteric and arcane rites of programming. While it's certainly true that top-level software engineers are impressively knowledgeable about the systems they code, these high priest types want you to believe that only a select group is capable of doing *any* kind of programming.

You're about to find out just how untrue that is. Coding, far from being a rarefied intellectual pursuit available only to an elite few, is a democratic craft that anyone can learn. As proof, I offer up this chapter, which demonstrates that true coding requires understanding just a handful of programming concepts: variables, data types, expressions, conditionals, loops, functions, and objects. Oh, sure, the high priests know probably know a few dozen more programming ideas. But with this chapter's accessibly small list of coding concepts, you can build a lifetime's worth of apps, websites, games, or whatever you like. Your path to becoming a true coder — ignore those blustering high priests over there — begins now.

Storing Stuff in Variables

By default, your programs live a life without the benefit of short-term memory. In the case of Python and JavaScript, the interpreter executes your code one statement at a time, until no more statements are left to process. It all happens in the perpetual present. Ah, but notice that I refer to this lack of short-term memory as the *default* state of your scripts. You have the power to give your scripts the gift of short-term memory.

But why would a script need short-term memory? Because one of the most common concepts that crops up when coding is the need to store a temporary value for use later. In most cases, you want to use that value a bit later in the same script. However, you may also need to use it in some other script, to populate an HTML form (if you're coding a web page) or as part of a larger or more complex calculation. For example, if you're constructing a shopping cart script, you may need to calculate taxes on the order. To do that, you must first calculate the total value of the order, store that value, and then later take a percentage of it to work out the tax.

In programming, the way you save a value for later use is by storing it in a *variable*. A *variable* is a small chunk of computer memory set aside for holding program data. The good news is that the specifics of how the data is stored and retrieved from memory happen well behind the scenes, so it isn't something you ever have to worry about.

Declaring variables

The process of creating a variable is called *declaring* in programming terms. All declaring really means is that you're supplying the variable with a name and telling the browser to set aside a bit of room in memory to hold whatever value you end up storing in the variable.

How you declare a variable depends on the programming language you're coding in. Python is nice and simple because you just set the name of the variable equal to the value you want it to store initially:

```
cookies_eaten = 3
```

This statement declares a variable named `cookies_eaten` and sets the variable's value to 3.

Most other languages require a bit more info. Here's a variable declared in Java (not the same as JavaScript; check out Chapter 3 if you don't believe me):

```
float interestRate = 0.05
```

The added `float` keyword declares the variable with the floating-point data type. Skip ahead to the "Dealing with Data Types" section to find out what on Earth the phrase *floating-point* is referring to.

REMEMBER

Variable names can't include spaces, so when a name requires two or more words, most coders smush the words together and capitalize the first letter of every word after the first. This combination of lowercase and uppercase letters is called *camelCase* (because it creates humps in the text; no, seriously).

Many languages enable you to declare a variable without also assigning it a value. Here's an example using the Go language:

```
var interestRate float32
```

Note the `var` keyword, which is short for *variable* and is a common keyword for declaring variables. You then assign a value to the variable later in your code:

```
interestRate = 0.05
```

Including variables in other statements

With a variable declared and assigned a value, you can then use that variable in other statements. When the interpreter comes across the variable, it goes to the computer's memory, retrieves the current value of the variable, and then substitutes that value into the statement. The following code presents an example:

```
interestRate = 0.05
interestRate = interestRate / 12
```

This code declares a variable named `interestRate` with the value `0.05`; it then divides that value by `12` and stores the result in the variable.

TECHNICAL STUFF

If the second statement is something you've never come across before, it probably looks a bit illogical. How can something equal itself divided by 12? The secret to understanding such a statement is to remember that the interpreter always evaluates the right side of the statement — that is, the expression to the right of the equals sign (=) — first. In other words, it takes the current value of `interestRate`, which is `0.05`, and divides it by `12`. The resulting value is what's stored in `interestRate` when all is said and done. For a more in-depth discussion of operators and expressions, fast-forward to the "Constructing Expressions" section.

Getting your head around arrays and lists

Variables are a fundamental aspect of coding, but it's easy to use them inefficiently. For example, consider the following declarations:

```
day1 = "Monday"
day2 = "Tuesday"
day3 = "Wednesday"
day4 = "Thursday"
day5 = "Friday"
day6 = "Saturday"
day7 = "Sunday"
```

These are string variables (check out "Dealing with Data Types" to learn what a string is), and together they store a collection of related things (days of the week, in this case). Whenever you find you have multiple variables storing related or similar items, you can group all those items into a single variable called an *array,* or in Python, a *list.*

You can enter as many values as you want into the array or list, and the programming language tracks each value using an *index number.* For example, the first value you add is given the index 0. (For obscure reasons, programmers since time immemorial have numbered lists of things starting with 0 instead of 1.) The second value you put into the array or list is index 1; the third value gets 2; and so on. You can then access any value in the array or list by specifying the index number you want.

You have to declare the array or list, and how you do that depends on the language. Here's an example list from Python:

```
days = ["Monday", "Tuesday", "Wednesday", "Thursday",
        "Friday", "Saturday", "Sunday"]
```

The square brackets ([and]) tell the interpreter that every item between the brackets is part of the list assigned to the variable `days`.

In most programming languages, you reference an array or a list item using the array or list name followed by the item's index number in square brackets. For example, `days[0]` refers to `"Monday"` and `days[6]` refers to `"Sunday"`. (A few languages — most notably Visual Basic and Visual Basic for Applications — use regular parentheses instead of square brackets.)

Dealing with Data Types

In programming, a variable's *data type* specifies what kind of data is stored in the variable. The data type is a crucial idea because it determines not only how two or more variables are combined (for example, mathematically) but also whether they can be combined at all. *Literals* are a special class of data type, and they cover values that are fixed (even if only temporarily). For example, consider the following variable assignment statement:

```
todaysQuestion = "Who let the dogs out?"
```

Here, the text `Who let the dogs out?` is a literal string value. All programming languages support three kinds of literal data types: numeric, string, and Boolean. The next three sections discuss each type.

Working with numeric literals

The two basic numeric literals are integers and floating-point numbers:

>> **Integers:** These numbers don't have a fractional or decimal part. So you represent an integer using a sequence of one or more digits, as in these examples:

```
0
42
2001
-20
```

>> **Floating-point numbers:** These numbers do have a fractional or decimal part. Therefore, you represent a floating-point number by first writing the integer part, followed by a decimal point, followed by the fractional or decimal part, as in these examples:

```
0.07
3.14159
-16.6666667
7.6543e+21
1.234567E-89
```

TECHNICAL STUFF

The last two floating-point examples require a bit more explanation. They use *exponential notation*, which is an efficient way to represent really large or really small floating-point numbers. Exponential notation uses an `e` (or `E`) followed by the *exponent*, which is a number preceded by a plus sign (+) or a minus sign (–).

You multiply the first part of the number (that is, the part before the e or E) by 10 to the power of the exponent. Here's an example:

```
9.87654e+5
```

The exponent is 5, and 10 to the power of 5 is 100,000. Multiplying 9.87654 by 100,000 results in the value 987,654.

Here's another example:

```
3.4567e-4
```

The exponent is –4, and 10 to the power of –4 is 0.0001. Multiplying 3.4567 by 0.0001 results in the value 0.00034567.

Working with string literals

A *string literal* is a sequence of one or more letters, numbers, or punctuation marks, enclosed in either double quotation marks (") or single quotation marks ('). Here are some examples:

```
"Coding For Dummies"
'Literally a string literal'
""
"What's the deal with airline peanuts?"
```

REMEMBER

The string "" (or '' — two consecutive single quotation marks) is called a *null string* or an *empty string*. It represents a string that doesn't contain any characters.

The final example shows that it's okay to insert — or *nest* — one or more instances of one of the quotation marks (such as ') inside a string enclosed by the other quotation mark (such as "). Being able to nest quotation marks comes in handy when you need to embed one string inside another, which is a common coding situation. Here's a JavaScript example:

```
onsubmit="processForm('testing')";
```

However, it's illegal to insert in a string one or more instances of the same quotation mark that encloses the string, as in this example:

```
"This is "illegal" in every programming language."
```

Working with Boolean literals

Booleans are the simplest of all the literal data types because they can assume only one of two values: `true` or `false`. That simplicity may make it seem as though Booleans aren't particularly useful, but the capability to test whether a particular variable or condition is true or false is invaluable in programming.

You can assign Boolean literals directly to a variable, like this:

```
taskCompleted = true
```

Alternatively, you can work with Boolean values implicitly by using expressions (refer to the section "Constructing Expressions" to learn more). For example, in most languages, you can test whether two items are *equal* by using the `==` operator:

```
currentMonth == "August"
```

The comparison expression `currentMonth == "August"` asks the following: Is the value of the `currentMonth` variable equal to the string `"August"`? If it is, the expression evaluates to the Boolean value `true` (or `True` in some languages); if it's not, the expression evaluates to `false` (or `False` in some languages).

REMEMBER

When you want to assign a value to a variable, you use a single equals sign (=), which is known in the programming trade as the *assignment operator*. When you want to compare two things to determine whether they're equal, you use two equals signs (==), which coders refer to as the *equal to operator*.

Constructing Expressions

An *expression* is a collection of symbols, words, and numbers that performs a calculation and produces a result. That's a nebulous definition, I know, so I'll make it more concrete.

When your check arrives after a restaurant meal, one of the first things you probably do is take out your smartphone and use the calculator to figure out the tip amount. The service and food were good, so you're thinking 20 percent is appropriate. With phone in hand, you tap in the bill total, tap the multiplication button, tap 20%, and then tap Equals. Voilà! The tip amount appears on the screen and you're good to go.

A programming expression is something like this kind of procedure because it takes one or more inputs, such as a bill total and a tip percentage, and combines them in some way — for example, by using multiplication. In expression lingo, the inputs are called *operands,* and they're combined by using special symbols called *operators:*

- ➤ **operand:** An input value for an expression. An operand is the raw data that the expression manipulates to produce its result. The operand could be a number, a string, a variable, a function result (refer to "Organizing Code into Functions," later in this chapter), or an object property (check out "Introducing Objects," later in this chapter).

- ➤ **operator:** A symbol that represents a particular action performed on one or more operands. For example, the ∗ operator represents multiplication, and the + operator represents addition.

Assuming that your code has already declared a variable named billTotal that holds the bill total, as well as a variable named tipPercentage that holds the percentage you want to tip, here's an expression that calculates a tip amount and assigns the result to a variable named tipAmount:

```
tipAmount = billTotal * tipPercentage
```

The expression is everything to the right of the equals sign (=). Here, billTotal and tipPercentage are the operands, and the multiplication sign (∗) is the operator.

Another analogy I like to use for operands and operators is a grammatical one — that is, if you consider an expression to be a sentence, the operands are the nouns (the things) of the sentence and the operators are the verbs (the actions) of the sentence.

Building numeric expressions

Calculating a tip amount on a restaurant bill is a mathematical calculation, so you may be thinking that code expressions are going to be mostly mathematical. If I were standing in front of you and happened to have a box of gold stars on me, I'd certainly give you one because, yes, math-based expressions are probably the most common type you'll come across.

A mathematical calculation is often called a *numeric expression,* and it combines numeric operands and arithmetic operators to produce a numeric result. Every programming language's basic arithmetic operators are more or less the same as those found in your smartphone's calculator app or on the numeric keypad of your computer's keyboard, plus a couple of extra operators for more advanced work. Table 2-1 lists the basic arithmetic operators you can use in your code expressions.

TABLE 2-1   ## Basic Arithmetic Operators

Operator	Name	Example, where n = 10	Result
+	Addition	n + 4	14
++	Increment	n++	11
–	Subtraction	n – 4	6
–	Negation	– n	–10
––	Decrement	n––	9
*	Multiplication	n * 4	40
/	Division	n / 4	2.5
%	Modulus	n % 4	2

REMEMBER

Although most programming languages (including JavaScript) support the increment (++) and decrement (––) operators, some languages (including Python) don't.

Almost all programming languages support a few extra operators that combine some of the arithmetic operators and the assignment operator, which is the humble equals sign (=) that assigns a value to a variable. Table 2-2 lists these *arithmetic assignment* operators.

TABLE 2-2   ## Arithmetic Assignment Operators

Operator	Example	Equivalent
+=	x += y	x = x + y
–=	x –= y	x = x – y
*=	x *= y	x = x * y
/=	x /= y	x = x / y
%=	x %= y	x = x % y

Building string expressions

A *string expression* is one where at least one of the operands is a string, and the result of the expression is another string. String expressions are straightforward in the sense that there is only one operator to deal with: the *concatenation* operator, which in most languages (including Python and JavaScript) is +. You use this operator to combine (or *concatenate*) strings in an expression. For example, the expression `"Java"` + `"Script"` returns the string `"JavaScript"`.

Yep, it's unfortunate that the concatenation operator is identical to the addition operator because this similarity can lead to some confusion. For example, the expression 2 + 2 returns the numeric value 4 because the operands are numeric. However, the expression `"2"` + `"2"` returns the string value 22 because the two operands are strings.

Building comparison expressions

You use *comparison expressions* to compare the value of two or more numbers, strings, variables, function results, object properties, or object method results. If the expression is true, the expression result is set to the Boolean value `true`; if the expression is false, the expression result is set to the Boolean value `false`. You'll use comparisons with alarming frequency in your code, so it's important to understand what they are.

Table 2-3 summarizes the comparison operators used in most programming languages.

TABLE 2-3   ## Comparison Operators

Operator	Name	Example	Result
==	Equal to	10 == 4	false
!=	Not equal to	10 != 4	true
>	Greater than	10 > 4	true
<	Less than	10 < 4	false
>=	Greater than or equal to	10 >= 4	true
<=	Less than or equal to	10 <= 4	false
===	Strictly equal to (JavaScript)	"10" === 10	false
!==	Strictly not equal to (JavaScript)	"10" !== 10	true

In Table 2-3, note that JavaScript uses === instead of == (and !== instead of !=). JavaScript supports == (and !=), but for too-geeky-to-get-into reasons, your JavaScript code should only ever use === (and !==).

Building logical expressions

You use *logical expressions* to combine or manipulate Boolean values, particularly comparison expressions. For example, if your code needs to test whether two different comparison expressions are both true before proceeding, you can do that with a logical expression.

Table 2-4 lists the most common logical operators.

TABLE 2-4   **Logical Operators**

Operator	Name	General Syntax	Returned Value
&& or and	AND	*expr1* && *expr2* or *expr1* and *expr2*	true if both *expr1* and *expr2* are true; false otherwise
|| or or	OR	*expr1* || *expr2* or *expr1* or *expr2*	true if one or both of *expr1* and *expr2* are true; false otherwise
! or not	NOT	!expr or not expr	true if *expr* is false; false if *expr* is true

In the Operator column of Table 2-4, note that most programming languages (JavaScript is one of them) use the symbols &&, ||, and !. Just a few languages (Python is one of them) use the words and, or, and not.

Making Decisions with Conditionals

One of the most common coding conundrums is controlling when part of your code runs. For example, you might want a particular set of statements to run only if today is Monday. Similarly, you might want some division code *not* to run if the divisor is equal to 0. Because constraints such as the day of the week and whether a value is a particular number are used as conditions that dictate when or if some code will execute, this programming logic is called *conditional execution,* and the language features you use are called *conditionals.*

Making simple true/false decisions

The most basic test is the simple true/false decision (which could also be thought of as a yes/no or an on/off decision). In this case, your program looks at a certain condition, determines whether it's currently true or false, and acts accordingly. Comparison and logical expressions (covered in the preceding section) play a big part here because they always return a `true` or `false` result.

In all programming languages, simple true/false decisions are handled by the `if` statement, which has a similar syntax in most languages. You can use the *single-line* syntax:

```
if (expression) statement
```

or the *block* syntax:

```
if (expression) {
    statement1
    statement2
    . . .
}
```

REMEMBER

Syntax refers to the symbols, keywords, and structures that define how code must be written and formatted in a particular programming language to be correctly interpreted and executed by a compiler or interpreter.

In both cases, *expression* is a comparison or logical expression that returns `true` or `false`, and `statement`, `statement1`, `statement2`, and so on represent the code to run if *expression* returns `true`. If *expression* returns `false`, the code doesn't run the statements.

For example, suppose your code includes variables named `totalCookies` and `totalApples` that hold, respectively, the number of cookies and the number of apples the user ate this week. In your analysis, it's vital that you calculate the user's cookies-to-apples ratio (hey, it's your analysis):

```
cookiesToApples = totalCookies / totalApples
```

That's fine, but your code will generate an error if totalApples equals 0 since dividing by 0 is illegal. To prevent that error, you can use an if statement:

```
if (totalApples != 0) {
    cookiesToApples = totalCookies / totalApples
}
```

If totalApples isn't 0, the expression totalApples != 0 returns true, so the division statement runs. If, instead, totalApples is 0, the expression totalApples != 0 returns false, so the division statement doesn't run and no error occurs.

TIP

Note that in the block syntax, I've been indenting the statements by four spaces. This increases the readability of the code by making it clear which statements belong to the block (that is, the part between the braces: { and }). Some programmers use two spaces, but four makes the indentation clearer. (If someone tells you to use tabs instead of spaces, ignore them.)

Branching with if. . .else statements

Using the if statement to make decisions adds a powerful new weapon to your coding arsenal. However, the simple version of if suffers from an important limitation: A false result only bypasses one or more statements; it doesn't execute any of its own. This is fine in many cases, but there will be times when you need to run one group of statements if the condition returns true and a different group if the condition returns false. To handle these scenarios, you need to use an if. . .else statement which, again, has a similar syntax in most languages:

```
if (expression) {
    statements-if-true
} else {
    statements-if-false
}
```

The *expression* is a comparison or logical expression that returns true or false. *statements-if-true* represents the block of statements you want your code to run if *expression* returns true, and *statements-if-false* represents the block of statements you want executed if *expression* returns false.

As an example, consider the following code:

```
if (currentDay == "Monday") {
    discountRate = 0.25
} else {
```

```
    discountRate = 0.1
}
discountedPrice = regularPrice * (1 - discountRate)
```

This code calculates a discounted price of an item, where the discount depends on whether the current day is Monday. Assume that earlier in the code, the script set the value of the current day (`currentDay`) and the item's regular price (`regular Price`). An `if. . .else` statement checks whether `currentDay` equals `Monday`. If it does, `discountRate` is set to `0.25`; otherwise, `discountRate` is set to `0.1`. Finally, the code uses the `discountRate` value to calculate `discountedPrice`.

Automating Repetitive Tasks with Loops

It's one thing to write code that gets the job done, but your goal as a coder should always be to write code that gets the job done as efficiently as possible. Efficient programs run faster, take less time to code, and are usually (not always, but usually) easier to read and troubleshoot.

One of the best ways to introduce efficiency into your coding is to look for areas where you're essentially repeating the same code over and over. For example, consider the following code:

```
total = 0
total = total + 1
total = total + 2
total = total + 3
total = total + 4
total = total + 5
total = total + 6
total = total + 7
total = total + 8
total = total + 9
total = total + 10
```

This code first declares a variable named `total` and sets it equal to `0`. The next line adds `1` to the total, the next line adds `2`, and so on down to the final line, which adds `10` to the total. Besides being a tad useless, this code reeks of inefficiency because most of the code consists of repeatedly adding a value to the `total` variable.

To make code such as this more efficient, you can use a *loop*, which is a programming structure that repeats one or more statements for as long as you need it to. Quite a few different loop types are available, which tells you how important loops are to the coding process. I won't go through the different loop types here. Refer to Chapter 5 to learn about looping in Python and to Chapter 11 to get the goods on JavaScript loops.

For now, I'll hint at the loop wonders to come by introducing you to one of the most common loop types: the `while` loop, which uses the following syntax:

```
while (expression) {
    statements
}
```

Here, *expression* is a comparison or logical expression (that is, an expression that returns `true` or `false`) that, as long as it returns `true`, tells your code to keep executing the *statements* in the block.

Essentially, the programming language interpreter handles a `while` loop as follows: "Okay, as long as *expression* remains `true`, I'll keep running through the loop statements, but as soon as *expression* becomes `false`, I'm out of there."

Here's a closer look at how a `while` loop works:

1. Evaluate the *expression* in the `while` statement.

2. If *expression* is true, continue with Step 3; if *expression* is false, skip to Step 5.

3. Execute each of the statements in the block.

4. Return to Step 1.

5. Exit the loop (that is, execute the next statement that occurs after the `while` block).

The following code demonstrates how to use `while` to rewrite the inefficient code I presented earlier in this section:

```
total = 0
num = 1

while (num <= 10) {
    total = total + num
    num = num + 1
}
```

The code begins by initializing the `total` variable to 0, as before. To control the loop, the code declares a variable named `num` and initializes it to 1, which means the expression `num <= 10` is `true`, so the code enters the `while` block, adds `num` to `total`, and then increments `num`. This is repeated until the 11th time through the loop, when `num` is incremented to `11`, at which point the expression `num <= 10` becomes `false` and the loop is done.

Organizing Code into Functions

Imagine, if you will, cooking a dish that you make up as you go along. You assemble the ingredients you need, perform all the prep work and cooking, and then enjoy the resulting meal. A month or so later, you remember that the meal you thought up was delicious, so you repeat the process: You assemble the ingredients (perhaps with some slight variations this time), perform all the prep work and cooking (hoping you remember the steps correctly), and then once again chow down on the resulting dish.

That second time also produced a good meal, but there's an extra cognitive load involved because you're trying to remember what you did the first time. If it's a meal you think you'll cook a lot, just making it up from scratch every time is hard. A much better and easier way to go would be to write a recipe that has the following characteristics:

» It has a name.

» It has a list of ingredients.

» It has a set of instructions.

» It produces a dish.

In coding, the equivalent of a recipe is called a function, and every programming function has recipe-like features:

» It has a name.

» It has a list of inputs called *arguments*.

» It has a set of statements that it runs.

» It produces a result.

A *function*, then, is a group of statements that are separate from the rest of the program and that perform a designated task. (Technically, a function can perform any number of chores, but as a rule it's best for each function to focus on a specific task.) When your program needs to perform that task, you tell it to run — or *execute,* in programming vernacular — the function.

The way you define a function varies depending on the programming language, but in the simplest case (used in languages such as JavaScript, PHP, and Visual Basic), the basic structure of a function looks like this:

```
function functionName([arguments]) {
    statements
}
```

where:

>> function identifies the block of code that follows it as a function. (Some languages use func, others use fun, Python uses def, and some languages don't bother with a keyword.)

>> *functionName* is a unique name for the function. In most languages, function names must begin with a letter or an underscore (_); the rest of the function name can include any letter, any number, or the underscore; and you can't use any other characters, including spaces, symbols, and punctuation marks.

>> *arguments* are zero or more values that are passed to the function and act as variables within the function. Arguments (or *parameters,* as they're sometimes called) are typically one or more values that the function uses as the raw materials for its tasks or calculations. You always enter arguments between parentheses after the function name, and you separate multiple arguments with commas. If you don't use arguments, you must still include the parentheses after the function name.

>> *statements* are the code that performs the function's tasks or calculations.

TIP

When I present the syntax of a function that includes one or more optional arguments, I surround those arguments with square brackets — [and] — to let you know.

TIP

Note how the statements line in the example is indented slightly from the left margin. This standard and highly recommended programming practice makes your code easier to read. This example is indented four spaces, which is enough to do the job but isn't excessive. Some programmers use two spaces.

Note, too, the use of braces ({ and }). These are used in many languages (including JavaScript) to enclose the function's statements within a block, which tells you (and the interpreter or compiler) where the function's code begins and ends.

Here's an example function:

```
function getDiscountedPrice (currentDay, regularPrice) {
    if (currentDay == "Monday") {
        discountRate = 0.25
    } else {
        discountRate = 0.1
    }
    discountedPrice = regularPrice * (1 - discountRate)

    return discountedPrice
}
```

This function is named `getDiscountedPrice` and accepts two arguments: `currentDay` and `regularPrice`. Inside the function, the code sets the `discountRate` based on the day of the week, performs the calculation, and then uses the `return` statement to send the result back. Back to where? Back to whichever statement executed — or *called* — the function.

Here's a slightly more complete example that demonstrates this function being called:

```
function getDiscountedPrice (currentDay, regularPrice) {
    if (currentDay == "Monday") {
        discountRate = 0.25
    } else {
        discountRate = 0.1
    }
    discountedPrice = regularPrice * (1 - discountRate)

    return discountedPrice
}

dayOfWeek = "Friday"
listPrice = 19.95
reducedPrice = getDiscountedPrice(dayOfWeek, listPrice)
```

The final three statements declare and initialize the `dayOfWeek` and `listPrice` variables, and then call the `getDiscountedPrice` function, passing the values of the `dayOfWeek` and `listPrice` variables as arguments. The value returned by the function is stored in the `reducedPrice` variable.

Introducing Objects

Only the simplest programs do nothing but assign values to variables and calculate expressions. To go beyond these basic programming beginnings — that is, to write truly useful programs — your code needs to manipulate things. Okay, I know *things* is annoyingly unspecific, but what your code manipulates depends on what the program was designed to do.

Take JavaScript as an example. JavaScript was designed from the start to manipulate the web page that it's displaying. That's what browser-based JavaScript is all about, and that manipulation can come in many forms:

>> Add text and HTML attributes to an **element**.

>> Modify a CSS **property** of a class or other selector.

>> Store some data in the browser's internal **storage.**

>> Validate a **form's** data before submitting it.

The bold items in this list are examples of the things you can work with, and they're special for no other reason than that they're programmable. In coding parlance, these programmable things are called *objects*.

You can work with objects in your code in any of the following three ways:

>> You can read and make changes to the object's *properties.*

>> You can make the object perform a task by activating a *method* associated with the object.

>> You can define a procedure that runs whenever a particular *event* happens to the object.

To help you understand objects and their properties, methods, and events, I'll put them in real-world terms. Specifically, consider your computer as though it were an object:

>> If you wanted to describe your computer as a whole, you'd mention things like the name of the manufacturer, the price, the size of the hard drive, and the amount of RAM. Each of these items is a *property* of the computer.

>> You also can use your computer to perform tasks such as writing letters, crunching numbers, and coding programs. These are the *methods* associated with your computer.

>> A number of things happen to the computer that cause it to respond in predefined ways. For example, when the On button is pressed, the computer runs through its Power On Self-Test, initializes its components, and so on. The actions to which the computer responds automatically are its *events*.

These properties, methods, and events give you an overall description of your computer.

But your computer is also a collection of objects, each with its own properties, methods, and events. The hard drive, for example, has various properties, including its speed and data-transfer rate. The hard drive's methods are actions such as storing and retrieving data. A hard drive event may be a scheduled maintenance task, such as checking the drive for errors.

In the end, you have a complete description of the computer: its appearance (its properties), how you interact with it (its methods), and to what actions it responds (its events).

In most programming languages, you reference an object's properties and methods using *dot notation,* as shown using the syntax in the following generic expressions:

```
object.property
object.method()
```

where

>> *object* is the object that has the property or method.

>> *property* is the name of the property you want to work with.

>> *method* is the name of the method you want to run. Note that some methods are function-like in that they accept one or more arguments.

For example, consider the following JavaScript expression:

```
document.location
```

This expression refers to the `document` object's `location` property, which holds the address of the document (usually a web page) currently displayed in the browser window.

Because a property always contains a value, you're free to use property expressions in just about any type of statement and as an operand in an expression. You can assign a property value to a variable and in many cases you can assign a new value to the object property.

Methods that return values are similar: You can use them in expressions and assign their results to variables.

Documenting Code with Comments

A program that consists of just a few lines is usually easy to read and understand. However, your programs won't stay that simple for long, and these more complex creations will be correspondingly more difficult to read. (This difficulty will be particularly acute if you're looking at the code a few weeks or months after you first wrote it.) To help you decipher your code, it's good programming practice to make liberal use of comments throughout the script. A *comment* is text that describes or explains a statement or group of statements. Comments are ignored by the interpreter or compiler, so you can add as many as you deem necessary.

For short, single-line comments, use either the double-slash (//) or a hash symbol (#). Most programming languages (including JavaScript) support //, but some (such as Python) require #.

Put the // (or the #) at the beginning of the line and then type your comment after it (with a space in between for readability). Here's an example:

```
// Calculate the discounted price
discountedPrice = regularPrice * (1 - discountRate)
```

It's fine to use // (or #) for two or three comment lines in a row. However, most programming languages support multiple-line comments that begin with the /* symbol and end with the */ symbol. Here's an example:

```
/*
This code is released under the Creative Commons Zero
v1.0 Universal (CC0 1.0) license. To the fullest extent
permitted by law, I (the author) have dedicated this work
to the public domain.

This means:
 - You are free to copy, modify, distribute, and use this
   code, for any purpose, even commercially.
 - No permission or attribution is required, but giving
   credit is appreciated.
```

```
   - This code is provided "as-is," without any warranties
     or guarantees.

For more details, refer to:
https://creativecommons.org/publicdomain/zero/1.0/
*/
```

WARNING

Although it's fine to add quite a few comments when you're just starting out, you don't have to add a comment to everything. If a statement is trivial or its purpose is glaringly obvious, forget the comment and move on. If you're not sure whether to comment some code, go ahead and add the comment, particularly while you're just getting started building a program. Adding copious comments to your new code is a great way to organize your thoughts and keep your code readable. You can always go back later and delete comments that you no longer need.

Debugging Code and Handling Errors

It usually doesn't take too long to get short scripts and functions up and running. However, as your code grows larger and more complex, errors inevitably creep in. In fact, it has been proven mathematically that any code beyond a minimum level of complexity will contain at least one error and probably quite a lot more.

Many of the bugs that crawl into your code will consist of simple typos that you can fix quickly, but others will be more subtle and harder to find. For the latter — whether the errors are incorrect values returned by functions or problems with the overall logic of a script — you need to be able to get inside your code to scope out what's wrong.

The good news is that most programming languages have a ton of top-notch tools that can remove some of the burden of program problem solving, which is known as *debugging* in the coding trade.

Understanding error types

When a problem occurs, you first need to determine what kind of error you're dealing with. The three basic error types are syntax errors, runtime errors, and logic errors:

>> **Syntax errors:** These errors arise from misspelled or missing keywords, incorrect punctuation, or mangled indentation in Python.

» **Runtime errors:** Runtime errors occur during the execution of a program. They generally mean that the interpreter or compiler has stumbled upon a statement that it can't figure out. A runtime error might be caused by trying to use an uninitialized variable in an expression.

» **Logic errors:** If your code zigs instead of zags, the cause is usually a logic error, which is a flaw in the logic of your script. It might be a loop that never ends or a function that doesn't return a value. Logic errors are usually the toughest to pin down because you don't get an error message to give you a clue about what went wrong and where.

Taking a look at some debugging techniques

Debugging effectively is closer to an art than a science and something you'll acquire an intuitive feel for as you become more experienced as a coder (which is the same thing as saying "as you become more experienced dealing with the inevitable errors in your code"). I talk about language-specific debugging techniques in Chapter 8 (Python) and Chapter 14 (JavaScript), but here's a general look at the three main debugging techniques:

» **Pausing code execution:** In this technique, you temporarily stop your code, which puts the code into *break mode* to let you examine certain elements, such as the current values of variables or object properties. Break mode also lets you execute program code one statement at a time (refer to the next item in this list) so that you can monitor the flow of the script. If you know approximately where an error or a logic flaw is occurring, you can enter break mode at a specific statement in the program by setting a *breakpoint* on that statement.

» **Stepping through your code:** One of the most common (and most useful) debugging techniques is to step through the code one statement at a time. Doing so lets you get a feel for the program flow to make sure that things such as loops and function calls are executing properly. You can use three main techniques:

  • *Step one statement at a time:* Executes the current statement and then pauses on the next statement. If the current statement to run is a function call, stepping takes you into the function and pauses at the function's first statement. You can then continue to step through the function until you execute the last statement, at which point the browser returns you to the statement after the function call.

- *Step over some code:* For a statement that calls a function, executes the function normally without stepping into it, and then resumes break mode at the next statement *after* the function call.

- *Step out of some code:* Takes you immediately out of a function that you've stepped into. This is handy when you've accidentally stepped into a function that you'd meant to step over.

» **Monitoring script values:** Many runtime and logic errors are the result of (or, in some cases, can result in) variables assuming unexpected values. If your program uses or changes these elements in several places, you'll need to enter break mode and monitor the values of these elements to figure out where things go awry.

More debugging strategies

Debugging your programs can be a frustrating job, even for relatively small apps. Here are a few tips to keep in mind when tracking down programming problems:

» **Indent your code for readability.** All code is immeasurably more readable when you indent the code in each statement block. Readable code is that much easier to trace and decipher, so your debugging efforts have one less hurdle to negotiate. How far you indent is a matter of personal style, but two or four spaces is typical:

```
function myFunction() {
    Each statement in this function
    block is indented four spaces.
}
```

If you nest one block inside another, indent the nested block by another four spaces:

```
function myFunction() {
    Each statement in this function
    block is indented four spaces.
    while (something <= somethingElse) {
        Each statement in this nested while
        block is indented another four spaces.
    }
}
```

Note that when you code in Python, nesting block statements four spaces is required.

>> **Break down complex tasks.** Don't try to solve all your problems at once. If you have a large program or function that isn't working right, test it in small chunks to try to narrow down the problem.

>> **Break up long statements.** One of the most complicated aspects of script debugging is making sense out of long statements (especially expressions). It's usually best to keep your statements as short as possible. After you get things working properly, you can often recombine statements for more efficient code.

>> **Comment out problem statements.** If a particular statement is giving you problems, temporarily deactivate it by turning the statement into a comment (check out "Documenting Code with Comments" for more info). If you have a number of consecutive statements you want to skip, you can turn them all into a multiline comment.

>> **Use comments to document your scripts.** Speaking of comments, it's a programming truism that good code — meaning (at least in part) code that uses clear variable and function names and a logical structure — should be self-explanatory. However, almost every piece of non-trivial code contains sections that, when you examine them later, aren't immediately obvious. For those sections, it's another programming truism that you can never add enough explanatory comments. The more comments you add to complex and potentially obscure chunks of your code, the easier your programs will be to debug.

Chapter **3**

Getting to Know Some Programming Languages

There are only two kinds of languages: the ones people complain about and the ones nobody uses.

—BJARNE STROUSTRUP (INVENTOR OF C++)

Long-time coders tend to be a tad, well, opinionated about certain aspects of programming. Some of these aspects are reasonably described as trivial, such as whether two or four spaces should be used to indent code and whether strings should be delineated with double quotes (") or single quotes ('). More substantively, most experienced coders will defend their choice of programming editor to the death (which is only a slight exaggeration). Coders spend an inordinate amount of time waging these and other so-called holy wars over non-holy subjects such as braces, semicolons, and commas.

But these battles have nothing on those that surround programming languages, which spark some of the most intense holy wars in tech. Coders can be fiercely loyal to their favorite languages, sometimes to the point of raving lunacy. The web is littered with the rubble of scorched-earth battles over the merits of C versus C++, Python versus Ruby, and JavaScript versus TypeScript.

Happily, this chapter doesn't rehash any of these ancient (and fundamentally irresolvable) language wars. What you *do* get in this chapter is an introduction to the most popular and the most useful languages around today. Although the rest of this book delves into Python and JavaScript in more depth, you really can't go wrong if you decide to learn any of the languages that I mention in this chapter (with a few noted exceptions).

Ranking Programming Languages

When it comes to choosing a programming language to learn, it's best to first decide what you want to make, then find a language that can make it happen, preferably with a learning curve that's not too long and not too steep.

If, after all that, you're still not sure, another useful angle for comparing languages is to look up where each language ranks in terms of popularity or usage. The web has tons of such rankings, but two are considered to be the most useful:

>> **TIOBE Index (www.tiobe.com/tiobe-index/):** Measures the popularity of programming languages by counting the number of search engine queries for each language (using data from Google, Bing, Yahoo!, Wikipedia, Amazon, YouTube, and Baidu), as well as the number of skilled engineers, courses, and third-party vendors mentioning a language. The TIOBE Index is updated monthly. (For what it's worth, TIOBE stands for *The Importance of Being Earnest*, which is the title of an Oscar Wilde play.)

>> **IEEE Spectrum (https://spectrum.ieee.org/):** Ranks programming languages based on usage and demand by aggregating data from GitHub (a site for code repositories), Stack Overflow (a site for code discussions), Google Search trends, social media mentions, Reddit, IEEE Xplore (academic papers), and Indeed (job postings). The IEEE Spectrum ranking is updated annually.

Neither is perfect, but together they give you a reasonable sense of the popularity of a programming language. I provide both rankings for each language I mention in this chapter. (The TIOBE Index rankings are from August 2025 and the IEEE Spectrum rankings are from 2024.)

Assembly: Close to the Machine

Back in Chapter 1, I talked about how computers use 1s and 0s internally and that, at the most fundamental level, computers respond to instructions written in machine code. But writing raw machine language is like trying to have a dinner conversation using only Morse code — sure, it's *technically* possible, but nobody in their right mind would think it's a good idea.

To get away from the inefficiency and tedium of trying to communicate with a computer in its native tongue, a British computer scientist named Kathleen Booth invented something called assembly language way back in the 1940s. Assembly language acts as a kind of bridge between human-understandable code and the raw binary instructions that a computer executes.

For example, a typical machine code instruction looks like this:

```
01001000 11000111 11000000 00000001 00000000 00000000 00000000
```

Yuck! Now here's the assembly code equivalent:

```
mov rax, 5
```

Hmm, well, okay, I guess that's every bit as incomprehensible to you as the machine code, but at least you're dealing with letters and with numbers beyond those unfathomable 1s and 0s.

The key point is that assembly language is easier to write than pure machine code because instead of memorizing binary patterns (as if!), you use short commands called *mnemonics,* such as mov for moving data and add for addition.

In the preceding example, the instruction is telling the computer to move (mov) the value 5 into the register (a small storage area in the CPU) named RAX (rax).

Here's a longer example:

```
mov rax, 5
mov rbx, 3
add rax, rbx
```

This code puts 5 into register RAX and 3 into register RBX, and then adds the contents of RBX to RAX, which in this case means that RAX now holds the value 8.

REMEMBER

Assembly allows for fine control over the computer's central processing unit (CPU). High-level languages such as Python hide the details of how the CPU executes code, but assembly lets you optimize performance and interact directly with hardware. Therefore, assembly is foundational for understanding how computers work. If you ever want to dive deep into cybersecurity, embedded systems (task-specific computers squirreled inside larger devices such as medical devices and industrial machines), or operating systems, you'll need to get your hands dirty with assembly code.

REMEMBER

Unlike Python or JavaScript, which work on any computer, assembly language is specific to the type of CPU you're using. An Intel x86 processor understands different assembly instructions than an ARM (Advanced RISC Machine) processor (like the one in most smartphones). This means that learning assembly is often tied to a particular CPU architecture.

If you want to give assembly a whirl (how brave of you!), here are some next steps:

>> **Decide which architecture you want to write for.** The architecture will be either x86 for Windows programs or ARM for M-series Macs, Raspberry Pi boards, and most smartphones and smart home devices.

>> **Look at simple examples, preferably *lots* of them.** Many online resources provide basic assembly programs.

>> **Get yourself an assembler.** An *assembler* is a compiler for translating assembly code into machine code. Examples include NASM (Netwide Assembler) and MASM (Microsoft Macro Assembler) for x86, and ARMASM (ARM Assembler) for ARM.

>> **Experiment in a sandbox.** Websites like Try It Online (https://tio.run/) and Compiler Explorer (https://godbolt.org/) enable you to choose an assembler, write assembly code for it, and compile the code. (It's called a *sandbox* because it's a place where you can play with the code without fear of wrecking anything.)

Since time immemorial, programming teachers have introduced students to a language by offering a "Hello, World!" program, which is generally used as an example of the simplest working program in the language. Who am I to break with tradition? Therefore, for each language I introduce in this chapter, I provide a "Hello, World!" example. Here's one for x86 (64-bit) assembly language written for the Linux operating system:

```
section .data
    msg db "Hello, World!", 0 ; Define the string to print

section .text
    global _start ; Set the program entry point

_start:
    mov rax, 1     ; Set syscall to 1 (sys_write)
    mov rdi, 1     ; Set the file descriptor to 1 (stdout)
    mov rsi, msg   ; Store a pointer to the message
    mov rdx, 13    ; Store the message length
    syscall        ; Execute the system call
```

```
mov rax, 60    ; Set syscall to 60 (sys_exit)
mov rdi, 0     ; Set the exit code to 0
syscall        ; Execute the system call
```

Note that, in assembly code, a semicolon marks the start of a comment. So in the preceding code, any text to the right of a semicolon is a comment describing the code to the left of the semicolon.

All the code in this chapter is available with this book's example files. Head back to the Introduction to learn how to get your mitts on those files.

REMEMBER

What about rankings? Not surprisingly, assembly doesn't rank near the top in any ranking, but neither is it mired anywhere near the bottom:

TIOBE Index: 20th

IEEE Spectrum: 33rd

Python: No Experience Required

By far the most common complaint I hear about learning programming is how finicky coding can be. Forget a brace ({ or }) or a semicolon (;) or some other rarely used punctuation mark and your program fails miserably. That's a valid criticism for most programming languages because they tend to be *syntax-heavy*, which means they have a seemingly endless list of complex and strict rules about what goes where.

Fortunately, there are exceptions to these exacting languages. One such exception is Python, one of the most popular and beginner-friendly programming languages in the world. Designed from the ground up to be easy to read and write, Python is the antithesis of all those persnickety languages.

Python's emphasis is on simplicity and readability, which makes it a great choice for anyone just getting started with coding. Unlike all those other programming languages that are defined by their labyrinthine syntax and overly meticulous rules, Python is forgiving and intuitive. That easygoing nature enables beginners to focus on learning core programming concepts and to get programs up and running quickly without getting bogged down by syntactical complexities.

To give you just the teensiest taste, here's a complete, working "Hello, World!" program in Python:

```
message = "Hello, World!"
print(message)
```

Here, `print()` is a built-in Python function that outputs text to the screen. After running this program, the text `Hello, World!` appears on your screen.

Because Python is so popular, a vast community of developers is out there ready to answer questions, write tutorials, offer coding challenges, and generally provide whatever support you need on your quest to learn the Python language. Python's popularity also means a rich ecosystem of prefabricated Python code — called *libraries* — exists to enable you to create programs that perform sophisticated tasks such as data analysis without having to code everything from scratch. Nice.

If Python was just easy to read and write, it would be a worthy candidate for your first programming language. But Python is also extremely flexible and versatile, which means you can use it for an eye-popping variety of tasks:

>> **Automate everyday tasks.** Python saves time by automating repetitive tasks. With just a few lines of code, you can rename multiple files at once, automatically send emails or reminders, or scrape information from websites.

>> **Work with and analyze data.** If you like numbers or want to explore data, Python makes it easy to create simple charts and graphs and analyze basic statistics (like averages, trends, or word frequency).

>> **Build simple games.** Python lets you dip your toes into game development. As a beginner, you can create a text-based adventure game or a guess-the-number game. With libraries such as Pygame, you can even start adding graphics to your games as you progress.

>> **Create simple apps.** Python makes it easy to build small applications that help you stay organized. For example, you could make a to-do list app to track your tasks or build a basic calculator.

>> **Interact with online data sources.** Even as a beginner, you can use Python to pull in real-time data from the internet, including live weather updates for your city, fun facts, random jokes, or recent news headlines.

>> **Experiment with AI and machine learning.** Python is a major player in AI, and beginners can start with simple chatbots that respond to user input, a program that predicts numbers based on past data, or a script that recognizes common words in text. Make no mistake: AI is an advanced topic, but Python makes it easy to experiment as you learn.

- » **Build your own websites.** Python is used in web development with frameworks like Flask and Django. (A *framework* is a library that makes it easy to build websites by providing prefabricated code to handle common tasks such as database interactions and user authentication.)

- » **Control hardware and IoT projects.** You can use Python to control a Raspberry Pi to make small gadgets, automate home devices (like turning lights on and off), and even read sensor data from small machines.

If Python sounds like the right choice for your first foray into coding, head on over to Part 2, where I take you through everything you need to know to get started with this beginner-friendly language.

Rankings:

TIOBE Index: 1st

IEEE Spectrum: 1st

JavaScript: The Glue that Binds the Web

When you surf the web, each page you visit consists of text, images, maybe a video or two. How all that data is structured on the page is the job of a technology called Hypertext Markup Language, or HTML. How all that data looks on the page is the job of a technology called Cascading Style Sheets, or CSS. Together, HTML and CSS make up the *front end* of the web.

REMEMBER

I don't cover HTML and CSS in depth in this book due to the proverbial space limitations, but you get a brief introduction to both in Chapter 17. If that quick look gets you hankering for more, may I suggest my book *HTML, CSS, and JavaScript All-in-One For Dummies*, which will tell you everything you need to know.

But have you ever wondered where all that data comes from? Sometimes the data is added directly to the page, but in this modern age more often than not the data comes from a database that resides on a special computer called a *web server*. The database and the code that works with the data make up the *back end* of the web.

JavaScript is the secret sauce that brings the front end and the back end together to create the vast majority of web pages you visit today. JavaScript is the default programming language used for coding websites today. JavaScript is, first and foremost, a front-end web development language. That is, JavaScript runs inside the web browser and has access to everything on the page: text, images, HTML tags, CSS properties, and more. Having access to all the web page stuff means that you can use code to manipulate, modify, and even add and delete web page elements.

But although JavaScript runs in the browser, it's also capable of reaching out to the server to access back-end stuff. For example, with JavaScript, you can send data to the server to store that data in a database and you can request data from the server and then use code to display that data on the web page.

JavaScript, then, is the backbone of the modern web, powering everything from interactive websites to web applications and even mobile and desktop apps. It's a versatile and beginner-friendly programming language that enables developers to add dynamic behavior to web pages, making it one of the most essential languages for anyone interested in coding.

What makes JavaScript a great starter language is that it enables beginners to write, run, and troubleshoot code directly in a web browser without needing any special setup or tools. As long as you have access to a web browser (it doesn't even have to be online), you can experiment with code and display the results instantly. But you need a special browser, right? Nope. JavaScript is the only programming language supported by all modern web browsers, so you can use any browser you like.

Happily, the syntax of JavaScript is straightforward, especially for fundamental coding constructs such as variables, loops, and conditionals. That straightforwardness makes JavaScript an excellent language for learning core programming concepts.

Want a sample? Okay: Here's a complete, working "Hello, World!" program in JavaScript:

```
let message = "Hello, World!";
console.log(message);
```

Here, `console.log()` is a built-in JavaScript function that prints messages to the console (an output area in a web browser's development tools). In this case, after running this program, the text `Hello, World!` appears in your browser's console.

JavaScript is one of the best programming languages for beginners because you can start creating fun and useful projects almost immediately. Whether you're interested in building websites, making interactive elements, or even experimenting with simple games, JavaScript has something exciting for you. Here's what you can expect to do as a beginner:

>> **Make web pages interactive.** If you've ever clicked a button on a web page and something changed — such as a menu appeared, a pop-up showed up,

or a form responded to your input — that's JavaScript at work. You can also show and hide sections of a page or create a simple image slideshow.

>> **Build fun mini-projects.** JavaScript enables you to quickly build small projects that you — and anyone else who has access to your site — can use. Need a countdown timer for an event? JavaScript can do it. Want a random joke generator that shows a new joke when you click a button? That's JavaScript at work.

>> **Create simple games.** Even as a beginner, you can start making basic games with JavaScript. With a bit of coding, you can create a number-guessing game where the user has to guess the correct number, a rock-paper-scissors game that plays against the computer, or a simple quiz where users can answer questions and get a score.

>> **Add cool features to your pages.** Once you get comfortable, you can start adding features that make your pages more dynamic and engaging. For example, you could add a dark mode toggle that switches between light and dark themes, or you could add a search bar that filters page content.

>> **Connect to online data.** JavaScript can pull information from the internet in real time. Even as a beginner, you can learn how to connect to online sources to display random facts or quotes, show the latest news headlines or weather updates, or build a simple app around online data (such as a list of movies or books).

If you're interested in exploring the possibilities of JavaScript, check out Part 3, where you can learn everything you need to know to get started in the world of JavaScript coding.

Rankings:

TIOBE Index: 6th

IEEE Spectrum: 3rd

Sneaking a Peek at a Few Other Popular Languages

By a conservative estimate, something like 700 programming languages are in existence, with at least 100 languages in active use. 100! That's way too many to get your head around, so in this section I offer potted descriptions of the ten languages that I think are the most useful to know about.

C

C is a powerful, low-level programming language that has been around since the 1970s. It's known for its speed, efficiency, and direct access to hardware (that's what *low-level* means), making it a foundational language in computer science. Lots of modern languages, including C++ (covered next), Java, and Python, are influenced by C.

C is a fast and efficient language, making it great for performance-critical applications. C doesn't have a bunch of fancy features, so its programs tend to be super-compact. All these features are why C is the code underlying many of today's most complex projects:

>> **Operating systems:** Windows, macOS, and Linux are all primarily written in C.

>> **Embedded systems:** Smart devices, IoT devices, and device firmware are routinely coded in C.

>> **Game development:** Game engines such as Unreal Engine are written in C.

>> **Compilers and interpreters:** Many programming language compilers and interpreters are written in C. For example, the most widely used Python interpreter, called CPython, is written in C.

>> **High-performance applications:** Many databases, networking tools, and scientific computing tools use C for maximum performance.

But coding in C is not for the faint of heart. There are no built-in safety features, so C, unlike newer languages, doesn't protect against common programming mistakes like buffer overflows (where a program writes more data to a memory area — called a *buffer* — than the area can hold, causing adjacent memory to be overwritten, often disastrously). Also with C, the developer has to allocate and free memory manually, which can lead to memory leaks (gradual increases in memory usage caused by failing to release no longer needed memory).

Here's a "Hello, World!" example in C:

```
#include <stdio.h>

int main() {
    char message[] = "Hello, World!";
    printf("%s\n", message);
    return 0;
}
```

Rankings:

TIOBE Index: 3rd

IEEE Spectrum: 9th

C++

As its name implies, C++ (pronounced "SEE-plus-plus") is an extension of C, adding object-oriented programming (OOP) features while maintaining the speed and efficiency of C. *OOP* is a programming philosophy based on the concept of objects (refer to Chapter 2) which, when used correctly, can make code more organized, easier to reuse, and easier to scale. Many modern languages use OOP principles, including Python, JavaScript (partially), C#, Kotlin, PHP, and Swift.

Like C, C++ runs close to the hardware, making it great for performance-critical applications. But with the addition of OOP features, C++ code is more reusable and more organized and supports both high-level and low-level programming. C++ is widely used for high-performance applications and system programming:

>> **Game development:** Lots of game-related code is written in C++ because game engines and interfaces have to be fast and require access to hardware.

>> **High-performance software:** Many financial trading systems and scientific computing applications are coded in C++ for high performance.

>> **Operating systems and embedded systems:** C++ is used to code many Windows components and the firmware for many IoT devices.

>> **Web browsers:** The core components of browsers such as Chrome and Firefox are written in C++.

>> **Graphics and virtual reality (VR) applications:** Many 3D rendering applications and VR simulations use C++.

On the downside, C++ has a huge learning curve and is far more complex than Python or even Java. As with C, developers must manually manage the allocation and release of memory, problems with which can lead to bugs and memory leaks. For these reasons, writing and debugging C++ code can take longer than in higher-level languages.

Here's a "Hello, World!" example in C++:

```
#include <iostream>

int main() {
    std::string message = "Hello, World!";
    std::cout << message << std::endl;
    return 0;
}
```

Rankings:

TIOBE Index: 2nd

IEEE Spectrum: 4th

C#

C# (pronounced "SEE-sharp") is a modern, high-level programming language developed by Microsoft. It's heavily used for Windows applications, game development, and web services, and runs on the .NET framework. (.NET — it's pronounced DOT-net — is a software development platform created by Microsoft. It provides the tools, libraries, and a runtime environment needed to build and run Windows applications, web apps, and services. .NET also supports cross-platform development across Windows, macOS, and Linux using the unified .NET platform.)

You might be thinking that since C++ was an extension of C, C# must be an extension of C++. Yes and no. C# does extend C++ by automating the allocation and release of memory, so it removes the burden of manual memory management. But C# also removes the features found in both C and C++ that give developers low-level access to the hardware.

C# is an OOP language that's relatively easy to learn (at least compared to C++) and has strong error checking. It's a must if you ever want to get into Windows application development because it works seamlessly with .NET. C# is popular today for not only Windows applications but also game development, Azure cloud computing services, enterprise software, and web development.

Here's a "Hello, World!" example in C#:

```
using System;

class Program {
    static void Main() {
```

```
        string message = "Hello, World!";
        Console.WriteLine(message);
    }
}
```

Rankings:

TIOBE Index: 5th

IEEE Spectrum: 7th

Go

Go (also called Golang) is a modern, open-source programming language developed by Google in 2009. It was designed to be a relatively easy language to learn by offering developers simple, clean, and easy-to-read code with a minimum of fussy rules (such as the semicolons that C and Java require at the end of each statement).

Go is a compiled language, so the resulting files are super-fast. Go is also cross-platform because you can compile your code to run on Windows, macOS, or Linux. That performance is why Go is very popular and is used for multiple areas of development:

>> **Cloud computing and DevOps:** Go is used by bigtime cloud concerns such as Docker, Kubernetes, and Terraform. (DevOps is a set of practices and tools that integrate software development — the Dev part — and IT operations — the Ops part — to improve collaboration, automate workflows, and accelerate software delivery.)

>> **Web development:** Go is a popular language for coding back-end application programming interfaces (APIs) and microservices. (An *API* is software that enables different apps to communicate with each other. A *microservice* is a program that performs a specific task — such as user authentication — and is part of a larger application consisting of multiple such services.)

>> **Networking and distributed systems:** Go code is fast and scalable (able to expand without running into problems), so it can handle large numbers of users.

>> **High-performance applications:** Go is the language-of-choice when companies such as Google, Uber, and Dropbox feel the need for speed.

>> **Command-line tools:** Go is great for building automation scripts that run from the command prompt.

Here's a "Hello, World!" example in Go:

```go
package main

import "fmt"

func main() {
    var message string
    message = "Hello, World!"
    fmt.Println(message)
}
```

Rankings:

TIOBE Index: 8th

IEEE Spectrum: 8th

Java

Java is a powerful and widely used programming language best known for enabling developers to create "write once, run anywhere" code. That is, Java programs can run as-is on different devices (Windows PCs, Macs, mobile devices, you name it). How is that possible? It's all thanks to a chunk of software called the Java Virtual Machine (JVM), which acts as a kind of translator between your Java code and each device's operating system.

REMEMBER

So, Java and JavaScript are close language cousins, right? Nope. Other than both being coding languages, the two have little in common. As I like to say, Java is to JavaScript what ham is to hamburger.

Java has a bit of a learning curve, is one of those syntax-heavy languages I mentioned earlier, and requires the installation of a special development kit to get started, so it's not an ideal language for beginners.

To give you a taste, here's a "Hello, World!" example in Java:

```java
public class HelloWorld {
    public static void main(String[] args) {
        String message = "Hello, World!";
        System.out.println(message);
    }
}
```

That code is quite a bit denser than the equivalent code in JavaScript and especially Python.

However, experienced Java developers love its clear syntax and strong error checking, which is why Java is a very popular language used all over the place:

>> **Android app development:** Many Android apps are built with Java.

>> **Web applications:** Java is used to build apps in banking, e-commerce, and enterprise systems.

>> **Game development:** Java is a very popular choice for mobile and desktop games.

>> **Big data and cloud computing:** Java is used in back-end services for handling large-scale applications.

Rankings:

TIOBE Index: 4th

IEEE Spectrum: 5th

Kotlin

Kotlin is a modern, concise, and safe programming language developed by JetBrains. Google has anointed Kotlin as the preferred language for Android app development. Kotlin is designed to be easier to read and write than Java while maintaining high performance. Kotlin is also fully interoperable with Java, which means it works seamlessly with existing Java projects.

Even though Kotlin code can be a bit slower than the equivalent Java code and even though Kotlin does have a relatively steep learning curve, it's one of the fastest growing languages today and developers are using it for lots of things:

>> **Android app development:** Kotlin is the primary language for coding modern Android apps.

>> **Web development:** You can use Kotlin libraries such as Ktor and Spring Boot to build back-end web applications, APIs, and microservices.

>> **Cross-platform apps:** With Kotlin Multiplatform, you can share code between Android, iOS, and web apps.

>> **Data science and machine learning:** You can use Kotlin libraries such as Kotlin for Data Science to crunch data and KotlinDL (where DL is short for deep learning) to build AI applications.

Here's a "Hello, World!" example in Kotlin:

```
fun main() {
    val message: String = "Hello, World!"
    println(message)
}
```

Rankings:

TIOBE Index: 19th

IEEE Spectrum: 17th

PHP

PHP (the name is a recursive acronym for PHP: Hypertext Processor) is a server-side scripting language designed for web development. (*Server-side* refers to operations that run on a server. The opposite is *client-side*, which refers to code that runs on a *client*, a system used to access a server. In web development, a web server represents the server side, and the web browser represents the client side.) PHP is widely used for building dynamic websites and web applications and is designed to work seamlessly with databases such as MySQL (pronounced "MY-ess-kew-ell" or sometimes "MY-sequel").

PHP is a beginner-friendly language with relatively simple syntax. Its syntax shares similarities with JavaScript, such as the use of braces and semicolons, so if you learn one, you'll be able to pick up the other quickly. (Someone who can code both the client-side and the server-side is well on their way to becoming what's known in the trade as a *full-stack developer.*)

Although PHP has been around forever (the first version was released way back in 1995!), it remains a powerful and popular language for many different uses:

>> **Server-side web development:** PHP is designed to handle web forms, user authentication, database chores, and pretty much anything else required for web development on the server. About 75 percent of websites use PHP, including WordPress, Facebook, and Wikipedia.

>> **Content management systems:** A CMS is software that enables users to create, edit, manage, and publish digital content, such as a blog. Many bigtime CMS platforms — including WordPress, Drupal, and Joomla — are built using PHP.

>> **Ecommerce websites:** PHP is the engine behind lots of sites that enable ecommerce, including WooCommerce and Magento.

>> **APIs and back-end services:** Many developers use PHP to create APIs, and a PHP framework called Laravel helps developers create web apps.

>> **Automating web tasks:** PHP is widely used for automating routine web chores such as form handling, file uploads, and sending email.

While newer languages like server-side JavaScript (Node.js) are growing in popularity, PHP still powers a massive chunk of the web and remains a great choice for anyone who wants to learn server-side web development.

TIP

Shameless plug: If you want to learn both PHP and JavaScript and how they can work together to build amazing web apps, may I not-even-remotely-humbly suggest my book *Web Coding & Development All-in-One For Dummies*, 2nd Edition?

Here's a "Hello, World!" example in PHP:

```php
<?php
$message = "Hello, World!";
echo $message;
?>
```

Rankings:

TIOBE Index: 15th

IEEE Spectrum: 13th

Rust

Rust is a systems programming language known for its speedy performance and memory safety. It was built originally by a team at Mozilla (developer of the Firefox web browser) but is now an open-source project led by the Rust Foundation. Rust is widely used for developing high-performance, safe, and reliable software. Unlike C and C++, Rust offers developers built-in tools for preventing memory leaks and memory-related program crashes.

The blazing speed of Rust programs (they're comparable to C and C++ programs) and the safety of the code mean that Rust is rapidly finding lots of adherents in the high-end coding world:

>> **Systems programming:** Rust is widely viewed as a modern alternative to C and C++ for operating system development.

>> **WebAssembly:** Rust is often used to create WebAssembly code, which is high-performance, compiled code that runs in the web browser.

>> **Embedded systems:** Rust provides safe and efficient code for IoT devices.

>> **Game development:** Rust is used in many high-performance game engines.

>> **Networking and cloud services:** Rust enables developers such as Amazon Web Services and Cloudflare to create fast, safe back-end services.

>> **Cybersecurity and blockchain:** Rust is popular with developers who need to build secure applications and cryptographic tools.

Rust is powerful and complex, but it's becoming very popular, so it would be a great language to learn if you want a career in coding. If you're interested, you can check out my book *Rust All-in-One For Dummies*.

Here's a "Hello, World!" example in Rust:

```
fn main() {
    let message = "Hello, World!";
    println!("{message}");
}
```

Rankings:

TIOBE Index: 18th

IEEE Spectrum: 11th

Swift

Released in 2014 by Apple, Swift is a modern, fast, and safe programming language created for coding apps across Apple's major operating systems: iOS, iPadOS, macOS, tvOS, and watchOS. Swift is designed to be easy for beginners while powerful enough for professionals. Swift combines a clean and readable syntax reminiscent of Python, the speed of C thanks to being a compiled language, and some of the modern features of JavaScript. If you want to code apps only in the Apple ecosystem, you might want to take a close look at Swift.

Here's a "Hello, World!" example in Swift:

```swift
let message = "Hello, World!"
print(message)
```

Rankings:

TIOBE Index: 25th

IEEE Spectrum: 21st

TypeScript

TypeScript is just JavaScript with extra features that enable you to specify a data type when you declare a variable and to warn you when you try to mix data types. To understand why this is useful, first check out a basic variable declaration in JavaScript:

```javascript
let message = "Hello, World!";
```

All is good: You're just storing a string literal in a variable named message. But later in the same program, your code could do this:

```javascript
message = 42;
```

Now, instead of a string literal, you're using the same message variable to store a numeric literal. JavaScript is totally fine with that.

JavaScript might not protest at this mixing of data types, but such mixing can lead to problems in complex programs or when you use a method that requires a particular data type (such as a string). To avoid such woes, Microsoft invented TypeScript, which enables developers to specify a data type when they declare a variable. Here's an example:

```typescript
let message: string = "Hello, World!";
console.log(message);
```

Here, message is the variable name and the extra : string characters specify that message can only contain string data. If, later in the same program, your code tried to assign a number to the message variable, TypeScript would display an error message.

Rankings:

TIOBE Index: 35th

IEEE Spectrum: 5th

Grokking the Difference between Interpreted and Compiled Languages

No matter which programming language you use, all programs must be translated into something that a computer can understand and execute. The coding world uses two different tools to do this translating: compilers and interpreters.

A *compiler* is a software program that translates the entire source code of a program into machine code (sometimes called *binary*) before execution. The resulting machine code file can then be run repeatedly without further translation. The main advantages of compiled code are that it runs very fast and the compiler will let you know if your code contains syntax errors. The main disadvantage of compiled code is that the larger and more complex the code, the longer the compilation time. Compiled languages include C, C++, Go, Rust, and Swift.

An *interpreter* is a software program that translates and executes the source code one statement at a time, rather than converting the entire program into machine code beforehand. The interpreter reads and executes source code directly, so interpreted code runs slower because the translation happens at runtime. The interpreter stops executing the code at the first error it trips over. Interpreted languages include Python, JavaScript, and PHP.

Some languages use both a compiler and an interpreter. That is, the original code is compiled and then the compiled code is executed using an interpreter. Languages that use both a compiler and an interpreter include C#, Java, and Kotlin.

2

Learning Python: The Beginner-Friendly Language

IN THIS PART . . .

Set up your Python environment.

Learn the basics of Python.

Explore lists, conditionals, and loops.

Level up with functions, files, and object-oriented programming.

Debug your Python programs.

Tackle some Python projects.

IN THIS CHAPTER

» **Installing Python on your computer**

» **Setting up your Python coding environment**

» **Executing Python code interactively**

» **Running your first Python program**

» **Starting your inevitable love affair with Python**

Chapter **4**

Getting Started with Python

Python is the most powerful language you can still read.

—PAUL DUBOIS

When you read the results of any of the billion or so developer surveys available online, Python is almost always in the top three and more often than not is number one. It doesn't matter whether the survey question is about which language developers use most often, which language they enjoy using the most, or even which language they want to learn next. In survey after survey, Python always ranks at or near the top. And if the survey is aimed at people who are just learning to code? Ah, then Python floats to the top almost without fail.

Why all the love for Python? Almost all of today's most-used languages have multiple quirks — such as requiring a semicolon at the end of every statement or using punctuation marks such as colons (:) or braces ({ and }) in idiosyncratic ways. These syntax oddities aren't mentally taxing, but they do serve as barriers that tend to put off beginners (and even many experienced coders). Python is mercifully free of all that syntax noise. A Python program is clean and clear, making it a pleasure to both write and read. But that simplicity doesn't mean that

Python is a toy language. No way. Once you know the language, you can use it for sophisticated applications such as data science and even artificial intelligence. Python programs pack a punch.

In this chapter, you run your first Python program. But before you get that far, this chapter also takes you on a brief but necessary trip to get your computer set up to do the Python thing.

Getting to the Command Line

Whether you use Windows or macOS, you're no doubt used to making things happen by using your mouse or trackpad to click or double-click icons, buttons, and other visual knickknacks. But every Windows PC and every Mac has an alternative tool for getting things done: the command line. The *command line* (also known as the *command-line interface,* or *CLI*) is a text-based interface that enables you to interact with the computer by typing commands rather than clicking and dragging graphical elements.

When you first start learning to code with Python, it all happens on the command line, so it can feel a little like having a chat with your computer. You say something like this:

```
print('Hello!')
```

and your computer instantly responds with this:

```
Hello!
```

It's not quite a conversation (since, via your code, you're telling the computer what to say or do), but as a coding process it's simple, direct, and super satisfying.

Okay, so where does this conversation take place? This style of coding — one statement at a time — is done in the Python interactive shell, also called REPL (read, evaluate, print, loop; I explain these a bit later in the "Running in interactive mode [REPL]" section). REPL is a safe and secure place for

>> Trying out new Python features

>> Test-driving little ideas

>> Making mistakes and learning fast

Sure, executing one statement at a time might not sound useful now, but it's a great way to get started. Eventually, you'll graduate to writing full Python scripts and building cool stuff in a code editor.

For now, most of what you'll do with Python will take place at your computer's command line, and how you get there depends on whether you're using Windows or macOS.

Launching Terminal on Windows

Windows offers a Terminal app with two command-line environments, and it doesn't matter which one you use to run your Python statements or scripts:

>> **Windows PowerShell:** Click Start, type **term**, and then click Terminal in the search results. Alternatively, right-click Start and then click Terminal in the shortcut menu that pops up. PowerShell is the default Terminal environment, so that's what appears whenever you launch Terminal.

>> **Command Prompt:** Click Start, type **cmd**, and then click Command Prompt in the results. Alternatively, right-click Start, click Run (or press Windows+R) to open the Run dialog box, type **cmd**, and then click OK.

REMEMBER

If you're running an older version of Windows that doesn't include Terminal, you can download the app from the Microsoft Store.

Figure 4-1 shows the Terminal window with Windows PowerShell as the command-line environment. Note that you can click the arrow pointed out in Figure 4-1 to switch between Command Prompt and PowerShell.

Click the arrow to display a menu of command-line environments

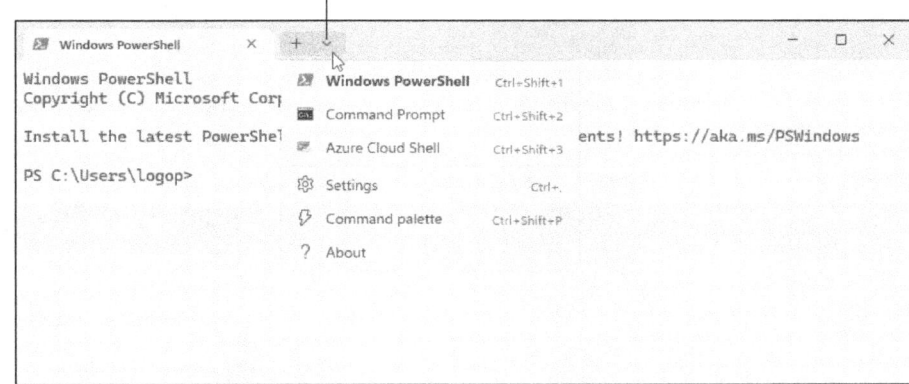

FIGURE 4-1:
The Windows
Terminal app
running Windows
PowerShell.

Launching Terminal on macOS

macOS offers the Terminal app for all your Mac-related command-line frolics. You have three main ways to get there:

>> **Spotlight Search:** Click the Spotlight Search icon in the menu bar (and shown in the margin) or press ⌘+Spacebar, type **term**, and then click Terminal in the search results.

>> **Launchpad:** Click Launchpad on the dock, click Other, then click Terminal.

>> **Finder:** Click Finder on the dock, and then click Applications ⇨ Utilities ⇨ Terminal.

Figure 4-2 shows the macOS Terminal app.

```
● ● ●                     paul — -zsh — 80×15
Last login: Mon Mar 24 15:51:35 on ttys000
paul@Pauls-MacBook-Pro ~ %
```

FIGURE 4-2:
The macOS
Terminal app.

Some useful Terminal shortcuts

You'll likely spend much of your Python career hanging around the command line, so you might as well learn a few handy keyboard shortcuts to make your terminal work easier and more efficient. To that worthy end, Table 4-1 presents a bunch of keyboard techniques and their Windows and macOS shortcuts.

TABLE 4-1   Terminal Keyboard Shortcuts

Action	Windows shortcut	macOS shortcut
Interrupt or stop current command	Ctrl+C	Control+C
Clear terminal screen	Ctrl+L	Control+L or Cmd+K
Exit terminal or session	Ctrl+D, or type **exit** then Enter	Control+D, or type **exit()** then Return
Cancel typed text or line	Esc	Control+U

Action	Windows shortcut	macOS shortcut
Autocomplete file or command	Tab	Tab
Cycle command history	Up arrow or down arrow	Up arrow or down arrow
Search command history	F8 or Ctrl+R	Control+R
Delete word (backward)	Ctrl+Backspace	Control+W
Delete line (cursor to start)	Ctrl+U	Control+U
Delete line (cursor to end)	Ctrl+K	Control+K
Move cursor word by word	Ctrl+left arrow or Ctrl+right arrow	Option+left arrow or Option+ right arrow
Move to start or end of line	Home or End	Control+A or Control+E
Paste from clipboard	Right-click or Ctrl+V	Cmd+V or Control+Y
Copy selected text	Right-click or Ctrl+C	Cmd+C
Scroll up or down terminal output	Ctrl+Up or Ctrl+Down	Shift+Page Up or Shift+Page Down

Installing Python

Programming languages evolve. New features are added, existing features are changed, no longer useful features are jettisoned, performance is improved, and security holes are patched. For many languages, new versions seem to arrive almost randomly, but not Python. Ever since version 3.9 was released in October 2020, a new version of the language has appeared faithfully every October. As I write this, Python 3.13 was released in October 2024, so that's the version I use in this book. More accurately, I use version 3.13.5. That extra ".5" tacked on at the end is there because Python releases minor versions (3.13.1, 3.13.2, and so on) regularly. Here's how to read a version number such as 3.13.5:

>> **3:** The major version number (some perhaps overly dramatic folks insist that we're currently in the "Python 3 era").

>> **13:** The feature release version number (the number bumped up by one each October).

>> **5:** The patch or bug fix version number (small fixes or improvements that are released every month or two).

The good news is that you don't have to worry about version numbers all that much because the Python folks are careful about releasing only proven versions of the language. When it's time to install Python, just use whatever the Python website says is the latest version and you'll always be fine.

Does your computer already have Python installed?

Before diving into the steps required to install Python, it's a good idea to check whether it's already installed and, if it is, to check which version you have.

Open a terminal in Windows or macOS, and then do the following:

» **Windows:** Type **python --version** and press Enter.

» **macOS:** Type **python3 --version** and press Return.

To be clear, there are two hyphens (–) before the word version in each command. One of three things will be true:

» **A recent version of Python is installed.** A message showing the Python version number appears, which will be similar to the following:

```
Python 3.13.5
```

As long as that number is 3.10 or higher, you're good to go. Feel free to skip over the upcoming instructions for installing Python. However, if you're a release or two behind, it's a good idea to install the most recent version, as I describe in that section.

» **An older version of Python is installed.** A message showing the Python version number appears, but it's older than version 3.10. For example:

```
Python 3.6.2
```

or even older:

```
Python 2.7.18
```

It's important to upgrade these older versions, so head down to the Python installation section for your operating system to learn how to get the latest version on your computer.

» **Python is not installed.** A message similar to the following appears:

```
Python was not found
```

In this case, saunter over to either the "Installing Python on Windows" section or the "Installing Python on macOS" section to get Python running on your machine.

WARNING

In Windows Terminal, the `Python was not found` message might be followed by this suggestion:

```
run without arguments to install from the Microsoft Store
```

Indeed, if you type **python** and press Enter, the Microsoft Store appears and displays a page prompting you to install the latest version of Python. I highly recommend that you *not* do this! The version of Python you get works fine, but it works with a configuration that can cause problems if you try to do anything but the most basic Python tasks. Do yourself a favor and get Python directly from the Python website. You'll thank me in the end.

Installing Python on Windows

If Python isn't installed, or if you want to upgrade to the latest version, here are the steps to follow on Windows:

1. **Point your favorite web browser to the Python website at** www.python.org/downloads.

The Python website should automatically detect that you're using Windows and display the message Download the latest version for Windows, as shown in Figure 4-3. If this message doesn't appear, click Downloads and then click Windows.

FIGURE 4-3:
The Python site is smart enough to detect that your PC is running Windows.

2. **Click the Download button (or link) for the latest version.**

In Figure 4-3, it's the Download Python 3.13.5 button.

Your web browser downloads the Python installation program, which will have a name along the lines of python-3.13.5-amd64.exe.

3. **When the download is complete, run the downloaded file.**

Your web browser might display a link such as Open File, which you can click. Otherwise, open File Explorer, navigate to your Downloads folder, and then double-click the downloaded file.

A Python Setup dialog similar to the one shown in Figure 4-4 shows up.

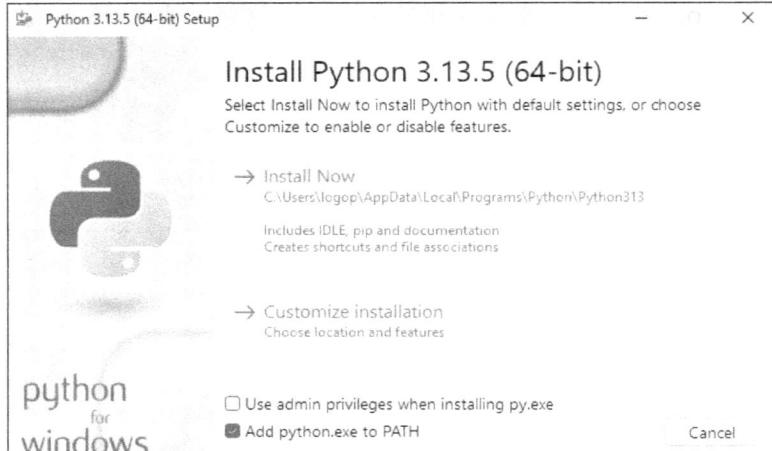

FIGURE 4-4:
The Python Setup dialog appears when you run the installer.

4. **Select the Add python.exe to PATH check box.**

WARNING

It's really important that you select this check box because doing so enables you to run Python from the command line and, later, enables a code editor such as VS Code editor to find Python automatically. If you forget to select this check box or you've already moved on, don't sweat it. Just run the Python installer again and be sure to select the check box this time.

5. **Click Install Now.**

The Python installation program does just that, which takes a minute or two. When the program is done, the Setup Was Successful dialog appears.

6. **Click Close.**

Python is ready to rumble!

To make sure, launch a new Terminal tab or window (if you had Terminal open before the Python installation, you need to close that window or start a new tab) and run the following command:

```
python --version
```

A response similar to the follow should appear:

```
Python 3.13.5
```

Installing Python on macOS

To install Python or upgrade to the latest version on macOS, follow these steps:

1. **Send your nearest web browser to the Python website at** www.python.
   org/downloads.

   The Python website should automatically detect that you're using macOS and display the message Download the latest version for macOS, as shown in Figure 4-5. If this message doesn't appear, click Downloads and then click macOS.

FIGURE 4-5:
The Python site is clever enough to detect that you're running macOS.

2. **Click the Download button (or link) for the latest version.**

   In Figure 4-5, it's the Download Python 3.13.5 button.

3. **If a dialog appears asking to allow downloads on** www.python.org,
   click Allow.

   Your web browser downloads the Python installer package, which will have a name along the lines of python-3.13.5-macos11.pkg.

4. **When the download is complete, run the downloaded installer.**

   Your web browser might display a link such as Open File, which you can click. Otherwise, open Finder, navigate to your Downloads folder, and then double-click the downloaded package file.

   The Install Python package runs and the Introduction dialog shows up.

5. **Click Continue in each dialog box that appears.**

6. **When you get to the Installation Type dialog, click Install.**

7. **If a prompt about your password shows up, use whatever method works best to authorize the installation.**

   The Python installer package performs the installation, which takes a minute or so. When the program is done, a Finder window pops up showing the installed Python files. Close that window because you don't need it.

8. **Click Close.**

   If a message appears wondering if you want the Python installer moved to the trash, go ahead and click Move to Trash because you don't need the installer file any longer.

   Python is ready for action!

To double-check that all is well, launch a new Terminal window (if you had Terminal open before the Python installation, you need to close that window and launch a new one) and run the following command:

```
python3 --version
```

A response like the following should appear on your screen:

```
Python 3.13.5
```

Running the Python Interpreter

Python is an interpreted language, which means Python code gets executed one statement at a time. So, when I talk about the "Python interpreter," I'm talking about the program that runs your Python code. However, the Python interpreter can do that job in two ways: in interactive mode or in script mode.

Running in interactive mode (REPL)

Interactive mode means that you open a terminal, launch Python (I explain how to do that shortly), and then enter your commands one at a time. Each time you enter a command, Python gives you a response related to what you entered. It's a bit like chatting with Python, and this conversational version of the interpreter is called REPL:

>> **Read:** After you press Enter or Return, the interpreter reads what you typed at the command line.

>> **Evaluate:** The interpreter examines your code. If there are no errors, the interpreter executes the code.

>> **Print:** The interpreter displays the result of your code. Note that some commands don't have results (for example, storing a value in a variable), so in these cases REPL displays nothing.

>> **Loop:** The interpreter waits for you to enter your next statement.

Suppose that you type the following and press Enter or Return:

```
>>> 2 + 2
```

Here, >>> is the REPL prompt; it isn't something you type. You type the $2 + 2$ part (shown in bold). The interpreter evaluates the code and then prints the result:

```
4
```

With its work done for now, the interpreter waits for the next command. That's REPL in action — it's Python's instant response playground. It's perfect for experimenting, testing ideas, and just poking around while you're learning.

TIP

When you're finished working in REPL, you need to close it to get back to the regular Terminal prompt:

>> **Windows:** Either press Ctrl+D or type **exit** and press Enter.

>> **macOS:** Either press Control+D or type **exit()** and press Return.

Running in script mode

REPL is a great place to get comfy with Python when you're just getting started, but very soon you'll graduate to more complex scripts that require many statements. In the Python world, you package those statements into a text file called a *script* that you save using the .py file extension.

To execute the commands in your script, you open a terminal, type **py** or **python** (on Windows) or **python3** (on macOS) followed by the name of your .py file. Here's an example:

```
python my_script.py
```

The Python interpreter gets to work and reads the script one line at a time, top to bottom, and executes each statement in order.

Running Python on Windows

To get the Python interpreter running on your Windows PC, you have two choices:

» **Command-line method:** Open Terminal and then type either python or py and press Enter. Wait! What? py? Where did that come from? py is a Python *launcher*, a special program used only to run Python. It offers some fancy tricks (such as being able to run different installed versions of Python), but there's no need to get into any of that. For our purposes, just think of it as a way to fire up the Python interpreter in four fewer characters.

» **Start menu method:** Click Start, click All, click the Python *version* folder, and then click Python *version*, where, in both cases, *version* is the version number of Python that you installed. For example, Figure 4-6 shows a Start menu with the Python 3.13 folder and Python 3.13 command.

Either way, the Python interpreter launches in the Terminal window and the following prompt appears (see Figure 4-7):

```
>>>
```

A cursor blinks on and off to the right of the prompt, which is your cue to type a command.

Running Python on macOS

To get the Python interpreter off the ground on macOS, open Terminal, type **python3**, and press Return. This method displays the Python interpreter's >>> prompt, as shown in Figure 4-8.

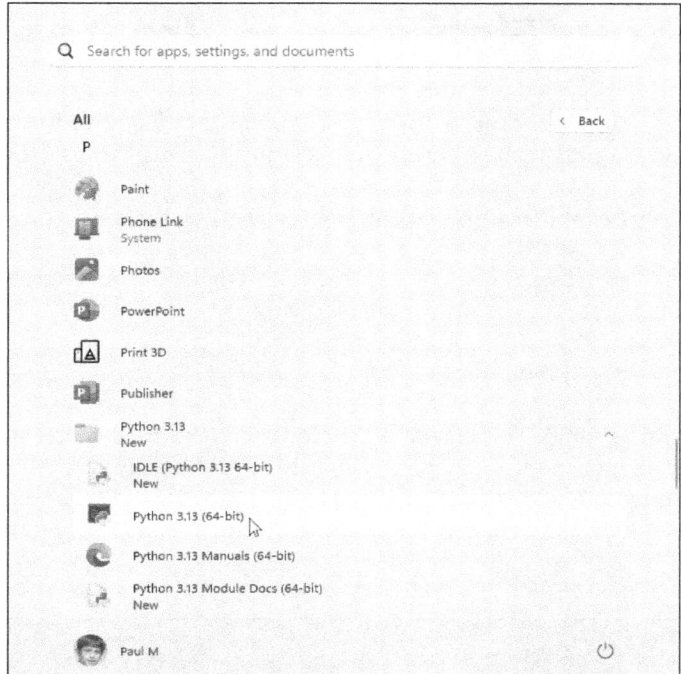

```
Windows PowerShell          ×    +  ∨                                        —    □    ×

Windows PowerShell
Copyright (C) Microsoft Corporation. All rights reserved.

Install the latest PowerShell for new features and improvements! https://aka.ms/PSWindows

PS C:\Users\logop> python
Python 3.13.5 (tags/v3.13.5:6cb20a2, Jun 11 2025, 16:15:46) [MSC v.1943 64 bit (AMD64)] on win32
Type "help", "copyright", "credits" or "license" for more information.
>>>
```

```
●  ◉  ◉                   📋 paul — Python — 80×24

Last login: Fri Jul  4 16:21:43 on ttys013
paul@Pauls-MacBook-Pro ~ % python3
Python 3.13.5 (v3.13.5:6cb20a219a8, Jun 11 2025, 12:23:45) [Clang 16.0.0 (clang-
1600.0.26.6)] on darwin
Type "help", "copyright", "credits" or "license" for more information.
>>> |
```

Running Your First Python Program

Assuming you have the Python interpreter running, give it a whirl by typing the following command (remember to type just the bold part, not the >>> prompt part):

```
>>> print("Hello, Python World!")
```

When you press Enter or Return, the Python interpreter runs your command, which in this case displays the following:

```
Hello, Python World!
```

Running single commands is fine for trying out basic stuff, but you can also use the Python interpreter to run multistatement programs. You can convince the Python interpreter to handle scripts with two or more statements in several ways. But before I get to those methods, following is an example script you can use:

```
name = input("What's your name? ")
print("Nice to meet you, " + name + "!")
chars = len(name)
print("Your name contains " + str(chars) + " characters.")
```

Here's a look at what this script does:

1. `name = input("What's your name? ")`

This statement uses Python's `input()` function (covered in Chapter 5) to display the prompt `What's your name?` on the screen. (Note the extra space at the end of the prompt, which is there to provide some daylight between the end of the prompt and what you type.) When you type your name and press Enter or Return, what you typed is stored in the `name` variable.

2. `print("Nice to meet you, " + name + "!")`

This statement takes the phrase `Nice to meet you,` appends the value of the `name` variable (in Python, you combine two strings using the + operator), and tacks on an exclamation point (`!`). The entire string is then displayed on the screen using the `print()` function.

3. `chars = len(name)`

This statement uses the `len()` function (it's short for *length*) to calculate the number of characters in the string that's stored in the `name` variable, and then stores that number in the `chars` variable.

4. `print("Your name contains " + str(chars) + " characters.")`

This statement takes the phrase `Your name contains`, appends the number stored in the `chars` variable, uses the `str()` function (it's short for *string*) to convert the number to a string to avoid an error, and adds the text `characters.` to the end. The `print()` function then outputs the entire string to the screen.

Running the program in interactive mode

In the Python REPL, you have two ways to run a multistatement program:

» **Add one statement at a time.** For each statement, type it (or copy it if you have it written down elsewhere and then paste it at the ››› prompt), and then press Enter or Return. Figure 4-9 shows the example program having been entered in REPL one statement at a time.

» **Paste the entire program.** Assuming you have the entire script available somewhere, copy the entire script, paste it at the ››› prompt, and then press Enter or Return. The Python interpreter goes through each statement one by one, starting from the first line.

```
● ● ●                          paul — Python — 80×13
>>> name = input("What's your name? ")
What's your name? Sue Flay
>>> print("Nice to meet you, " + name + "!")
Nice to meet you, Sue Flay!
>>> chars = len(name)
>>> print("Your name contains " + str(chars) + " characters.")
Your name contains 8 characters.
>>> |
```

FIGURE 4-9: Running the example program one statement at a time in the REPL.

Running the program in script mode

Another way to run the program — and by far the most common way once your Python programs get beyond just a few statements — is to save the code to a `.py` file and then ask the Python interpreter to execute the file.

So, the first step is to use your favorite text editor to start a new text file, type your code into that file, and then save the file using the `.py` file extension. Figure 4-10 shows the example program (with a few added comments — the lines beginning with #) saved as the `whats_your_name.py` file in the VS Code editor.

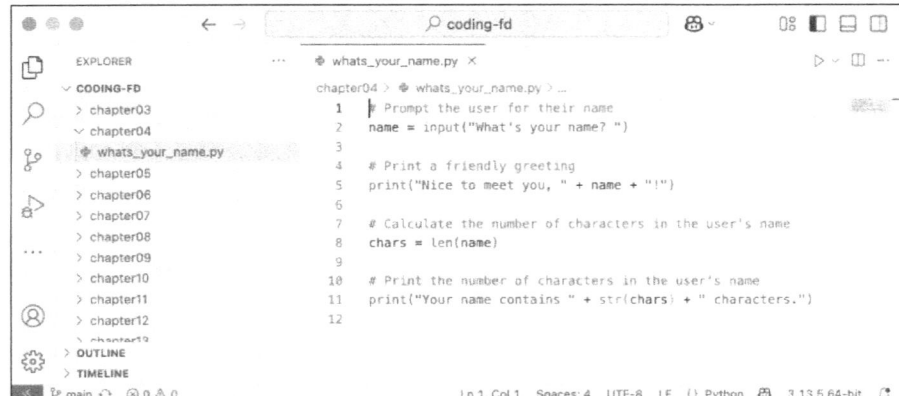

FIGURE 4-10:
The example
Python program
saved to a .py
file in the VS
Code editor.

From here, how you proceed depends on whether you're using Windows or macOS.

Running a script file in Windows

To run a script file in Windows, you need to use your terminal window to navigate to the same folder as the one you used to save your .py file. Here's how:

1. **Open File Explorer.**

2. **Navigate to the folder that contains the subfolder where your .py file is stored.**

   For example, if your file is in Documents\PythonStuff, navigate to the Documents folder.

3. **Right-click the subfolder that contains your .py file, and then click Open in Terminal.**

   A new Terminal tab appears and switches to the folder you right-clicked.

Now you're ready to tell the Python interpreter to run the file in script mode:

```
python file_name.py
```

Replace file_name.py with the name of your script file. Here's an example:

```
python whats_your_name.py
```

The Python interpreter loads the .py file, and then reads and runs each line from top to bottom without pausing between statements — unless your script includes one or more input() functions.

Running a script file in macOS

To run your script file in macOS, you need to navigate Terminal to the same folder as the one you used to save your `.py` file. Here are the steps to plow through:

1. **Arrange the Terminal and Finder windows so that both are visible on your desktop.**

2. **In Terminal, type** `cd` **followed by a space.**

    The `cd` command is short for *change directory,* which is what you'll be doing any second now. And, yep, you really do need to add a space after `cd`.

3. **Switch over to Finder.**

4. **Navigate to the folder that contains the subfolder where your** `.py` **file is stored.**

    For example, if your file is in Documents\PythonGoodies, navigate to the Documents folder.

5. **Drag the subfolder that contains your** `.py` **file and drop it inside the Terminal window.**

    The path of the folder now appears after the `cd` command.

6. **Press Return.**

    Terminal switches to that folder.

Now, at long last, it's time to get the Python interpreter to run the `.py` file in script mode:

```
python3 file_name.py
```

Replace `file_name.py` with the name of your script file. Here's an example:

```
python3 whats_your_name.py
```

The Python interpreter reads the `.py` file and then runs each statement one at a time.

Chapter **5**

Getting Comfy with Some Python Fundamentals

It's humbling to start fresh. It takes a lot of courage. But it can be reinvigorating. You just have to put your ego on a shelf and tell it to be quiet.

—JENNIFER RITCHIE PAYETTE

P ython's reputation as a benign language for beginners comes in part because Python mostly does away with the annoying rules (I'm looking at *you*, "End every statement with a semicolon") and oddball syntactic symbols (I'm looking at *you*, curly braces) that festoon other languages. But Python is also a great first language to learn because you don't have to learn much of it to do useful things.

In this chapter, I hope to prove how far you can get by learning just a few Python fundamentals. In the pages that follow, you explore Python variables, data types, and expressions. You also investigate what you can do with strings and how to get input from the user. By the time this chapter is done, you'll know just enough to be dangerous, er, I mean, just enough to write some useful little programs.

Declaring Variables

In most programming languages, you need to let the compiler or interpreter know that you're declaring a variable by starting off with a special keyword, such as var or let. (JavaScript, as I show in Chapter 10, is one of these languages.)

In Python, thankfully, you don't need any kind of keyword to declare a variable. Instead, you just get right down to it by thinking up a name for the variable and assigning it a value using the appropriately named *assignment operator* — =:

```
name = "Alice"
price = 9.95
is_cool = True
```

If you're assigning a string literal, surround it with either double quotation marks (") or single quotation marks ('). If you're assigning a numeric literal, just type the number. If you're assigning a Boolean value, use True or False. That's it! No fuss. This is one reason why Python has a reputation for being beginner-friendly.

Not that we're in "anything goes" territory, mind you, because there's a short list of rules you need to follow. In Python, variable names

>> **Must start with a letter or an underscore (_):** The other characters can be a letter, an underscore, or a number.

>> **Can't have spaces:** If you need to use multiple words to make a variable name more descriptive, it's traditional in Python to use snake_case, where you separate the words using underscores. For example, user_name or high_score.

>> **Are case-sensitive:** For example, the names total, Total, and TOTAL refer to three different variables.

REMEMBER

Although using all lowercase letters in your variable names isn't a requirement, I recommend that you do so. Lowercase names are faster to type, and you never have to worry about what capitalization you used when you declared the variable. Also, it's best to use descriptive names when you can. A name such as temp_celsius is clearer and easier to read than t_c or just t.

TIP

Python doesn't mind if you declare multiple variables in a single statement, which is useful when you need to initialize two or more variables with the same value, such as:

```
player1_health = player2_health = 100
```

Exploring Python Data Types

Like any programming language, Python has a relatively long list of data types. Happily for you, there are just three main types that you'll use most often as you're getting your Python feet wet:

» **String:** A text value, which can be a string literal such as "kumquat" or 'rutabaga', a value returned by one of Python's string methods (check out "Messing Around with Strings," later in this chapter), or text returned by a custom function or an object property. The Python interpreter uses the str keyword to refer to the string data type.

» **Number:** A numeric value, which can be either an integer such as 42 or a floating-point decimal such as 3.14159. A number can be a literal, the result of an expression, the return value of a function, or the value of an object property. The Python interpreter uses the int (for integer) and float (for floating point) keywords to refer to the number data type.

TIP

When your code requires a large number, you can make the number more readable by inserting an underscore (_) where you'd normally use a thousands separator if you were writing the number in the real world:

```
preferred_salary = 1_500_000
```

» **Boolean:** The value True or the value False. A Boolean can be an expression result, a function return value, or an object property value. The Python interpreter uses the keyword bool to refer to the Boolean data type.

When you declare a variable, as I describe in the preceding section, Python automatically figures out what type of data you're storing: a string, a number, or a Boolean. Nice.

REMEMBER

Python defines quite a few more data types, but most of them can be filed under the "For Nerds Only" category. Some other data types that I cover in Chapter 6 and that you'll use often are the list, the range, and the tuple and dictionary.

Mixing data types

Python is generally pretty easygoing about data types, meaning that however you use a string, a number, or a Boolean, the interpreter will do its best to figure out what you mean. Not that what the interpreter figures out is always obvious. For example, Python is fine mixing numbers and Booleans because internally Python represents True as 1 and False as 0. For example, you could enter the following (remember: just the bold text) at the REPL prompt:

```
>>> 3 + True
```

The result is 4, because 3 + True is equivalent to 3 + 1.

Yep, Python allows Booleans and integers to overlap, but mixing them intentionally in complex logic can confuse your future self — or anyone reading your code. It's best to use Booleans just for logic and integers just for math.

As another example, you might wonder what will happen here:

```
>>> "ho" * 3
```

Somewhat surprisingly, this is the result:

```
'hohoho'
```

That is, when the Python interpreter comes across "*string*" * *number*, it repeats *string*, *number* times.

However, sometimes mixing data types just doesn't work. For example, in Python you combine — or *concatenate* — two strings using the + operator. The expression "lolla" + "palooza" produces the string "lollapalooza". However, suppose you enter the following statement at the REPL prompt:

```
>>> account_number = "ac" + 12345
```

Instead of what you might expect — that the value ac12345 is now stored in the account_number variable — you instead the following error appears:

```
TypeError: can only concatenate str (not "int") to str
```

This error is saying, "Hey, whoa, wait just a second. You're only allowed to concatenate a string with another string. You tried to concatenate a string with an integer. Sorry, no can do."

Converting data types

Despite the Python interpreter's objections, sometimes your code really does need to mix data types in a particular way. To work around any errors that might crop up, you can use some built-in Python functions to convert — or *coerce,* in programming lingo — one data type into another:

>> **str(*number*):** Converts *number* into a string.

>> **int(*string*):** Converts *string* into a number. This conversion works only if *string* contains a valid integer written in digits and surrounded by quotation marks, like "42". If it says "forty-two" or includes any letters or symbols, Python will throw a tantrum.

>> **float(*value*):** Converts *value* from a string or an integer into a floating-point number. Again, if *value* is a string, it must be a valid integer or floating-point number in quotation marks.

>> **bool(*value*):** Converts *value* to a Boolean. Non-zero numbers and non-empty strings are converted to True; 0 and " " (the empty string) are converted to False.

For example, from the preceding section, I showed that the following throws an error because you can't concatenate a string with an integer:

```
>>> account_number = "ac" + 12345
```

To make this work, you need to convert the number 12345 into a string, like so:

```
>>> account_number = "ac" + str(12345)
```

Now the value ac12345 gets stored properly in the account_number variable.

Constructing Expressions

Okay, so you've got your variables, and each one has a data type that Python has noted for you behind the scenes. Maybe you've stored your name in a variable. Or maybe you've stored the number of cookies you've eaten in one variable and how many uneaten cookies are left in another. What happens next? What can you actually *do* with those variables?

One of the most common uses of variables is to use them in expressions. A Python *expression* is a bit of code that combines one or more operands, such as variables or literal values, with one or more operations, such as addition or multiplication, to produce a result.

For example, here's a simple expression you could type at the REPL prompt:

```
>>> 2 + 2
```

The Python interpreter reads that and says, "Easy. That's 4." It evaluates the expression and displays the result onscreen.

Expressions get a whole lot more interesting and useful once you start using variables as operands. Here's an example (in this book's example files, refer to chapter05/example01.py):

```
cookies_eaten = 3
cookies_not_eaten = 2
total_cookies = cookies_eaten + cookies_not_eaten
print(total_cookies)
```

Here, `cookies_eaten + cookies_not_eaten` is the expression. The result — 5, in this case — is stored in the `total_cookies` variable.

Basic math operators in Python

Python comes with a toolbox of common mathematical operators that you can wield to build your arithmetic expressions. Table 5-1 lists the available math operators.

TABLE 5-1   **Python's Math Operators**

Operator	Name	What It Does	Example	Result
+	Addition	Adds values	2 + 3	5
–	Subtraction	Subtracts values	5 – 2	3
*	Multiplication	Multiplies values	4 * 2	8
/	Division	Divides values	8 / 2	4.0
//	Floor division	Returns only the integer portion of a division	7 // 2	3
%	Modulo	Returns the remainder after a division	7 % 2	1
**	Exponentiation	Raises one number to the power of another	2 ** 3	8

TECHNICAL STUFF

If two numbers divide evenly, regular division (/) doesn't return an integer result, as you might expect. It always returns a floating-point result.

Python also comes with a few extra operators that combine some of the arithmetic operators and the assignment operator (=). Table 5-2 lists these *arithmetic assignment* operators.

TABLE 5-2

Python Arithmetic Assignment Operators

Operator	Example	Equivalent
+=	x += y	x = x + y
-=	x -= y	x = x - y
*=	x *= y	x = x * y
/=	x /= y	x = x / y
**=	x **= y	x = x ** y
%=	x %= y	x = x % y

Comparison operators in Python

When you need an expression that compares one value with another, Python has your back by offering a complete list of comparison operators, as shown in Table 5-3.

TABLE 5-3 **Python's Comparison Operators**

Operator	Name	Example	Result
==	Equal to	5 == 5	True
!=	Not equal to	5 != 3	True
>	Greater than	7 > 3	True
<	Less than	2 < 1	False
>=	Greater than or equal to	4 >= 4	True
<=	Less than or equal to	3 <= 2	False

You'll use these operators a ton when writing conditionals and loops in Chapter 6 (refer to "Conditionals in Python" and "Python Loops," respectively).

Building logical expressions in Python

You use logical expressions to combine or manipulate Boolean values, particularly comparison expressions. For example, your code might need to know whether two comparison expressions are both True before continuing. That kind of test is the province of the logical expression, which you build in Python using the logical operators listed in Table 5-4.

TABLE 5-4   **Python's Logical Operators**

Operator	What It Does	Example	Result
and	Returns True if both expressions are True; returns False, otherwise	True and False	False
or	Returns True if at least one expression is True; returns False otherwise	True or False	True
not	Returns True if the expression is False; returns False otherwise	not True	False

Here's an example (chapter05/example02.py):

```
hungry = True
has_cookies = False
if hungry and has_cookies:
    print("Time to munch!")
else:
    print("No cookies for you!")
```

To learn how Python `if` statements work, head over to the "Conditionals in Python" section in Chapter 6.

A quick peek at order of operations

Python follows the standard math rules for the order of operations — also known in the coding trade as PEMDAS:

1. Parentheses

2. Exponents

3. Multiplication and division

4. Addition and subtraction

For example, what value is stored in the `result` variable?

```
>>> result = 2 + 3 * 4
```

If you just process the expression from left to right, you might come up with 20 as the answer (2 + 3 = 5, then 5 * 4 = 20). But the Python interpreter, following PEMDAS, performs the multiplication first, and then the addition to get the correct result of 14 (3 * 4 = 12, then 2 + 12 = 14).

To force Python to perform the addition first, surround that part of the expression with parentheses:

```
>>> result = (2 + 3) * 4
```

In this case, the Python interpreter, still avidly following PEMDAS, performs the addition first (2 + 3 = 5) because it appears within parentheses, and then it performs the multiplication (5 * 4 = 20) to get a result of 20.

Messing Around with Strings

Earlier in this chapter in the "Exploring Python Data Types" section, I provide the following facts about Python strings:

» A string is text surrounded by double (") or single (') quotation marks.

» You can smush two strings together by using the concatenation operator (+). For example, "Cowa" + "bunga" produces "Cowabunga".

» You can repeat a string by using the multiplication operator (*). For example, "yadda" * 3 produces 'yaddayaddayadda'.

» You can convert a number to a string using Python's built-in str() function. For example, str(1812) produces the string "1812".

» The special string "" (or ' ') is called the empty string because nothing is between the two quotation marks.

That's a pretty good start, but there's much more to know about strings, as the following sections show.

Understanding string indexes

For a given string, the position of a single character in that string is called the *index* of the character. Like just about every programming language under the sun, Python's indexes are *0-based,* which means the index of the first character is 0, the index of the second character is 1, and so on. This is weird, I know, but you'll be surprised how quickly you get used to it.

Indexes are useful when you need to grab a chunk of a string in your code. For a single character, you use the following syntax:

```
string[index]
```

where:

» *string* is the string you're working with.

» *index* is the index number of the character you want.

Here's an example (chapter05/example03.py):

```
greeting = "hello"
print(greeting[0])
print(greeting[1])
```

The first `print()` statement returns h; the second `print()` statement returns e.

If you need a bigger slice of a string, you can use the following syntax to get the job done:

```
string[start:stop]
```

where:

» *string* is the string you're working with.

» *start* is the index number of the first character you want.

» *stop* is the index number that is one more than the last character you want.

Here's an example (chapter05/example04.py):

```
word = "rutabaga"
print(word[0:3])
print(word[4:7])
```

The first `print()` statement returns rut; the second `print()` statement returns bag.

If you ever need to know how many characters are in a string, use the `len()` function:

```
len(string)
```

where *string* is a reference to some string value. For example, `len("rutabaga")` would return 8.

Mixing strings with variables

One of the most common coding problems occurs when you want to create a string, but part of the string is stored inside a variable. One solution is to use concatenation, as in this example (chapter05/example05.py):

```
name = "Alphonse"
total = 7
print("I hear " + name + " ate " + str(total) + " cookies.")
```

Here's the output:

```
I hear Alphonse ate 7 cookies.
```

So, yep, it works, but getting all those quotation marks right is harder than it seems, and the string is super-hard to read.

A better solution is to use an *f-string* — short for *formatted string* — where you slap an f in front of the string and surround each variable with braces ({ and }). Here's the same example, this time using an f-string (chapter05/example06.py):

```
name = "Alphonse"
total = 7
print(f"I hear {name} ate {total} cookies.")
```

Ah, better. Not only are there just the two quotation marks to worry about, but the string is much more readable *and* you don't have to convert the total variable to a string. You're welcome!

String methods

In Python, a string is an object, so like any object worthy of the name, a string comes with various methods that you can use to perform operations on that string. For each method, you use the following general syntax:

```
string.method([parameter(s)])
```

where:

» *string* is the string object on which you want to perform the operation.

» *method* is the name of the method.

» *parameter(s)* represents one or more optional parameters that you use as input for the method.

There are tons of these methods, so Table 5-5 just summarizes the most useful ones.

TABLE 5-5   ## Useful String Methods

Method	What It Does	Example	Result
count()	Returns the number of instances of a substring within a string	fruit = "papaya" print(fruit.count("a"))	3
endswith()	Returns True if a string ends with the specified substring; returns False, otherwise	veg = "kumquat" print(veg.endswith("k"))	False
find()	Returns the position of the first instance of a substring within a string	fruit = "papaya" print(fruit.find("p"))	0 (find() returns −1 if the substring isn't found)
lower()	Converts a string to lowercase letters	my_str = "TOO LOUD!" print(my_str.lower())	too loud!
replace()	Replaces one substring with another within a string	message = "Hello, world!" print(message.replace("world", "Python"))	Hello, Python!
title()	Capitalizes just the first letter of each word in a string	print("the beaches".title())	The Beaches
upper()	Converts a string to uppercase letters	message = "Hello, world!" print(message.upper())	HELLO, WORLD!
startswith()	Returns True if a string begins with the specified substring; returns False, otherwise	veg = "kumquat" print(veg.startswith("k"))	True

TIP

If you just want to know whether a particular substring exists anywhere within a larger string, use the following

substring in *string*

where:

>> *substring* is the characters or characters that you want to check for in *string*.

>> *string* is the string in which you want Python to look for *substring*.

Python returns `True` if *substring* is **anywhere** in *string*; it returns `False`, otherwise.

Splitting and joining strings

One of the most popular use cases for Python code is working with text, which might be user input, data trapped in a comma-separated values (CSV) text file, data scraped from the web, and much more. To work with text, Python offers a couple of super-useful string object methods: `split()` and `join()`.

The split() method

The `split()` method chops up a string into smaller bits for easier processing:

```
string.split([separator])
```

where:

>> *string* is the string object on which you want to perform the split.

>> *separator* is an optional character that defines how you want the string to be split. If you don't include `separator`, Python uses the space character.

Here's an example (chapter05/example07.py):

```
sentence = "I love Python"
words = sentence.split()
print(words)
```

The result is the following list (check out the section "Storing Stuff in Lists" in Chapter 6 to learn more about Python lists):

```
['I', 'love', 'Python']
```

Alternatively, you can tell Python where you want the splits to occur in the string (chapter05/example08.py):

```
csv_data = "apple,banana,cherry"
fruits = csv_data.split(",")
print(fruits)
```

Here's the resulting list:

```
['apple', 'banana', 'cherry']
```

The join() method

The `join()` method is kind of the opposite of `split()` in that it glues two or more strings into a single string:

```
separator.join(list)
```

where:

- >> *separator* is the string you want Python to use to separate each substring. If you don't want a separator, use the empty string.

- >> *list* is a comma-separated list of the strings you want to join, surrounded by square brackets ([and]).

Here's an example (chapter05/example09.py):

```
parts = ["Coding", "For", "Dummies", "rules!"]
message = " ".join(parts)
print(message)
```

Here I'm asking Python to join the strings in the `parts` list by separating each with a space (" "). Here's the result:

```
Coding For Dummies rules!
```

Ah, thanks!

Getting input from the user

Python uses a built-in function called `input()` to get information from the user:

```
input([prompt])
```

The *prompt* is an optional message that appears on the screen followed by a colon and is used to tell the user what to type. (You can leave out *prompt*, but then the user just gets a blinking cursor, which might be confusing; it's best to always use a prompt.) Note that it's good practice to include a space at the end of your prompt so that the user's typing doesn't butt up against the prompt text.

When your program runs `input()`, Python displays the prompt, pauses the program, and waits for the user to type something and press Enter or Return. Python grabs whatever the user types as a string, which you usually store in a variable for later use in your program.

Here's an example (chapter05/example10.py):

```
name = input("What's your name? ")
print(f"Hello, {name}!")
```

When you run this program, the output will look something like this:

```
What's your name? Bartholomew
Hello, Bartholomew!
```

It's important to remember that whatever the user types is returned as a string, even if it looks like a number. To understand why this can be a big deal, consider the following code (chapter05/example11.py):

```
age = input("How old are you? ")
age_next_year = age + 1
print(f"Next year, you'll be {age_next_year}!")
```

Running this program produces the following output:

```
Traceback (most recent call last):
  File "example11.py", line 2, in <module>
    age_next_year = age + 1
                    ~~~~^~~
TypeError: can only concatenate str (not "int") to str
```

Ouch! Can you figure out the problem? That's right: Python interprets `age + 1` as concatenation, but you can't combine a string and an integer. If you want to do math on whatever the user inputs, you need to convert the string to the appropriate numeric data type. Here's a revised version of the code (chapter05/example12.py):

```
age = input("How old are you? ")
age_next_year = int(age) + 1
print("Next year, you'll be " + str(age_next_year) + "!")
```

This code uses int(age) to convert the input string to an integer. Now when you execute the program, it runs error-free:

```
How old are you? 99
Next year, you'll be 100!
```

TIP

You can convert the user's input to another data type right away by using the input() function itself as the argument for whatever conversion function you want to use:

```
age = int(input("How old are you? "))
```

Chapter **6**

Storing Data and Controlling Your Code

There should be one — and preferably only one — obvious way to do it.

—TIM PETERS

C oders — from grizzled veterans to the greenest rookies — love Python. They take to it because Python code is clean, clear, and easy to write and read (at least compared to other programming languages). But coders stay with Python because the language has an inherent elegance, an undeniable grace that sets it apart from other languages. Python code sparks joy.

In this chapter, you get your first glimpse at just how delightfully different Python is from other languages by looking at three common coding structures that Python implements uniquely: lists, conditionals, and loops.

Storing Stuff in Lists

A variable usually stores a single item of data, such as a grade, a day of the week, or the name of a Kardashian. But it's extremely common for your code to work with two or more (usually many more) items of related data, such as the grades for an entire class, every day of the week, or the names of everyone in a particular family.

Sure, you *could* create a separate variable for each item, but Python offers a faster, simpler, *and* more powerful way: the list. A *list* is a collection of items that resides in a single container. That description might sound underwhelming at the moment, but as I hope to show in the sections that follow, lists are a big deal in the Python world.

Making a list

You construct a list by starting with a pair of square brackets [and] , and then filling those brackets with the values you want to store, separated by commas. A list can hold just about anything: numbers, strings, Booleans — even other lists (chapter06/example01.py):

```
shopping_list = ["milk", "eggs", "bread", "Snickerdoodles"]
lucky_numbers = [7, 11, 548834]
mixed_bag = ["hello", 3.14, True, 42]
```

You can store as many items as you want and, as demonstrated in the third example, the items don't need to be the same data type (though using a single data type per list usually makes your coding life easier).

If you ever need to know how many items are in a list (that actually comes up a lot), use the len( ) function:

```
len(list)
```

Where *list* is the name of the list. Here's an example (chapter06/example02.py):

```
>>> print(len(shopping_list))
4
```

Making a list from a range of numbers

When you need a list that's a collection of numbers, the range( ) function is a great tool:

```
range(stop)
range(start, stop[, step])
```

where:

- » *start* is the first number you want in the range. If you specify only the *stop* argument, Python uses 0 as the *start* value.

- » *stop* is the last number you want in the range, minus one. For example, if you set *stop* to 10, the last number in the range will be 9.

- » *step* is the difference between each number in the range. The default value is 1.

range() gets you a range data type, so to turn that object into a proper list, use the range() function as an argument for the list() conversion function. Here are some examples (chapter06/example03.py):

```
>>> list(range(10))
[0, 1, 2, 3, 4, 5, 6, 7, 8, 9]
>>> list(range(1, 6))
[1, 2, 3, 4, 5]
>>> list(range(2, 20, 2))
[2, 4, 6, 8, 10, 12, 14, 16, 18]
```

To reverse the range, use the reversed() function:

```
>>> list(reversed(range(10)))
[9, 8, 7, 6, 5, 4, 3, 2, 1, 0]
```

Getting an item from a list

In the same way as I described earlier for a string (check out Chapter 5), list items are numbered according to their position in the list, and that number is called the *index*. The first item in the list has index 0, the second item has index 1, and so on.

So, you can grab something from a list by specifying the item's index number in square brackets after the list name. Here are some examples (chapter06/example04.py):

```
>>> print(shopping_list[0])
milk
>>> print(shopping_list[2])
bread
```

To get multiple items, you can *slice* the list with `list[start:end]`, where `list` is the name of the list, `start` is the index of the first item you want, and `end` is the index of the item that comes after last item you want. Python returns the items as a list:

```
>>> print(shopping_list[1:3])
['eggs', 'bread']
```

If you ask for an index that doesn't exist, Python throws a little tantrum:

```
>>> print(shopping_list[5])
IndexError: list index out of range
```

Changing an item in a list

Once you create a list, its items aren't set in stone. Python geeks like to say that lists are *mutable,* which is an eyeroll-inducing way of saying they're changeable. To change an item in a list, you set that item to the new value, like so (chapter06/example05.py):

```
>>> shopping_list[1] = "chocolate"
>>> print(shopping_list)
['milk', 'chocolate', 'bread', 'Snickerdoodles']
```

Adding and removing list items

Another way that lists are changeable is that you're free to add new items to the list and remove existing items from the list. Python offers a couple of ways to mess with the contents of a list in these ways, as I describe in the next two sections.

Adding list items

In Python, you can use the `append()` method to add an item to the end of the list or the `insert()` method to shoehorn an item into a list at a specific index:

```
list.append(item)
list.insert(index, item)
```

where:

- >> *list* is the list object in which you want to add the item.

- >> *item* is the item you want to add.

- >> *index* is the position within *list* where you want *item* to appear when using the insert() method.

Here are some examples (chapter06/example06.py):

```
>>> shopping_list = ["milk", "eggs", "bread", "Snickerdoodles"]

>>> shopping_list.append("butter")
>>> print(shopping_list)
['milk', 'eggs', 'bread', 'Snickerdoodles', 'butter']

>>> shopping_list.insert(1, "coffee")
>>> print(shopping_list)
['milk', 'coffee', 'eggs', 'bread', 'Snickerdoodles', 'butter']
```

Removing list items

If you need to prune a list, you can use the pop() method to either remove the item that's at the end of the list or remove an item at a specified index, or you can use the remove() method to remove the first item that matches a value that you specify:

```
list.pop([index])
list.remove(item)
```

where:

- >> *list* is the list object from which you want to remove the item.

- >> *index* is the position within *list* of the item you want to expunge. If you leave out *index*, pop() removes the last item in the list.

- >> *item* is the item you want to remove.

REMEMBER

Note that pop() not only removes an item from the list but also returns that item, which you could then store in a variable for later use.

Here are some examples (chapter06/example07.py):

```
>>> shopping_list = ["milk", "eggs", "bread", "Snickerdoodles"]

>>> last_item = shopping_list.pop()
>>> print(last_item)
Snickerdoodles

>>> print(shopping_list)
['milk', 'eggs', 'bread']

>>> first_item = shopping_list.pop(0)
>>> print(first_item)
milk

>>> print(shopping_list)
['eggs', 'bread']

>>> shopping_list.remove("eggs")
>>> print(shopping_list)
['bread']
```

Searching in a list

Want to know if something's in a list? Use the `in` keyword:

```
item in list
```

where:

- » *item* is the item you're looking for.
- » *list* is the list object in which you're looking.

If the item does appear somewhere in the list, the `in` expression returns `True`; otherwise, you get `False`. Here's an example (chapter06/example08.py):

```
>>> shopping_list = ["milk", "eggs", "bread", "Snickerdoodles"]

>>> print("bread" in shopping_list)
True

>>> print("rutabaga" in shopping_list)
False
```

More Ways to Store Stuff: Tuples and Dictionaries

When you're just getting started, there are two other Python data structures that you probably won't use all that often but are worth knowing in case you come across them in someone else's code. As you get more experienced with Python, you'll come to rely on these useful data structures (they're also Python data types): the tuple and the dictionary.

Storing unchanging data in a tuple

A *tuple* is a data structure that enables you to store multiple items in a single variable. Yes, I know, that sounds just like a list. However, there's one big difference: Tuples can't be changed (yep, the nerds insist on describing them as *immutable*). Once you forge a tuple, it's locked in. No changing items, no adding items, and no removing them. That sounds restrictive, but a tuple is a useful thing to have around when you're working with data that must never change.

For example, if you're making a game in which you have to track player positions on a 2D plane using (x, y) coordinates (where x is the horizontal position and y is the vertical position), the following conditions are true:

>> A given position only has just two values: x and y.

>> You don't want either x or y to be changed accidentally.

>> You don't want a third value added to the position.

>> You do want the capability to change both values at once (for example, when a player's position changes).

You can meet all these conditions by storing a player's current position in a tuple:

```
player_position = (125, 280)
```

Tuple values can be any valid Python data type, including strings, numbers, Booleans, lists, dictionaries (discussed in the next section), functions (refer to Chapter 7), and even other tuples. And, yes, you're free to mix and match data types within a single tuple.

As with lists, tuple values are indexed, with the first value at index 0, the second at index 1, and so on. You use the index in square brackets to extract that value from a tuple. Here's an example (chapter06/example09.py):

```python
player_position = (125, 280)
x = player_position[0]
y = player_position[1]
print(f"The player is at position ({x}, {y}).")
```

Python supports tuple *unpacking* where you assign variables to each item in the tuple. That is, rather than this:

```python
x = player_position[0]
y = player_position[1]
```

You can do this:

```python
x, y = player_position
```

You can't change a single element in a tuple, nor can you add elements to or delete elements from a tuple. What you *can* do is replace the entire tuple. So, for example, if the player's position changes, you can update the entire tuple:

```python
player_position = (160, 210)
```

What else can you do with a tuple? You can find out how many items it contains using len():

```python
>>> print(len(player_position))
2
```

Also, you can *iterate* (a fancy-schmancy programming term that means *loop*) through a tuple using a for loop, as in this example (chapter06/example10.py):

```python
quiz_answers = (
    "Rumpelstiltskin",
    "bullet bra",
    "antidisestablishmentarianism",
    "Senegalese",
    42)
for answer in quiz_answers:
    print(answer)
```

Looking up data in a dictionary

A *dictionary* is a data structure that enables you to store multiple items in a single variable. Yes, I know, that sounds just like a list or a tuple. However, in a dictionary, each item is actually a pair: the value you want to store and a label that describes the value. That label is called a *key*, so these pairs are known as *key-value pairs*.

That label is important because it can make your code more readable. For example, it's not at all clear what the following refers to:

```
person[0]
```

But even without looking at the rest of the code, it's pretty obvious what the following means:

```
person["age"]
```

Here are the general steps to follow to build a dictionary:

1. **Type an opening curly brace ({).**
2. **Type a key, which can be a string surrounded by quotation marks, a number, or a tuple.**

    You'll almost always use a string for the key. Also note that within a dictionary, the keys must be unique.
3. **Type a colon (:), a space, and then type the value, which can be any valid Python data type, including a string, number, Boolean, list, tuple, or even a dictionary.**
4. **Type a comma, then press Enter or Return.**
5. **Repeat Steps 2 through 4 for each item you want to store in the dictionary.**
6. **Type a closing curly brace (}).**

Here's an example to make things more concrete (chapter06/example11.py):

```
person = {
    "name": "Alice",
    "age": 30,
    "is_student": False
}
```

The keys are `"name"`, `"age"`, and `"is_student"`, and the values are `"Alice"`, 30, and `False`.

To get a value from a dictionary, use the key in square brackets:

```
>>> print(person["age"])
30
```

Dictionary values are changeable, and you update a value by setting its key to the new value:

```
>>> person["age"] = 31
```

You can also add a new key/value pair on-the-fly:

```
>>> person["email"] = "alice@somewhere.com"
```

You can use del to remove a key:

```
>>> del person["is_student"]
```

To iterate through a dictionary, you have a couple of choices. First, you can loop through just the keys:

```
for key in person:
    print(key)
```

Or you can loop through both the keys and the values:

```
for key, value in person.items():
    print(key, "=", value)
```

TECHNICAL STUFF

YET ANOTHER DATA STRUCTURE: SETS

One of the reasons pros such as data analysts and data scientists love Python is that it offers a seemingly endless menu of ways to store and mess around with data. So far in this chapter I've covered lists, tuples, and dictionaries. But you may hear Pythonistas talking about the "big four" data structures that every coder should know. What's missing? An occasionally handy data structure called the *set*, which stores only unique values and doesn't impose any order on its items.

You create a set by surrounding a comma-separated list of items (which can be numbers, strings, Booleans, or tuples) with braces ({ and }):

```
fave_fruits = {"peach", "apple", "orange", "cherry"}
```

You can then check if a value is in the set:

```python
if "apple" in fave_fruits:
    print("Apple is a favorite fruit!")
```

But perhaps the handiest use of sets is to extract just the unique values from a collection by running set(*collection*), where *collection* is a list, string, range, or tuple. Here's an example:

```python
str = "it was the best of times it was the worst of times"

# Extract the individual words into a list
words = str.split()

# Use set() to get just the unique words
unique_words = set(words)

print(unique_words)
```

Here's the output:

```python
{'best', 'was', 'the', 'worst', 'it', 'of', 'times'}
```

Conditionals in Python

As I mention in Chapter 2, the way you make your code do something smart is to create a conditional statement, where your code executes one or more statements only if a certain condition is met. In Python, you use three keywords to set up your conditionals: if, else, and elif.

The basic if statement

The simplest Python conditional involves using if all by itself:

```python
if expression:
    statement1;
    statement2;
    . . .
```

Here, *expression* is a comparison or logical expression that returns True or False, or a Boolean value. Note, too, that Python requires a colon (:) immediately after *expression*. Next, *statement1*, *statement2*, and so on represent the Python statement or statements the interpreter will run if *expression* returns True. If *expression* returns False, Python skips over the statements.

Here's an example (chapter06/example12.py):

```
score = int(input("What was your score? "))
if score >= 80:
    print(f"Wow, your score was {score}.")
    print("Nice job!")
```

If the condition (score >= 80) returns True, Python runs the two indented print() statements; otherwise, Python skips them.

REMEMBER

How does Python know which statements to run if the condition returns True? Those statements form the *if block*, and that block is defined as every statement after the colon (:) that is indented by the same number of spaces from the beginning of the if statement. In other words, in Python, indentation isn't an optional stylistic choice to make your code more readable — it's how Python knows what belongs to the if block.

REMEMBER

Python doesn't care how many spaces you use to indent, just as long as you use the same number of spaces within the block. For ideal readability of your code, the recommended number of indentation spaces is four.

Consider the following example (chapter06/example13.py):

```
is_raining = input("Is it raining (if not, just press Enter)? ")

if is_raining:
    print("Bring an umbrella!")
print("Have a great day!")
```

Pressing Enter (or Return) at the input() prompt returns an empty input that's equivalent to False; any other input (such as y, yes, or cats and dogs!) is equivalent to True. When the variable is_raining is True, the if statement prints Bring an umbrella! to the screen. However, since the next print() statement (the one that prints Have a great day!) isn't indented, it's not part of the if block, so it will run no matter whether the is_raining variable is True or False.

Adding an else statement

An if statement all by its lonesome runs one or more statements when its condition returns the value True and lightly leaps over those statements if the condition returns False. But what if, when the condition returns False, you want Python to run a *different* set of statements? Ah, to handle that scenario you need to augment the if statement with an else statement:

```
if expression:
    statement-if-true1;
    statement-if-true2;
    . . .
else:
    statement-if-false1;
    statement-if-false2;
    . . .
```

The *expression* is either a comparison or logical expression that returns True or False, or a Boolean. *statement-if-true1*, *statement-if-true2*, and so on define the block of statements that Python executes if *expression* returns True; *statement-if-false1*, *statement-if-false2*, and so on define the block of statements that Python executes if *expression* returns False.

Here's an example (chapter06/example14.py):

```
score = int(input("What was your score?"))

if score >= 80:
    print(f"Wow, your score was {score}")
    print("Nice job!")
else:
    print(f"Too bad, your score was {score}")
    print("Keep practicing!")
```

Even more choices with the elif statement

Making a this-or-that decision using if/else statements is extremely common in programming, so you'll turn to that structure again and again in your projects. But sometimes the world presents you with multiple conditions that your code has to somehow take into account. With a test score, for example, it's not enough to just check whether the score was greater than or equal to 80. Your code probably also has to check for scores greater than or equal to 90, 70, and so on.

When you need to check multiple conditions, that's where Python's `elif` (short for "else if") statement shines:

```
if expression1:
    statement-if-expression1-true1;
    statement-if-expression1-true2;
    ...
elif expression2:
    statement-if-expression2-true1;
    statement-if-expression2-true2;
    ...
else:
    statement-if-false1;
    statement-if-false2;
    ...
```

Python first tests *expression1*. If *expression1* returns True, Python runs the *statement-if-expression1-true* block and skips over everything else. If *expression1* returns False, Python then tests *expression2*. If *expression2* returns True, Python runs the *statement-if-expression2-true* block and skips over everything else. Otherwise, if all the `if` and `elif` tests return False, Python runs the *statement-if-false* block.

Feel free to add as many `elif` statements as you need. Here's an example (chapter06/example15.py):

```python
score = int(input("What was your score? "))

if score > 90:
    print(f"Woot, your score was {score}.")
    print("You get an A+")
elif score >= 80:
    print(f"Wow, your score was {score}.")
    print("You get an A.")
elif score >= 70:
    print(f"Not bad, your score was {score}.")
    print("You get a B.")
elif score >= 60:
    print(f"Okay, your score was {score}.")
    print("You get a C.")
elif score >= 50:
    print(f"Hmm, your score was {score}.")
    print("You get a D.")
```

```
else:
    print(f"Oh, snap, your score was {score}.")
    print("You get an F.")
```

Python Loops

As you code larger and more complex programs, one conundrum that will come up again and again is repetitious code. Here's an example (chapter06/example16.py):

```
shopping_list = ["milk", "eggs", "bread", "Snickerdoodles"]

print(f"Don't forget to buy {shopping_list[0]}")
print(f"Don't forget to buy {shopping_list[1]}")
print(f"Don't forget to buy {shopping_list[2]}")
print(f"Don't forget to buy {shopping_list[3]}")
```

This code displays the following:

```
Don't forget to buy milk
Don't forget to buy eggs
Don't forget to buy bread
Don't forget to buy Snickerdoodles
```

So, yep, the code works just fine, but all those `print()` statements are a drag to type. Imagine if the shopping list had a dozen items on it or *two* dozen. Forget about it!

Whenever you come across repetitive code like this, it's time to get Python to do some of the heavy lifting by using a *loop,* which is code that handles all the repetition for you.

Looping through a collection of things

One of the main types of Python loop is the `for` loop, which goes through every item in a collection, which could be just about any set of things you can define in Python, including a list, a string, a tuple, a dictionary, a set, or a range of numbers. Here's the general syntax:

```
for item in collection:
    statement1;
    statement2;
    ...
```

Here, *item* is a variable that stores an item from *collection* (which is a list, a string, a range, or another Python collection), and *statement1*, *statement2*, and so on represent the Python statements the interpreter will run for each item. These statements must be indented four spaces from the `for` statement.

Any item that you can loop through using `for` is known in the Python trade as an *iterable*.

Here's an example (chapter06/example17.py):

```
shopping_list = ["milk", "eggs", "bread", "Snickerdoodles"]

for product in shopping_list:
    print(f"Don't forget to buy {product}")
```

This code displays the following:

```
Don't forget to buy milk
Don't forget to buy eggs
Don't forget to buy bread
Don't forget to buy Snickerdoodles
```

Look at that: You get the same output as before, but you had to type the `print()` statement only once. Sweet! What's happening here is that Python is going through the items in `shopping_list` one by one. For each item, it stores the item's value in the `product` variable, which is then available to your code within the `for` block. The first time through the loop, `product` is given the value `milk`, the second time through `product` is set to `eggs`, and so on.

You can loop through strings too (chapter06/example18.py):

```
for letter in "Hello":
    print(letter)
```

Here's the output:

```
H
e
l
l
o
```

When you need to loop a set number of times, the range( ) function will get the job done (chapter06/example19.py):

```
for i in range(5):
    print(f"Loop number {i}")
```

Here's the output:

```
Loop number 0
Loop number 1
Loop number 2
Loop number 3
Loop number 4
```

Looping while a condition is True

The other main type of Python loop is the while loop, which repeats one or more statements as long as a specified condition returns True:

```
while expression:
    statement1;
    statement2;
    ...
```

Here, *expression* is a comparison or logical expression that returns True or False, or a Boolean value. *statement1*, *statement2*, and so on represent the Python statements the interpreter will run as long as *expression* returns True. (These statements must be indented four spaces from the while statement.) The general idea is something in the while block will update a value used in *expression*, such as a counter variable. Eventually, one pass through the while block will update that value in such a way that *expression* now returns False instead of True, and the while loop ends.

Here's an example (chapter06/example20.py):

```
counter = 0

while counter < 3:
    print(f"The loop counter is now: {counter}")
    counter += 1
```

This code initializes a variable named `counter` to 0. In the `while` statement, the expression `counter < 3` returns `True`, so Python runs the statements inside the `while` block: The current value of `counter` is printed and then the value of `counter` is increased by 1. The code then loops back to the `while` statement, rechecks the `counter < 3` expression, and repeats for as long as that expression returns `True`. After the third time through the loop, the value of `counter` is now 3, which means `counter < 3` returns `False` and the loop shuts down.

Here's the output

```
The loop counter is now: 0
The loop counter is now: 1
The loop counter is now: 2
```

Interrupting loop execution

TIP

If you ever need to exit a loop before it's finished, use the `break` statement (chapter06/example21.py):

```python
while True:
    value = input("Type a number (or q to quit): ")
    if value == "q":
        break
    else:
        print(f"The cube of your number is {int(value) ** 3}")
```

This code uses `while True` to set up an endless loop. After getting a value from the user, the code uses `if` to check whether that value was `"q"` (for quit). If it was, the code uses `break` to quit the loop; otherwise, it continues with the rest of the loop.

A slightly different case is when you need a loop to skip the rest of the code in the current loop because of some condition. To skip the rest of a loop and return to the beginning, use the `continue` statement (chapter06/example22.py):

```python
tax_factors = [1.05, 1.08, 1.04, 0.00, 1.03]
price = 100.00
for factor in tax_factors:
    if factor == 0:
        continue
    else:
        original_price = price / factor
        tax_rate = int((factor - 1) * 100)
        print(f"The price less {tax_rate}% tax is ${original_price:.2f}")
```

This code loops through the items in the `tax_factors` list. If it comes across an item that equals 0, it uses `continue` to skip the rest of the loop (and thereby avoid an illegal division by zero) and return to the beginning for the next item. Here's the output:

```
The price less 5% tax is $95.24
The price less 8% tax is $92.59
The price less 4% tax is $96.15
The price less 3% tax is $97.09
```

Adding Comments to Your Code

I discuss comments in general in Chapter 2. Python keeps comments simple by offering just a single symbol to indicate the start of a comment: #, the hash or pound sign.

You can add single-line comments that appear on their own line in your code, or inline comments which appear on the same line as some code. The following example (chapter06/example23.py) demonstrates both types:

```
# Initialize the counter
counter = 0

# Loop as long as the counter is less than 3
while counter < 3:
    print(f"The loop counter is now: {counter}")
    counter += 1  # Increment the counter
```

Example: Build Your Own Survey Bot

To complete this chapter, I offer the following example (chapter06/example24. py), which demonstrates most of the concepts I present in this chapter and Chapter 5, including variables, data types, expressions, strings, lists, conditionals, and loops. I added lots of comments to help you understand what the code is doing.

```
# Simple Survey Analyzer

print("Welcome to the Super Quick Survey!")
```

```python
print("---------------------------------")

# Store the survey questions in a list
questions = [
    "What's your name? ",
    "How old are you? ",
    "What's your favorite programming language so far? "
]

# Create an empty list to store the answers
answers = []

# Loop through the questions
for question in questions:

    # Get the answer to the next question
    answer = input(question)

    # Add the answer to the answers list
    answers.append(answer)

# Unpack the answers into variables
name = answers[0]
age = int(answers[1])
language = answers[2]

# Respond based on their input
# The \n in the string prints a blank line
print(f"\nThanks, {name}! Here's your survey summary:\n")

print(f"You are {age} years old.")

# Add some conditional feedback
# about their age
if age < 18:
    print("You're off to an early start - awesome!")
elif age > 60:
    print("Proving it's never too late to learn!")
else:
    print("Perfect time in life to be learning something new!")
```

```python
print(f"\nYou enjoy coding in {language}.")

# Add some conditional feedback about
# their programming language choice
if language.lower() == "python":
    print("Great choice - Python is beginner-friendly and powerful!")
elif language.lower() == "javascript":
    print("Nice! JavaScript makes the web come alive.")
else:
    print(f"{language}? Very cool. Every language has its own superpower.")

print("\nThanks for taking the survey!")
```

IN THIS CHAPTER

» **Defining and calling functions**

» **Wrapping your head around variable scope**

» **Installing and importing Python modules**

» **Working with external code libraries**

» **Reusing data stored in files**

Chapter **7**

Reusing Code

Good programmers know what to write. Great ones know what to reuse.

— ERIC S. RAYMOND

One of the secrets to programming productivity is also one of the oldest pieces of advice in the world: *Don't reinvent the wheel!* If you or someone else has already solved a particular programming puzzle, use that solution instead of re-solving the puzzle every time you come across it.

Avoiding reinventing wheels in coding generally involves reusing existing code as much as possible. If you've already written some code, you can structure it so that you can easily reuse it elsewhere. If you find code in one of Python's public code repositories, you can bring that code into your Python file.

This chapter marks a turning point in your Python path where you go from writing the one-off bits of code in Chapters 5 and 6 to creating efficient, reusable, and powerful programs. This chapter is all about teaching you how to use functions to break your code into reusable chunks; how to use modules to expand your Python toolkit without having to write new code; how to use libraries to borrow useful tools that others have made; and how to reuse data by writing it to and reading it from files.

Making Your Code More Efficient with Functions

One of the superpowers of a good coder is to always be on the lookout for inefficient places in your code. If you've declared a bunch of variables for similar data, perhaps you could bring all those variables into a single list (covered in Chapter 6). If you have to repeat some code for each item in a string or list or for a specified number of times, write the code once and wrap it in a `for` or `while` loop (also covered in Chapter 6).

Another way to write ridiculously efficient code is to look for a collection of statements that you need to run frequently. For example, suppose your program, given a price, needs to calculate a final cost that includes tax and shipping. Here's an example (in this book's example files, check out chapter07/example01.py):

```python
# Get the price
price = float(input("Enter the price: "))

# Calculate 7% tax
tax = price * 0.07

# Is the price at least $50?
if price >= 50:

    # If so, charge a flat rate for shipping
    shipping = 5.00
else:

    # Otherwise, charge 10% of the price for shipping
    shipping = price * 0.1

# Calculate the total
total = price + tax + shipping

print(f"Total with tax and shipping: ${total:.2f}")
```

TIP

You might be wondering what the symbols `:.2f` are doing in the f-string in the final statement. The colon (`:`) indicates formatting instructions are coming up; the `.2` tells Python to output exactly two digits after the decimal; and the `f` formats the number as a floating-point value.

That code works fine for a single price, but what if you have to calculate the total for ten prices, or a hundred? Not fun! The efficient solution is to wrap the code inside a function, which has the following general syntax in Python:

```
def function_name([arguments]):
    statement1
    statement2
    ...
    return value
```

where:

- >> def: Identifies the block of code that follows it as a function. def is short for *define*.

- >> *function_name*: A unique name for the function. The naming rules and guidelines that I outline for variables in Chapter 5 also apply to function names.

- >> *arguments*: Optional one or more comma-separated values that are passed to the function and act as variables within the function. If you don't use arguments, you must still include the parentheses after the function name.

- >> *statement1*, *statement2*, and so on: The code that performs the function's tasks or calculations.

- >> return *value*: Sends *value* back as the result of the function, where *value* is something calculated or in some other way determined by your function statements. Note that if the function doesn't use a return value, you can forgo the return statement.

As with conditionals and loops (refer to Chapter 6), you tell Python which statements are included in the function by indenting them (four spaces is the standard indentation).

To run a function, your code uses the function name, followed by the arguments in parentheses, if any. (If the function doesn't require arguments, you still need to include the parentheses.) Here's an example (chapter07/example02.py):

```
def get_user_name():
    name = input("What's your name? ")
    return name

your_name = get_user_name()
print(f"Nice to meet you, {your_name}!")
```

This code defines a `get_user_name()` function, which prompts the user for their name and then returns that name. When the function is called using `get_user_name()`, the return value is store in the `your_name` variable, which is then printed to the screen.

For the earlier example of calculating a total including tax and shipping, all the calculation code can go inside a function. In the following code (chapter07/example03.py), I shoehorned the calculations inside a function named `calculate_total()`:

```python
def calculate_total(price):

    # Calculate 7% tax
    tax = price * 0.07

    # Is the price at least $50?
    if price >= 50:

        # If so, charge a flat rate for shipping
        shipping = 5.00
    else:

        # Otherwise, charge 10% of the price for shipping
        shipping = price * 0.1

    # Calculate the total
    total = price + tax + shipping

    # Return the total
    return total

counter = 0

while (counter < 3):
    # Get the price
    price = float(input("Enter the price: "))

    # Get the total with tax and shipping
    total = calculate_total(price)

    print(f"Total with tax and shipping: ${total:.2f}")

    counter += 1
```

Following the function, a `while` loop asks for a price and then calls `calculate_total()` with `price` as the argument. The function result is stored in the `total` variable, which is then printed to the screen as before. The loop repeats this two more times before quitting. I added the loop to demonstrate that with the calculation code handily stored in the `calculate_total()` function, you can reuse that function as many times as you need.

WARNING

Because Python is an interpreted language, it reads your code from top to bottom, like reading a recipe as you cook. So, if you try to call a function before it's defined, Python will look confused and throw an error. That's why, in the examples I've shown so far, the statements that call the function come after the function.

Getting the Hang of Variable Scope

You may be tempted to think that once you declare a variable, you can then use that variable anywhere later in the same program. It makes sense. For example, suppose you declare a variable as the first statement of a function inside your program. Python is an interpreted language that processes one statement at a time from top to bottom, so once Python has processed your function variable declaration, you should be able to use that variable as needed anywhere later in the program, all the way to the end of the file. Right?

Nope. Welcome to the world of variable scope, where you learn who can access what, when, and where.

What is variable scope, anyway?

Variable scope — often shortened to just *scope* — defines where in the program a variable can be used and where it can't be used. To put it another way, a variable's scope determines which statements and functions can access and work with the variable. Scope, then, is just a fancy way of saying, "Where does this variable exist?" or "Where can this variable be used?"

You definitely want to care about scope in your Python scripts for several reasons:

>> **You may need to use the same variable in multiple functions.** For example, a function may use a variable to store the result of a calculation, and other functions may also need to use that result. In this case, you'd set up the scope of the variable so that it's accessible to multiple functions.

>> **You may want to use the same variable name in multiple functions.** If these variables are otherwise unrelated, you'll want to make sure that there is no confusion about which variable you're working with. In other words, you'll restrict the scope of each variable to the function in which it is declared.

>> **It helps with debugging.** When a Python program zigs instead of zags, understanding the scope of the variables involved can be crucial to figuring out the problem.

Python lets you establish two types of scope for your variables:

>> Global scope

>> Function scope

The next two sections describe each type in detail.

Global: The "everyone's invited" scope

When a variable has *global scope*, the variable has the following properties:

>> The variable is declared outside any function.

>> The variable is available to be used in any statement after the declaration.

>> In particular, the variable is available to be used inside any function defined after the variable declaration.

Here's an example (chapter07/example04.py):

```
message = "Hello, scope world!"  # global variable

def greet():
    print(message)  # works just fine

greet()
```

Here, even though the `print(message)` statement resides in the `greet()` function, that function can still access the `message` variable because it was defined outside any function and therefore has global scope.

Local: The "for function eyes only" scope

When a variable has *local scope*, the variable has the following properties:

» The variable is declared inside a function.

» The variable is available to be used in any statement that comes after the declaration in the same function.

» The variable is unavailable to any statements outside that function.

Here's an example (chapter07/example05.py):

```python
def greet():
    user_name = input("What's your name? ") # local variable
    print(f"Hi, {user_name}!")  # works just fine

greet()

print(user_name)  # Not gonna happen
```

Here's a sample output:

```
What's your name? Dweezil
Hi, Dweezil!
Traceback (most recent call last):
  File "chapter07/example05.py", line 7, in <module>
    print(user_name)  # Not gonna happen
          ^^^^^^^^^
NameError: name 'user_name' is not defined
```

Whoops! Here, the `user_name` variable is declared in the `greet()` function. This declaration makes `user_name` a local variable, so the `print()` statement in the `greet()` function works as expected. However, when the code tries to use the `user_name` variable outside the function in the final `print()` statement, the Python interpreter implodes with `NameError: name 'user_name' is not defined` because outside the function, Python has no idea what `user_name` is — that variable lives and dies inside `greet()`.

WARNING

So why not just make everything a global variable? That may seem like a reasonable way to go, and it's true that global variables can be handy. However, if you use them too much, your code gets messy and hard to manage. It's like leaving all your clothes on the floor instead of putting them in drawers. If a variable is only ever used inside a function, make it a local variable and save global variables for those relatively rare times you need a value throughout your program.

Here's an example (chapter07/example06.py) that demonstrates when you should use a global variable:

```python
app_title = "Awesome App"   # Global variable

def show_welcome():
    print(f"Welcome to {app_title}!")

def show_goodbye():
    print(f"Thanks for using {app_title}! Goodbye!")

show_welcome()
show_goodbye()
```

Here's the output:

```
Welcome to Awesome App!
Thanks for using Awesome App! Goodbye!
```

In this example, the `app_title` variable has global scope, so both functions can use the variable without any problem.

Avoiding Wheel Reinvention with Modules

When you get some experience with Python, you'll start noticing all kinds of puzzles in the form of what appear to be gaps in the language. How do you calculate how many days are between two dates? How do you calculate the square root of a number? How do you find the mean or the standard deviation of a list of numbers? How do you generate a random number between 1 and 6 to simulate a dice roll for a game?

Sure, with a lot of effort and a lot of Googling you might be able to solve these puzzles yourself, but you'd just be reinventing some very difficult wheels. That's because Python comes with an impressively large toolbox full of prewritten code, all of which is available for you to use in your Python programs. This toolbox is called the *standard library,* and you access this library using special Python files called modules.

A *module* is a file containing prefab Python code — such as functions or constants — that you can bring into any project instead of writing the code from scratch. There are modules available to plug all the "gaps" I just mentioned:

>> The datetime module enables you to work with dates and times, including calculating the number of days between two dates.

>> The math module offers a huge number of math-related functions, including one that calculates the square root of a number.

>> The statistics module provides a ton of stats functions, including ones that calculate the arithmetic mean and the standard deviation of a sample.

>> The random module offers functions for generating random values, including one function that can generate a random integer between any two values.

REMEMBER

Who codes all these modules? Most of what you'll find in the standard library is created and maintained by the Python Software Foundation (PSF) and a team of core Python developers from around the world. It's a community-driven effort, and many of the modules have been around (and evolving) for years. So, as you dive into these modules, if you ever find yourself thinking, "Dang, this is handy," remember that you're standing on the shoulders of giants — dedicated and skilled Python coders who built a bunch of useful tools so you don't have to.

TIP

To browse a complete list of the modules available in the standard library, surf to https://docs.python.org/3/library/. Here you find modules organized by category, including data types, numeric and mathematical modules, generic operating system services, and internet data handling.

Want a sneak peek? Here's a tiny sample:

Module	Used For
math	Math functions and constants
random	Random numbers and choices
datetime	Manipulating dates and times
os	Interacting with the operating system
sys	Getting info about the Python system
time	Sleep, timestamps, and more
statistics	Calculating mean, median, and other stats
json	Working with JSON data (refer to Chapter 8)

Importing a module

Python's standard library modules are separate parts of the language, and to use any module you must import it into your Python program. To *import* a module means to make the module's code available to your Python program.

To import an entire module, you have two choices:

```
import module
import module as alias
```

where:

>> *module* is the name of the module in the standard library.

>> *alias* is a nickname that you use to refer to the module instead of the name *module*. In most cases, your alias will be something shorter or easier to type (or both) than the module's name.

For example, to import the statistics module, you'd include the following in your Python program (usually at the top of the file):

```
import statistics
```

Alternatively, you can import statistics using an alias, such as stats:

```
import statistics as stats
```

TIP

After you import a module, you can display a list of all the stuff inside that module by running the print(dir(*module*)) statement, where *module* is the name of the imported module:

```
import math
print(dir(math))
```

Using a module

Once you've imported a module, it's available to your program as an object. That means you can use Python's standard dot notation to access all the goodies the module provides, such as functions, constants, data structures (such as lists), and classes (refer to Chapter 8):

```
module.function()
module.constant
module.list
module.class
```

Here, `module` is the name of the imported module or its alias, and `function()`, `constant`, `list`, or `class` is the name of the module element you want to use.

For example, the `statistics` module offers a `mean()` function that returns the arithmetic mean of some collection of numbers. The following code (chapter07/example07.py) puts that function through its paces:

```
# Import the statistics module to use the mean() function
import statistics

# Store the test scores in a list
test_scores = [77, 65, 82, 71, 90, 53, 68, 79, 47, 77]

# Calculate the mean value of the test scores
test_mean = statistics.mean(test_scores)

print(test_mean) # Output: 70.9
```

WHAT HAPPENS WHEN YOU IMPORT A MODULE?

TECHNICAL STUFF

Suppose you include something like the following in your code:

```
import math
```

What's really happening here? Behind the scenes, Python performs the following steps:

1. It finds the `math.py` file in the standard library.

2. It loads and runs the `math.py` code.

3. It creates a module object, which acts like a container full of whatever functions, classes, and constants are defined in the module.

4. It assigns the name `math` to that container. If you specify an alias with the `import` statement, Python assigns that alias to the container, instead.

Now your module is ready for action.

The key here is the second-last statement, which uses `statistics.mean(test_scores)` to run the `statistics` module's `mean()` function on the `test_scores` list.

Similarly, a common bit of logic needed in certain games is calculating the distance between two points on the 2D plane. If both points are represented as (x, y) tuples (refer to Chapter 6), you take the difference between the x values, square that difference, take the difference between the y values, square that difference, sum those two squares, and then take the square root of that sum. This is the good old Pythagorean theorem in action. Here's some code (chapter07/example08.py) that implements this algorithm:

```python
# Import the math module to use the sqrt() function
import math

# Define two points as (x, y) tuples
point1 = (3, 4)
point2 = (7, 1)

# Calculate the difference between the x values
dx = point2[0] - point1[0]

# Calculate the difference between the y values
dy = point2[1] - point1[1]

# Apply the Pythagorean theorem:
# distance = √(dx² + dy²)
distance = math.sqrt(dx**2 + dy**2)

print(f"The distance between the points is: {distance:.2f}")
```

Importing part of a module

You don't always have to import an entire module. Your code will be a little cleaner and easier to understand if you import just the part of the module — such as a particular function, constant, or class — you need:

```python
from module import element
```

Here, `module` is the name of the module and `element` is the name of the module element you want to import. When you import only part of a module, you no longer need to use the dot notation; just refer to the `element` name directly.

For example, the previous code (chapter07/example08.py) requires only the `sqrt()` function, so the `import` statement could have been this:

```
from math import sqrt
```

In that case, the distance calculation changes to this:

```
distance = sqrt(dx**2 + dy**2)
```

TIP

You can specify more than one element. If you do, be sure to separate them with commas, as in this example:

```
from math import sqrt, pi, pow
```

As a final example, here's some code (chapter07/example09.py) that uses the `date` class of the `datetime` module to get the user's birth date, and then calculates the user's age, in days:

```
# Import just the date class from the datetime module
from datetime import date

# Get today's date
today = date.today()

# Ask the user for their birth date
year = int(input("Enter the year you were born (e.g., 1990): "))
month = int(input("Enter the month you were born (1-12): "))
day = int(input("Enter the day you were born (1-31): "))

# Create a date object for the birth date
birth_date = date(year, month, day)

# Calculate the difference between today and the birth date
days_old = (today - birth_date).days

print(f"You are {days_old} days old!")
```

Here are the main highlights of this code:

>> Just the `date` class is imported from the `datetime` module.

>> The `date.today()` function returns today's date.

>> The user is asked to input their birth year, month, and day.

>> The `date()` constructor creates a new `date` object from the user's input.

>> The birth date is subtracted from today to produce a `timedelta` object, which represents the difference between two dates.

>> The `timedelta` object's days property returns how many whole days are in that difference.

Here's a sample output:

```
Enter the year you were born (e.g., 1990): 2000
Enter the month you were born (1-12): 1
Enter the day you were born (1-31): 1
You are 9322 days old!
```

Rolling your own modules

Although you'll usually import modules from Python's standard library, nothing is stopping you from building your own library of reusable Python code and using `import` to bring any part of that library into your projects.

Creating and using your own modules requires just three steps:

1. **Create a text file and populate it with the functions, constants, lists, and other data that you want to make available to other Python files.**

2. **Save your text file as a Python (`.py`) file.**

   For simplicity's sake, save this module in the same folder as whatever file or files you'll be using to import the module.

3. **In another Python file, import your module by adding the statement `import` *module*, where *module* is the name of the file you saved in Step 2 minus the `.py` extension.**

For example, suppose I copy the `calculate_price()` function (from the "Making Your Code More Efficient with Functions" section) and save it in a file named `my_module.py` (chapter07/my_module.py):

```
def calculate_total(price):

    # Calculate 7% tax
    tax = price * 0.07

    # Is the price at least $50?
```

```
        if price >= 50:

            # If so, charge a flat rate for shipping
            shipping = 5.00
        else:

            # Otherwise, charge 10% of the price for shipping
            shipping = price * 0.1

        # Calculate the total
        total = price + tax + shipping

        # Return the total
        return total
```

Here's the code from a separate file (chapter07/example10.py):

```
import my_module

counter = 0

while (counter < 3):
    # Get the price
    price = float(input("Enter the price: "))

    # Get the total with tax and shipping
    total = my_module.calculate_total(price)

    print(f"Total with tax and shipping: ${total:.2f}")

    counter += 1
```

This code imports `my_module`, and then uses `my_module.calculate_total()` to call the module's `calculate_total()` function.

Reuse Heaven: Installing External Libraries

Python comes with a ton of useful built-in features, and importing modules from Python's standard library (which I cover in the preceding section) gives you access to a wide range of powerful tools. Depending on the types of projects you're looking to build, having these two code sources at your disposal may give you everything you need.

But probably not.

If you have a project that grabs data from a website or a server; displays attractive charts; works with Excel files; involves building a chatbot; or is related to creating any kind of reasonably sophisticated game, you're going to need some help.

Fortunately, that help is almost always just a few clicks away in the form of an external library. An *external library* is custom Python code that someone wrote and shared with the world. These libraries aren't included with Python by default, nor are they part of Python's standard library, but you can download and install them in seconds. Think of them as plug-ins or expansion packs for your Python powers.

Most Python libraries live on the Python Package Index (PyPI), which is like the App Store for Python code. You can browse and search the entire index of libraries by steering your favorite browser to https://pypi.org. Be warned, though: The site is home to hundreds of thousands (yes, you read that right: *hundreds of thousands*) of libraries — everything from game engines to machine learning toolkits.

Installing a library

Python includes a tool called pip (short for Pip Installs Packages; yep, it's another one of those recursive acronyms; refer also to PHP in Chapter 3). pip is your personal library installer.

To install a library, you open your terminal or command prompt, exit the Python REPL if you have a session running, and type the following:

```
pip install library
```

In macOS Terminal, you may need to run this command, instead:

```
pip3 install library
```

Here, replace *library* with the name of the Python library you want to install. For example, one of the most popular libraries is requests, which enables a Python program to make requests to websites and application programming interfaces (APIs). Refer to Chapter 8 for the details about APIs and the request library. For now, know that you install requests by running the following command at the terminal:

```
pip install requests
```

Or, in macOS Terminal:

```
pip3 install requests
```

Importing and using a library

Once you've convinced `pip` to install a library, you use the library in your Python code just as though it was a module. That is, you first import the library using the `import` statement:

```
import library
import library as alias
```

where:

>> `library` is the name of the installed library.

>> `alias` is a nickname that you use to refer to the library instead of the name `library`. In most cases, your alias will be something shorter or easier to type (or both) than the library's name.

For example:

```
import requests
```

You then use dot notation to access the library's functions, constants, lists, and classes:

```
library.function()
library.constant
library.list
library.class
```

Here's an example (check out chapter07/example11.py) that uses `requests.get` to connect to the Random Joke API:

```
import requests

# Get a random joke
```

```
response = requests.get("https://official-joke-api.appspot.com/random_joke")

if response.status_code == 200:
    print("I was able to connect to the API no problem.")
else:
    print("Something went wrong. This is not a joke.")
```

For a version of this code that not only explains what's happening here but also gets and displays a random joke, refer to Chapter 8.

Reusing Data by Writing and Reading Files

In Chapter 6 I talk about storing data in a list, a tuple, and a dictionary. These data structures are extremely useful, but their utility ends when the program's done. That is, if you've plopped some data in a list or whatever, that data evaporates as soon as the Python interpreter executes the final statement of the program.

This chapter has been all about reusing code both to make your programs more efficient and more powerful and to make coding those programs much faster and easier. But all the benefits of reusing code apply equally to reusing data — and the more data you have, the greater the benefit.

But how do you reuse data? The key is to store that data in its own file outside any Python program. You can use Python to write the data to its own file, or you might already have data in some format, such as a text file. Python also offers ways to read the data in that file, which enables you to reuse the data by bringing it into any Python program.

Reading and writing files turns your little Python script into something that can

>> Save data between runs

>> Keep a log of user activity

>> Save and load settings or configurations

>> Store progress in a game or project

>> Generate reports

>> Build real-world tools like notepads or file converters

In this section, you learn how to work with files on your computer using Python, so your programs can save and retrieve — in short, *reuse* — data, just like the pros.

Opening a file

In Python, you work with files using the open( ) function:

```
open(file, mode)
```

where:

» *file* is the name of the file you want to work with, surrounded by quotation marks. If the file is in the same folder as your program, just provide the filename. Otherwise, you need to specify the path to the file.

» *mode* is an optional letter, surrounded by quotation marks, that indicates how you want Python to open the file. Most of the time, you'll use either w (for write mode; refer to "Writing data to a file") or r (for read mode, which is the default; refer to "Reading data from a file").

You always use open( ) in the following context:

```
with open(file, mode) as alias:
    statement1
    statement2
    ...
```

where:

» *alias* is a temporary name you use in your code to refer to the file you opened.

» *statement1*, *statement2*, and so on represent the code you use to manipulate the open file in some way. Note that each of these statements must be indented from the with statement by the same number of spaces.

When the with block is complete, Python automatically closes the file.

Writing data to a file

To write some data to a file, the open( ) function uses "w" (short for *write*) as the *mode* argument and the with block uses the open file object's write( ) method to write a string to the open file. Here's an example (chapter07/example12.py):

```
with open("limerick.txt", "w") as file:
    file.write("Limerick #1\n")
    file.write("There once was a coder named Ray\n")
    file.write("Who wrote Python all night and day\n")
```

```
file.write("Through one missing colon\n")
file.write("His sanity was stolen\n")
file.write("Now code just makes him run away\n")
file.write("\n")
```

This code opens a file named `limerick.txt` in write mode ("w") using the alias `file`. If `limerick.txt` doesn't exist, Python creates it; if `limerick.txt` does exist, Python overwrites it (so you want to be careful here that you don't overwrite a file you don't want to trash). Then a series of `file.write()` methods writes a few strings to the open file. The \n text at the end of each string is called the *newline* character and ensures that the next string added to the file begins on its own line.

TIP

If you have an existing file, you may prefer to add new content to it rather than overwriting it. No problem! Just open the file in append mode, where your `open()` function uses `"a"` (short for *append*) as the *mode* argument (chapter07/example13.py):

```
with open("limerick.txt", "a") as file:
    file.write("Limerick #2\n")
```

Reading data from a file

If you have an existing file that has data you want to use in a program, you can read the contents of that file by using the `open()` function with `"r"` (short for *read*) as the *mode* argument. The `with` block uses the open file object's `read()` method to grab the entire contents of the open file. Here's an example (chapter07/example14.py):

```
with open("limerick.txt", "r") as file:
    content = file.read()
    print(content)
```

This example opens the `limerick.txt` file from the preceding section in read mode ("r") using the alias `file`. The `file.read()` method grabs everything from the file and stores it in the `content` variable, which is then printed.

REMEMBER

Read mode is the default, so if you leave out the *mode* argument, Python assumes you want to open the file in read mode.

Sometimes it's better to read a file one line at a time. You can do that with ease using a `for` loop that runs through each line in the open file (chapter07/example15.py):

```
with open("limerick.txt", "r") as file:
    for line in file:
        no_newline = line.strip()
        print(no_newline)
```

The `strip()` method removes whitespace characters at the beginning and end of a string. In this case, `strip()` removes each newline character that Python automatically adds to the end of each line, so you don't get empty spaces between lines.

It's often useful to read all the file data at once and append each line of the file as an item in a list. You can do that with the file object's `readlines()` method. Here's an example (chapter07/example16.py):

```
with open("limerick.txt", "r") as file:
    lines = file.readlines()
    for line in lines:
        print(line.strip())
```

Example: Building a Quotations Archive

To complete this chapter, this section presents some code for an example program that creates and maintains an archive of quotations. The archive is stored in a text file, uses several modules from the standard library, and corrals most of the code into functions to keeps things organized and readable.

Here's the full code (chapter07/example17.py):

```
# Import the necessary modules
import random
from datetime import date

# Create a constant for the name of the text file
QUOTATIONS_FILE = "quotations.txt"

# This function displays the app menu
```

```python
def show_menu():
    print("\nWelcome to the Quotations Archive!\n")
    print("What would you like to do?")
    print("1. View all quotations")
    print("2. Add a new quotation")
    print("3. Get a random quotation")
    print("4. Quit")


# This function reads the quotations from the file
# and returns them as a list
def read_quotations():
    # Start with an empty list
    quotations = []

    # Check if the file exists before trying to read it
    if not file_exists(QUOTATIONS_FILE):
        # If the file doesn't exist, return an empty list
        return quotations

    # Open the file in read mode
    with open(QUOTATIONS_FILE, "r") as file:
        # Read each line from the file
        for line in file:
            # Strip whitespace and add the line to the list
            quotations.append(line.strip())

    # Return the list of quotations
    return quotations


# This function checks if the file exists
# and returns True or False
def file_exists(filename):

    # Import the os module to check for file existence
    import os

    # Use os.path.exists to check if the file exists
    # and return the result
    return os.path.exists(filename)


# This function saves a new quotation to the file
def save_quotation(quotation):
    # Open the file in append mode
    with open(QUOTATIONS_FILE, "a") as file:
```

```python
        # Get the current date and format it
        # and format it as YYYY-MM-DD
        today = date.today().isoformat()

        # Write the quotation and the date to the file
        file.write(f"{quotation} (added on {today})\n")

# This function asks for a new quotation
def add_new_quotation():

    # Prompt the user for a new quotation
    quotation = input("Enter your quotation: ")

    # Save the quotation to the file
    save_quotation(quotation)

    # Inform the user that it has been saved
    print("Quotation saved!")

# This function displays all saved quotations
def view_all_quotations():

    # Read the quotations from the file
    quotations = read_quotations()

    # Check if there are any quotations
    if not quotations:
        # If not, inform the user
        print("No quotations saved yet.")
    else:
        # If there are, display them
        print("\nYour saved quotations:")
        for quotation in quotations:
            print(f"- {quotation}")

# This function displays a random quotation
def show_random_quotation():
    # Read the quotations from the file
    quotations = read_quotations()
```

```python
    # Check if there are any quotations
    if not quotations:
        # If not, inform the user
        print("No quotations to show. Try adding some first!")
    else:
        # If there are, choose one at random
        # and display it
        print("\nHere's a random quotation:")
        print(random.choice(quotations))


# This function is the main loop of the program
def main():
    # Loop until the user chooses to quit
    while True:

        # Show the menu and get the user's choice
        show_menu()
        choice = input("Choose an option (1-4): ")

        # Check the user's choice,
        # then call the appropriate function
        if choice == "1":
            # Display all the quotations
            view_all_quotations()
        elif choice == "2":
            # Prompt for a new quotation
            add_new_quotation()
        elif choice == "3":
            # Display a random quotation
            show_random_quotation()
        elif choice == "4":
            # Exit the program
            print("Goodbye! Keep those quotations coming.")
            # Exit the loop to quit the program
            break
        else:
            # Handle a choice that's not 1-4
            print("Invalid option. Please try again.")


# Run the main function to start the program
main()
```

The code is liberally sprinkled with comments, so it should be straightforward to follow what it's doing. Here are a few not-so-straightforward things to watch out for:

» The archive file (quotations.txt) must be in the same folder as the Python file.

» The name of the archive file (quotations.txt) is used several times in the code. To avoid having to edit all those instances if you decide to change the filename, the program defines the constant QUOTATIONS_FILE and sets it equal to the filename as a string. Using all-uppercase letters for the names of constants is standard programming practice.

» The file_exists() function imports the os module and uses the path object's exists() method to determine whether the quotations archive file exists.

» In the show_random_quotation() function, the random module's choice() function is used to grab a random item from the list of quotations.

» The main() function defines the overall logic of the program, which is a common Python organizing structure. In this program, main() uses a while True loop to display the menu, prompt the user to choose a menu option, and handle the input by calling the appropriate function. Using while True means the loop runs until the user cancels the program by choosing the Quit menu option. At that point, the while loop is exited by running the break statement.

» Coding the Pythonic way

» Swooning over list comprehensions

» Hitting the big-time with object-
oriented programming

» Connecting with APIs

» Debugging your code

Chapter **8**

Expanding Your Python Skills

The code you write makes you a programmer. The code you delete makes you a good one. The code you don't have to write makes you a great one.

—MARIO FUSCO

P ython fundamentals such as variables, lists, conditionals, and loops (the topics of Chapters 5 and 6), and ever-so-slightly-more-advanced topics such as functions, modules, libraries, and file handling (the topics of Chapter 7), enable you to create a wide variety of honest-to-goodness programs. Even if you never learn another speck of Python, you now have coding skills that will last you a lifetime.

But with that nicely stocked Python toolbox at your disposal, the programs you code may lack a certain something and feel a bit, well, limited. I'm pretty sure you're not going to the trouble of reading this book just to write limited code! On the contrary, my assumption is you picked up this book because you have ambitions that include writing powerful programs that do useful things.

That, I'm happy to report, is totally doable! What has to happen now is that you need to expand your Python repertoire to match your ambitions. And adding to your Python toolkit is what this chapter is all about. In this chapter, you dive into the deep end of Python by exploring list comprehensions, object-oriented programming, APIs, handling errors, and debugging your programs. By the time you're done, you might need to level up your ambitions to match your new skills!

Waxing Pythonic

If you spend even a little time around Python coders either online or off, you'll come across the adjective *Pythonic* quite a bit. *Pythonic* describes code that follows the spirit, style, and best practices of Python. In other words, Pythonic code is

>> **Clean,** meaning the code is easy to read and understand.

>> **Concise,** meaning the code does what it needs to with minimal fuss.

>> **Expressive,** meaning the code clearly shows the intent of the author.

>> **Elegant,** meaning the code avoids clunky, repetitive patterns.

A collection of guiding principles for writing Python code called the Zen of Python also reflects the Pythonic way:

Beautiful is better than ugly.

Explicit is better than implicit.

Simple is better than complex.

Complex is better than complicated.

Readability counts.

There should be one — and preferably only one — obvious way to do it.

TIP

To see the full list of principles in the Zen of Python, head over to the terminal, start a new Python interpreter session, type **import this,** and press Enter or Return.

For example, suppose you have a list named `recipe` that includes all the ingredients in a recipe. The unPythonic way to loop through the list is to use a counter, which is a common structure in many other programming languages:

```
for i in range(len(recipe)):
    print(recipe[i])
```

It takes a bit of effort to figure out what this code is even doing! Now check out the Pythonic version:

```
for ingredient in recipe:
    print(ingredient)
```

Ah, that's better. That's straightforward, efficient, readable — in a word, *Pythonic* — code.

Comprehending List Comprehensions

By now, you've probably spent some quality time with `for` loops. Maybe you've even used one to build up a list of things — like squares of numbers, filtered words, or your top five pizza toppings in alphabetical order. Well, Python has a handy shortcut for that sort of thing. It's called a *list comprehension*, and once you get the hang of it, you'll find a thousand and one ways to use it.

Setting up a basic list comprehension

Let's say you want to make a list of the squares of numbers 0 through 10. You could code it like so (refer to chapter08/example01.py in this book's example files):

```
squares = []
for x in range(11):
    squares.append(x ** 2)
```

That works just fine. But Python says, "Why not do all that in a single statement?" With a list comprehension, you can do this (chapter08/example02.py), instead:

```
squares = [x ** 2 for x in range(11)]
```

Wild, huh? You get the same result, but with far less typing, no `append` calls (so it's faster), and fewer chances for typos or indentation mishaps. Just one rather lovely little line of logic.

TECHNICAL STUFF

What's up with the word *comprehension* here? It sounds like a highfalutin term you'd hear in an English exam, not in Python code. The term *comprehension* come from *set comprehension* in mathematics (also called *set abstraction*). In math, you can define a set like this:

The set of all y such that y is a square number between 0 and 100.

That's a set comprehension. Python borrowed the idea and turned it into a more readable way of constructing lists. So, a *Python list comprehension* is just a way of expressing what you want your list to contain, based on some rule or pattern.

A list comprehension follows this basic recipe:

```
[do_this for each_thing in some_collection]
```

where:

» *do_this* is an expression that performs some operation on *each_thing* and returns a value. In the squares example, *do_this* is the expression x ** 2.

» *each_thing* is an item from *some_collection*. In the squares example, *each_thing* is x.

» *some_collection* is anything Python can loop through, such as a list, a string, a range, a tuple, or a dictionary. In the squares example, *some_collection* is range(11), which returns a range of numbers from 0 to 10.

Here's another example (chapter08/example03.py):

```
words = ["aardvark", "clunker", "kludge", "moist", "razz"]
word_lengths = [len(word) for word in words]
print(word_lengths)
```

This list comprehension applies the len() function to determine the number of characters in each word in the words list. Here's the output:

```
[8, 7, 6, 5, 4]
```

Adding a filter

By default, a list comprehension creates a new list that has the same number of items as the collection it iterates over. In the squares example from the preceding section, the list comprehension collection range(11) contains eleven values (0 through 10), so the list of squares also has eleven values:

```
[0, 1, 4, 9, 16, 25, 36, 49, 64, 81, 100]
```

What if you want the squares of only even numbers? No problem. List comprehensions support if statements, and a particular item in the collection is operated on only if the logical expression defined for the if statement returns True:

```
[do_this for each_thing in some_collection if condition]
```

Here, the added *condition* part tells Python to perform the *do_this* operation on the current item in *some_collection* only if *condition* returns True when it's applied to that item.

The following example (chapter08/example04.py) adjusts the squares code to square only even numbers:

```
even_squares = [x ** 2 for x in range(11) if x % 2 == 0]
```

The if at the end acts as a filter that says, "Only square x if x is divisible by 2." (The % operator — it's called *modulo* — returns the remainder when the left side is divided by the right side. If the remainder is 0 when a number is divided by 2, it means the number is even.) This means you can build and filter a list at the same time — which is kind of like baking a cake and slicing it in the same pan: efficient *and* delicious!

TIP

Sometimes the *do_this* part of a list comprehension returns just the *each_thing* part. That may sound weird, but it's useful for a common list comprehension task: extracting the items in a collection that match some condition, such as starting with a particular letter.

Suppose you want to extract from a list of names all those that start with *A*. Here's how you could do this using regular code (chapter08/example05.py):

```
matches = []
for name in names:
    if name.startswith("A"):
        matches.append(name)
```

Now here's the list comprehension version (chapter08/example06.py):

```
matches = [name for name in names if name.startswith("A")]
```

This list comprehension is saying, "For each name in the names collection, add name to the matches list if the name starts with the letter *A*." All that in one line? Now *that* is some efficient code!

Introducing Object-Oriented Programming (OOP)

Once you start tackling larger projects, you may get to a point that's familiar to all programmers: It feels like your code is getting out of control. Maybe you have dozens of variables floating around or functions that feel disconnected from the data they're supposed to work on. You're copying and pasting the same code over and over with tiny tweaks. You're starting to feel like you're juggling spaghetti.

If you've never experienced this state, believe me when I tell you that one day you will. It happens even to the most experienced coders. But those coders — and, soon, you — know the solution to messy, redundant code: object-oriented programming, or OOP for short.

The problem: Everything's scattered

Let's say you're building a little pet-tracking app for an animal shelter. You might start out like this (chapter08/example07.py):

```
pet1_name = "Chase"
pet1_species = "dog"
pet1_age = 3

pet2_name = "Whiskers"
pet2_species = "cat"
pet2_age = 1

pet3_name = "Hammy"
pet3_species = "hamster"
pet3_age = 2
```

Then, later in your code, you write a function to print the pet info:

```
def print_info(name, species, age):
    print(f"{name} is a {age}-year-old {species}.")

print_info(pet1_name, pet1_species, pet1_age)
print_info(pet2_name, pet2_species, pet2_age)
print_info(pet3_name, pet3_species, pet3_age)
```

Here's the output:

```
Chase is a 3-year-old dog.
Whiskers is a 1-year-old cat.
Hammy is a 2-year-old hamster.
```

It works! But now imagine that the shelter has not three pets, but three *dozen* pets. That's a lot of variables. Okay, fine, it's for a good cause, so you create all those variables. But now the shelter has asked that the app also track vaccinations and show which pets are due to be vaccinated. Later they come back to you and ask you to track adoption status, including which pets having been waiting the longest to be adopted. Now you have a huge pile of unwieldy variables and functions, all loosely connected, and your code starts to look like a junk drawer of pet facts.

The solution: Bring it all together with OOP

Rather than having a large number of variables supported by a bunch of functions located in various places of your code, your program would be easier to read and maintain if you could bring together all those variables and functions. That, in a nutshell, is what object-oriented programming is all about. It enables you to group related data and functions into something called a class.

To understand what a class does, imagine putting together a blueprint for a car. Those specs would include properties that describe the car — such as the make, model, and color — and a list of what the car can do — such as start, accelerate, and brake. With a detailed enough blueprint in hand, you could (theoretically, at least) create a car.

In OOP, a *class* is a kind of blueprint for a real or virtual thing you want to represent in your code, such as a pet, a car, or a character in a game. The class includes two types of items:

>> **Properties:** These describe the thing. For a pet, the properties could be the pet's name, species, and age. (In OOP circles, properties are often referred to as *attributes*.)

>> **Methods:** These specify either what the thing can do or what can be done with the thing. For a pet, a method could be to print the pet's info.

Once you have a class, you can use it to create data for your program based on that blueprint. Each piece of data you create with a class is called an *object*.

Okay, it's time to brush all that theory aside and do some OOP coding by learning how to build a class. Before I show you the general syntax involved, however, I take you through building a pet class for the shelter project.

Here's what that might look like in Python (chapter08/example08.py):

```
class Pet:

    def __init__(self, name, species, age):
        self.name = name
        self.species = species
        self.age = age

    def print_info(self):
        print(f"{self.name} is a {self.age}-year-old {self.species}.")
```

Yep, I hear you: There's a lot going on here. The key with OOP is that you put a bunch of work into building a class; then creating objects for your program is a breeze.

Okay, here's an overview of what's going on in this class:

» The class keyword tells Python you're building a class with, in this case, the name Pet.

» The __init__() function defines the properties for the class, which in this example are name, species, and age.

» The print_info() function defines a method for the class, which in this example prints info about a pet.

Remember that the class is just a blueprint. Once you've defined that blueprint, you can use it to make the objects that you'll use in your code. To that end, it's time to make a few pet objects (chapter08/example08.py [continued]):

```
chase = Pet("Chase", "dog", 3)
whiskers = Pet("Whiskers", "cat", 1)
hammy = Pet("Hammy", "hamster", 2)

chase.print_info()
whiskers.print_info()
hammy.print_info()
```

Here's the output:

```
Chase is a 3-year-old dog.
Whiskers is a 1-year-old cat.
Hammy is a 2-year-old hamster.
```

Same results as before, but now the data and the behavior are in one neat package (the class), which makes your code more readable, more organized, less repetitious, easier to expand, and easier to maintain. Win, win, win, win, win.

Okay, I skipped over all kinds of details in this example, so now it's time to put meat on these OOP bones.

Building a class

All your OOP adventures start with building a class, which you can think of as a kind of blueprint or set of instructions for building something you want to work with in your code.

A class begins, appropriately enough, with a class statement:

```
class ClassName:
```

Here, *ClassName* is the name you want to use for your class. In Python, class names follow these conventions:

- » If the name is one word, capitalize just the first letter of the word.
- » If the name is multiple words, capitalize just the first letter of each word and smush them all together (that is, don't separate the words with underscores or any other character).

For the record, this way of writing class names is called CapWords (or sometimes Pascal Case or UpperCamelCase). Note, as well, the colon at the end, as also seen in this example:

```
class Pet:
```

Now you can define the code that you want Python to run every time it uses the class to create an object. That startup code is a method called the class *initializer*, and it's one of Python's weirder-looking features:

```
def __init__(self, initial_values):
```

where:

>> __init__ is the special name for the method (the init part is short for *initializer*).

>> self refers to the object being created. The class uses self to refer to the object's properties (such as self.name) or the object's methods (such as self.print_info()).

>> *initial_values* refers to one or more comma-separated values that the initializer uses to set the object's properties.

Note that the initializer isn't required. So if you're creating a class that requires no initialization code, feel free to skip the __init__ method.

You'll mostly use the __init__ method to initialize the properties of the object you're creating. (An object is said to be an *instance* of the class, so these properties are often referred to as *instance attributes.*) In the following code, the properties are name, species, and age:

```
class Pet:

    def __init__(self, name, species, age):
        self.name = name
        self.species = species
        self.age = age
```

If you want, you can also populate the initializer with other code you want to run each time you create an object. For example, you might test a property value to make sure it's valid.

After the class statement, you have the option of declaring one or more *class attributes,* which are class-level variables that apply to every object you create from the class. Here's an example:

```
class Pet:
    adoption_fee = 75

    def __init__(self, name, species, age):
        self.name = name
        self.species = species
        self.age = age
```

Presumably the shelter's adoption fee is the same for every pet; this code includes that value as the class-level adoption_fee attribute.

Okay, you're getting there! The final piece of the class puzzle involves adding whatever methods you want to make available to each object. You do this by defining a function in the class and passing that function the `self` argument. Here's the `Pet` class with the `print_info()` method added (chapter08/example09.py):

```python
class Pet:
    adoption_fee = 75

    def __init__(self, name, species, age):
        self.name = name
        self.species = species
        self.age = age

    def print_info(self):
        print(f"{self.name} is a {self.age}-year-old {self.species} and costs
${self.adoption_fee} to adopt.")
```

Note that by passing `self` to the method as an argument, the method can now refer to both the class attribute (`self.adoption_fee`) and the class properties (such as `self.name`).

Creating an object

Once you have a class defined (which is the hard part of OOP), you're ready to use that class to create — or, as the nerds like to say, *instantiate* — objects in your code. You create an object from a class by calling that class and passing it the initial values you want to apply to the new object's properties:

```
ClassName(initial_values)
```

where:

>> *ClassName* is the name of the class.

>> *initial_values* refers to one or more comma-separated values that you want passed along to the class `__init__()` method.

Want some examples? You got 'em:

```python
chase = Pet("Chase", "dog", 3)
whiskers = Pet("Whiskers", "cat", 1)
hammy = Pet("Hammy", "hamster", 2)
```

Here's what's going on behind the scenes when you create an object in this way:

1. Python calls the class Pet.

2. The class creates a new object.

3. The class runs its __init__() method on the new object, using the values you passed in.

4. The class returns a shiny, new, and ready-to-use Pet object that your code would store in a variable, a list, or another data structure.

Using an object in your code

After you create an object from a class, that object has access to the properties, methods, and class attributes defined in the class.

You access an object property using dot notation:

```
object.property
```

Here, *object* is a reference to the object (such as a variable name) and *property* is the name of the property. For example:

```
print(chase.name)    # Chase
print(whiskers.age)  # 1
```

You call an object method using dot notation:

```
object.method()
```

Here, *object* is a reference to the object (such as a variable name) and *method()* is the name of the method. For example:

```
chase.print_info()  # Prints the info for Chase
hammy.print_info()  # Prints the info for Hammy
```

And, finally, you access an object's class attributes using dot notation on either the class or the object:

```
Class.attribute
object.attribute
```

Here, *Class* is the name of the class; *object* is a reference to the object (such as a variable name); and *attribute* is the name of the class attribute. For example:

```
print(Pet.adoption_fee)        # 75
print(whiskers.adoption_fee)   # Also 75
```

Working with APIs

Okay, it's Friday night, you just got home from work or school, and you're hungry. But you don't want to chow down on just anything. No, tonight it has to be pizza. What do you do? Well, one possibility would be to crank up the oven, roll out some dough, throw on some sauce and toppings, and cook your own pie.

Hah, as if! No, you're much more likely to peruse the website of your local pizza joint, place your order, and then a bit later — voilà! — your pizza arrives at your door.

Your Python programs face a similar choice. On the one hand, you could supply your program with the particular data or services or both it needs, but on the other hand you can "order" what you need and have it "delivered" to your app.

That's essentially what an application programming interface does. An API is just a set of rules that lets one program ask another program for something, such as data, and get a response. An API is a way for two programs to talk to each other. For our purposes, an API is a way for your Python code to order data from another program and get it delivered.

Let's say you have a Python program that requires today's weather. In the make-your-own-pizza version, you'd do something like this:

1. Open your favorite web browser.

2. Google your local weather.

3. Copy the weather info you need.

4. Switch to your Python code and paste the weather data.

5. Repeat Steps 1-4 every day for the rest of your life.

Or you could do the "takeout" version where you replace all five steps with code that connects to a weather API. Doesn't that sound easier? It is! In fact, with just a few lines of Python, you can request the current weather, and the API sends it back, usually in a nice, computer-friendly format that you can work with in your code.

Using APIs means your code can

>> Get live data from the internet, including weather, sports scores, stock prices, and cat facts.

>> Use powerful services, such as translating text, recognizing images, or even sending emails.

>> Pull in fun stuff for projects, such as jokes, trivia, movie info, or Pokémon stats.

APIs turn your humble Python script into something that feels way bigger because now it can connect with the real world.

Talking to an API with Python

As an example over the next couple of sections, I'll use a fun, free API that serves up a random joke each time you call it. Can't we all use a little more humor in our lives these days?

Okay, the API lives at this URL:

```
https://official-joke-api.appspot.com/random_joke
```

Try pasting that address into your browser and you'll see a random joke that looks something like this:

```
{"type":"programming","setup":"What do you call a computer mouse that swears a lot?","punchline":"A cursor!","id":435}
```

Probably not what you were expecting, right? That response is in a special format that's commonly used for sending API data. I explain it a bit later in the "Working with the data you get back" section. For now, it's time to show you how to get that same data in Python.

The easiest way to talk to an API in Python is by using a handy tool called the `requests` library. (Refer to Chapter 7 to learn how to install it using pip.) Think of it as your program's personal delivery driver: It handles the pickup and brings the data back.

To use `requests` in your code, you import it:

```
import requests
```

This gives your code access to functions that can send requests to APIs and handle the responses. For an API, you cajole it into returning data by submitting a GET request, which is a nerdy way of saying, "Yo, API, please give me some data." You send a GET request using the `requests.get()` method:

```
requests.get(URL)
```

Here, *URL* is the address of the API. The API will send back a response, and you always store that response in a variable, like so:

```
response = requests.get("https://official-joke-api.appspot.com/random_joke")
```

As part of the response, the API will return a status code, which is a number that represents how the transaction went. The only status code you need to worry about is 200, which means OK. The `response` object includes a `status_code` property that should be the first thing your code checks (chapter08/example10.py):

```
import requests

# Get a random joke
response = requests.get("https://official-joke-api.appspot.com/random_joke")

# Check the status code
if response.status_code == 200:
    print("I was able to connect to the API no problem.")
else:
    print("Something went wrong. This is not a joke.")
```

Assuming you received an OK status code, you can now do something useful with the returned data.

Working with the data you get back

If the connection went well, you're ready to work with the data the API sent back. The most basic way you can do that is to work with the `response` object's `text` property:

```
print(response.text)
```

Here's what you see:

```
{"type":"general","setup":"What cheese can never be yours?","punchline":"Nacho
    cheese.","id":156}
```

Why, look at that: It's in the same format as the text that appears in the web browser if you surf directly to the URL. This text format is known as JavaScript Object Notation, or JSON (it's pronounced like the name *Jason*). Despite the JavaScript in the name, it's a popular format for transmitting text in most programming languages.

To help you understand JSON a bit better, let me rearrange the response text a bit:

```
{
"type": "general",
"setup": "What cheese can never be yours?",
"punchline": "Nacho cheese.",
"id": 156
}
```

Now you can see that JSON is a collection of *property-value* pairs where, on each line, the item to the left of the colon is the property name and the item to the right of the colon is the value.

This format is similar to the Python dictionaries I cover in Chapter 6. In fact, the response object comes with a json() method that converts the JSON returned by the API into a Python dictionary:

```
joke = response.json()
```

If you run print(joke), here's what you see:

```
{'type': 'general', 'setup': 'What cheese can never be yours?', 'punchline':
    'Nacho cheese. ', 'id': 156}
```

Yep, that's a Python dictionary! The difference is that the dictionary is a set of key-value pairs, with the key to the left of the colon and the value to the right. To extract a value from the dictionary, you put the key in square brackets after the dictionary name. For example, to use the value of the setup key, you'd do this:

```
joke["setup"]
```

Here's a complete example (chapter08/example11.py):

```python
import requests

# Get a random joke
response = requests.get("https://official-joke-api.appspot.com/random_joke")

# Check the status code
if response.status_code == 200:

    # Convert the JSON to a dictionary
    joke = response.json()

    print("Here's a joke for you:")

    # Print the joke setup
    print(joke['setup'])

    # Wait for the user to press Enter
    input("...")

    # Print the joke punchline
    print(joke['punchline'])
else:
    print("Something went wrong. This is not a joke.")
```

REMEMBER

If the response isn't valid JSON, calling `.json()` will raise an error. I show you how to catch these kinds of runtime errors a bit later in the "Handling Program Errors" section.

A few API repositories

If you're convinced that APIs are a great way to enhance your Python programs, you'll be happy to know that tons of them are available. Here are some useful API repositories to check out:

>> **Public APIs** (https://github.com/public-apis/public-apis): A huge, community-curated list of free APIs on GitHub. It's organized by category (from Animals to Weather). This is a great site if you're just getting started with APIs.

>> **RapidAPI** (https://rapidapi.com/): A marketplace for APIs, so it's sort of like the App Store for APIs. The site enables you to search, test, and connect to APIs from a single dashboard. There are lots of free APIs, but you need to set up an account because some APIs require payment.

>> **API List** (https://apilist.fun/): A quirky, fun collection of APIs with lots of interesting ideas for small projects and experiments. Categories to check out include Humor, Meme, and Random.

Handling Program Errors

The Python interpreter runs through a program one statement at a time, starting from the top line. Ideally, the interpreter will make it all the way to the last statement without a hiccup, but what happens if the interpreter comes across some code that it can't figure out? Ah, that's when the interpreter has a little tantrum, stops processing the code, and chastises you with an error message.

Decoding Python traceback messages

The specific message you see depends on the program and the error, but a typical example will suffice to give you the idea. First, here's a program (chapter08/example12.py):

```
age = input("How old are you? ")
age_next_year = age + 1
print(f"Next year, you'll be {age_next_year}!")
```

Running this program produces the following output:

```
Traceback (most recent call last):
  File "example12.py", line 2, in <module>
    age_next_year = age + 1
                    ~~~~^~~
TypeError: can only concatenate str (not "int") to str
```

Well, okay, *that's* a little intimidating! But there's actually a ton of useful information here to help you solve the problem. Let me break it down for you:

>> Traceback: This output is a report from the interpreter that shows the path your program took right before it ran into an error.

» `most recent call last`: The report traces your program's path back from the error, beginning with the most recent line of code or function call to the first call that began the path that led to the error.

» `File "example12.py", line 2`: There are no function calls in the example code, so the interpreter just shows the name of the file and which line caused the error. In more complicated cases, you'd see a series of these statements tracing back the logic that caused the error to the beginning.

» `in <module>`: The error happened in the main part of your file, not inside a function or class. If the error or trace points to something inside a function or class, you'd see in `function` or in `class` (where `function` and `class` are names) instead of in `<module>`.

» `age_next_year = age + 1`: This code contains the statement that caused the error.

» `~~~~^~~`: The tildes (~) "underline" the part of the code where the problem lies and the caret (^) points at the specific spot where the interpreter ran into trouble.

» `TypeError: can only concatenate str (not "int") to str`: This line displays the error type and the error message. This part of the traceback tells you what exactly went haywire in your program. In this example, the interpreter is letting you know that your code seems to be trying to concatenate a string value (age) and an integer value (1), which is illegal. Changing the expression to `int(age) + 1` will make the interpreter happy again.

So, in short, a traceback is Python's "what, where, and how" error report because it shows you *what* went wrong (such as a `TypeError`), *where* it went wrong (such as line 2 of your Python file), and *how* it got there (if the logic that led to the error went through one or more functions or files).

Table 8-1 lists a few of the most common error types that you're likely to stumble upon.

Handling errors with try and except

If you're just running your code for yourself, dealing with tracebacks is par for the Python course. But if you want other people to run your programs, you certainly don't want them having to come face-to-face with some gnarly error message *and* you almost certainly would prefer that your program keep running instead of crashing. You can accomplish both goals — hide tracebacks and avoid program crashes — by using special Python code to handle any errors that crop up.

TABLE 8-1

Common Python Error Types

Error Type	What It Means	Example
`ValueError`	You used some invalid data.	`int("three")`
`TypeError`	You used the wrong type of data (such as adding a string to a number).	`"hello" + 3`

`NameError`	Python doesn't recognize the name you typed.	Typo in a variable name:
		
		`age = input("How old are you? ")`
		
		`age_next_year = int(agw) + 1`

`IndexError`	You asked for an item in a list that doesn't exist.	`my_list[5]` when the list has only three items
`KeyError`	You asked for a dictionary key that's not there.	`my_dict['pizza']` when `'pizza'` doesn't exist
`ZeroDivisionError`	You tried to divide by zero, which is illegal.	`10 / 0`
`RequestException`	Something went wrong with your API call.	Server is down, bad URL, and so on

For example, suppose your code includes the following statement:

```
number = int(input("Enter a number: "))
```

What happens if the user enters, say, a number with text characters instead of digits? Let's see:

```
Enter a number: three
Traceback (most recent call last):
  File "<python-input-1>", line 1, in <module>
    number = int(input("Enter a number: "))
ValueError: invalid literal for int() with base 10: 'three'
```

Yuck! A more robust and user-friendly way to handle this task would be to ask Python to watch for such an error and then display a message to the user when the error occurs. You accomplish this by using `try` and `except` blocks (chapter08/example13.py):

```
try:
    number = int(input("Enter a number: "))
    print(f"The square of your number is {number ** 2}.")
    print(f"The cube of your number is {number ** 3}.")
except ValueError:
    print("Oops! That wasn't a number.")
```

Here's what this code does:

1. Python enters the `try` block.

2. Python executes the next statement in the `try` block.

3. Python checks to see if an error occurred:

   - If no error occurs and there are more statements to execute in the `try` block, Python returns to Step 2. If no error occurs and the current statement is the last one in the `try` block, Python skips over the `except` block and continues with Step 5.

   - If an error does happen, Python enters the `except` block.

4. Python executes each statement in the `except` block, and then continues with Step 5.

5. Python executes the rest of the program.

Here's a sample output with no errors:

```
Enter a number: 6
The square of your number is 36.
The cube of your number is 216.
```

Here's a sample output when an error occurs:

```
Enter a number: three
Oops! That wasn't a number.
```

Look, ma, no traceback!

Handling API errors

Using `try` and `except` blocks is an especially handy technique when you're making an API call because that call could fail if the website is down, the address is wrong, or the internet disappears into the void.

Here's how to handle such failures gracefully (chapter08/example14.py):

```
import requests

try:
    response = requests.get("https://catfact.ninja/fact")
```

```
    # Check for an error
    response.raise_for_status()

    data = response.json()
    print(data['fact'])
except requests.exceptions.RequestException:
    print("There was a problem contacting the API.")
```

The key addition here is the `raise_for_status()` method, which checks the response status code and raises an exception if the response was an error. If the response code is in the 400s (indicating a client error) or the 500s (indicating a server error), your code will be diverted to the `except` block. This way, if something goes wrong, your program doesn't crash. Instead, it calmly alerts the user to what happened.

Debugging Your Code

Debugging is the process of finding and fixing coding errors — known semi-affectionately in the coding trade as bugs — so your program runs the way you expect it to. (Some wag once wrote that if debugging is defined as the process of removing bugs from code, programming must be defined as the process of putting them in!)

If you're thinking that your programs may have a few bugs now because you're just getting started but eventually you'll be a proficient enough programmer to write bug-free code, think again. Everyone — from the rawest rookie to the most polished pro — writes buggy code. Debugging isn't some technique that you'll use less and less as you gain experience; it's a normal, ho-hum aspect of coding that all developers do every day.

In fact, for many developers, debugging code is *more* interesting than writing it in the first place. These developers don't see program glitches as failures; they see them as a chance to don their virtual deerstalker hats and switch into detective mode.

When it comes to debugging Python code, you have three main routes to take:

» Follow the general debugging strategies that I list in Chapter 2.

» Use VS Code's Python Debugger.

» Run through a few Python-specific debugging techniques, which are coming right up.

When your Python code zigs instead of zags, returns the wrong result, or goes up in digital flames, it's time to crack your knuckles and get down to the labor of figuring out what went wrong and then patching the problem. It's not glamorous, but it's one of the most important coding skills you'll learn.

So, without further delay, here's a four-step Python-specific procedure to follow to understand what went wrong, find out where it went wrong, and fix what's wrong:

1. **Read the error message.**

    If your program blows up, the Python interpreter gives you a traceback, as I describe in the preceding section. That message contains a fistful of debugging gold because it tells you the type of error, specifies the line number and file where the error happened, and shows the operation Python was trying to execute when things went south.

    Most of the time, the error message contains enough info to debug the problem.

2. **Use** `print()` **to monitor program values.**

    By far the most common Python debugging technique is to add `print()` statements that output the current value of whatever variable, expression, or function result you want to monitor.

    For example, here's some code (chapter08/example15.py) that prompts the user for their age and then uses a `print()` statement to output the value of the age variable:

    ```python
    # Prompt for an age
    age = input("How old are you? ")

    # Print the age variable value
    print(f"The value of age is {age}.")

    age_next_year = int(age) + 1
    print(f"Next year, you'll be {age_next_year}!")
    ```

    Here's a sample output from this code:

    ```
    How old are you? 29
    The value of age is 29.
    Next year, you'll be 30!
    ```

3. **Use `type()` to check data types.**

A major cause of program errors is when your code is expecting a variable or function result to have a particular data type, but it ends up with some other type that wreaks havoc at execution time. You can take advantage of Python's `type()` function to find out the data type of something in your code.

For example, here's some code (chapter08/example16.py) that prompts the user for their age and then uses a `print()` statement to output the data type of the age variable:

```
# Prompt for an age
age = input("How old are you? ")

# Print the age variable data type
print(f"The data type of age is {type(age)}")

age_next_year = int(age) + 1
print(f"Next year, you'll be {age_next_year}!")
```

Here's a sample output from this code:

```
How old are you? 29
The data type of age is <class 'str'>
Next year, you'll be 30!
```

4. **Use `print()` to locate errors.**

Another good use of `print()` statements for debugging is when your Python code fails, but you don't get an error message. Now you have no idea where the problem lies, so what's a developer to do? You can gradually narrow down where the error occurs by adding a `print()` statement to your code that outputs a message like `Made it this far!`. If you see that message, you move the `print()` statement a little further down the code, repeating this procedure until you don't see the message, meaning the code failed before getting to the `print()` statement.

Don't worry about "cluttering" your code with a bunch of `print()` statements; you can delete them after you've squashed the bug.

Example: Cat Fact Cards

Here's a fun little example (chapter08/example17.py) that combines OOP, APIs, and handling errors in one program that creates, for each of three cats, a card with a random cat-related fact from the Cat Fact API:

```python
# Bring in requests for API calls
import requests

# Define the CatFactCard class
class CatFactCard:

    # Initializer
    def __init__(self, name):
        self.name = name
        self.fact = self.get_fact()

    # Get a random cat fact
    def get_fact(self):

        # Store the Cat Facts API URL
        url = "https://catfact.ninja/fact"

        # Try to get a fact from the API
        try:
            response = requests.get(url)

            # Check for an error
            response.raise_for_status()

            # If we're good, get the response
            data = response.json()

            # Send back the returned cat fact
            return data['fact']

        # Did an error occur?
        except:
            # If so, send back a message
            return "Sorry, couldn't fetch a fact right now."

    # Display the card's data
    def show(self):
        print(f"{self.name} says:")
        print(f"\"{self.fact}\"")
        print()

# Create some cat fact cards
cat1_card = CatFactCard("Whiskers")
```

```
cat2_card = CatFactCard("Peanuts")
cat3_card = CatFactCard("Slyvester")

# Display the cards
cat1_card.show()
cat2_card.show()
cat3_card.show()
```

Here's a sample output:

```
Whiskers says:
"A group of cats is called a clowder."

Peanuts says:
"A cat's nose pad is ridged with a unique pattern, just like the
    fingerprint of a human."

Slyvester says:
"Neutering a cat extends its life span by two or three years."
```

If you happen to get the same fact more than once, don't worry about it because that's just how this API works sometimes. You could say it's like herding cats!

IN THIS CHAPTER

» **Opening, reading, and massaging project data files**

» **Handling user input**

» **Cleaning data for analysis**

» **Analyzing words and sentences**

» **Analyzing text sentiment**

Chapter **9**

Building Some Useful Python Projects

Not only is example the best way to teach, it is the only way.
—ALBERT SCHWEITZER

The best way to learn coding is to be exposed to tons of small examples that illustrate whatever new programming concept is being introduced, type that code yourself (to get that "fingertip feeling" I mention in the Introduction), run it, and then play around with it to get a feel for how things work. Ideally, these small code snippets should be what I like to call "maximally trivial." That is, the code does more than just print "Hello, World!," but not so much that the underlying programming concept gets lost.

But there comes a time in every new coder's education when those training wheels need to come off so you can tackle something significant. That's what this chapter is all about. My assumption is that you know the fundamentals of Python and all about data structures, loops and conditionals, and files and modules. With that knowledge in your head, this chapter expands your coding horizons with two lar-geish projects that you build from scratch: an anagram guessing game and a text analysis app. Both scripts are well over 100 statements long, so these will be by far the biggest projects you've worked on so far. But I wouldn't have come up with these projects if I didn't think you could handle them, so let's get coding!

Project 1: Anagram Guessing Game

The first project is a game called Guessagram, where you're given a randomly selected word and your mission is to find as many anagrams of that word as you can. Which of your shiny, new Python skills will you use? Quite a few:

>> Reading data from a file and catching errors

>> Working with lists and dictionaries

>> Filtering with list comprehensions

>> Making random selections

>> Building a game loop using `while`

>> Working with strings

>> Interacting with users using `input()`

>> Keeping score and giving hints

The next few sections take you through the major sections of the code, so you can follow along and build your own version of the game.

Loading a list of words from a CSV file

The game data comes from a CSV file named `word_list.csv`, which has four columns of data:

>> **Word:** A list of English words, in uppercase, from AAH to ZYGOTES. Over 65,000 words are in the full list.

>> **Alpha:** The letters from the Word column arranged alphabetically. This format is useful in anagram coding because when two or more words are anagrams of each other, they'll have identical alphabetical letter arrangements. For example, the words DESPAIR, DIAPERS, and PRAISED are anagrams, and the Alpha value for each is ADEIPRS.

>> **Rank:** A number from 1 to 4, where the higher the number, the less common the word. This ranking comes from the Corpus of Contemporary American Usage.

>> **AnagramCount:** The number of anagrams each word has in the list.

Here's a sample from `word_list.csv`:

```
Word,Alpha,Rank,AnagramCount
AAH,AAH,3,1
AAHED,AADEH,3,1
AAHING,AAGHIN,3,0
AAHS,AAHS,3,0
AARDVARK,AAADKRRV,3,0
```

To read this data into the game, you import a module named `csv`, which offers methods for reading from and writing to CSV files:

```
import csv
```

Now you need to define a function to load the CSV data:

```
def load_words(path):
    try:
        with open(path, newline='') as csv_file:

    except FileNotFoundError:
        print(f"Whoops! The file {path} wasn't found!")
        print("Make sure it's in the same folder as this script.")
        sys.exit()
```

The `load_words()` function takes the location (`path`) of the CSV file and, in a `try` block, runs `open()` to open the file in read mode (not specified here because it's the default mode). The `newline=''` argument tells the `csv` library to handle line endings on its own, which you should always do with CSV files.

If the file specified by the `path` argument wasn't found, a `FileNotFoundError` is raised and the code jumps to the `except` block, where it displays a message and exits the program using `sys.exit()` (which comes from the `sys` module that the program imports at the top of the code).

Assuming no error was raised, now the code can read the CSV data:

```
reader = csv.DictReader(csv_file)
```

This statement uses the `DictReader()` method, which reads the CSV data into a collection of Python dictionaries, where each dictionary represents a row in the

CSV file with the items in the CSV header as the dictionary keys. Here's a partial look at that collection:

```
{'Word': 'AAH', 'Alpha': 'AAH', 'Rank': '3', 'AnagramCount': '1'}
{'Word': 'AAHED', 'Alpha': 'AADEH', 'Rank': '3', 'AnagramCount': '1'}
{'Word': 'AAHING', 'Alpha': 'AAGHIN', 'Rank': '3', 'AnagramCount': '0'}
{'Word': 'AAHS', 'Alpha': 'AAHS', 'Rank': '3', 'AnagramCount': '0'}
{'Word': 'AARDVARK', 'Alpha': 'AAADKRRV', 'Rank': '3', 'AnagramCount': '0'}
```

Now you *could* leave things here and work with every word, but that doesn't suit the purposes of our game. In fact, it would be best to filter the complete list to exclude the following:

» Words that are too short (less than 4 letters)

» Words that are too long (more than 10 letters)

» Words that are too obscure (Rank = 4)

Filtering the collection sounds like a job for a list comprehension:

```
words = [row for row in reader
        if len(row['Word']) >= 4
        and len(row['Word']) <= 10
        and row['Rank'] != '4']
```

With that done, the code can then return the words list and move on. Here's what we have so far:

```
import sys
import csv


def load_words(path):

    try:
        with open(path, newline='') as csv_file:
            reader = csv.DictReader(csv_file)
            words = [row for row in reader
                    if len(row['Word']) >= 4
                    and len(row['Word']) <= 10
                    and row['Rank'] != '4']
            return words
```

```
    except FileNotFoundError:
        print(f"Whoops! The file {path} wasn't found!")
        print("Make sure it's in the same folder as this script.")
        sys.exit()

words = load_words('word_list.csv')
```

Finding anagrams

Later, after the game chooses a random word from the filtered word list (check out "Getting a random word and its anagram," a bit later), the code needs to determine all the anagrams of that word. Since finding anagrams happens frequently, it makes sense to plop that code in its own function:

```
def find_anagrams(word, word_list):
```

Here, `word` is the word to be anagrammed and `word_list` is the filtered list of words returned by the `load_words()` function in the preceding section.

Recall that any two anagrams will have identical alphabetic orderings of their letters, so the first thing the `find_anagrams()` function needs to do is sort the letters of the `word` argument:

```
sorted_word = ''.join(sorted(word.upper()))
```

Here, `sorted()` is a Python function that returns a sorted list of the items in whatever iterable it was passed, such as a string in this case. (The words in the CSV are all uppercase, so that's why the preceding statement uses `word.upper()`.) The code needs a word, not a list, so the `join()` method combines the sorted letters, which are stored in the `sorted_word` variable.

Grabbing all the anagrams is straightforward; we search the `word_list` collection for items where the `Alpha` key value is the same as the `sorted_word` value. Once again, a list comprehension does it in a single statement:

```
anagrams = [w['Word'] for w in word_list
            if w['Alpha'] == sorted_word
            and w['Word'] != word]
```

The condition w['Word'] != word is required so that the code doesn't return the word as its own anagram. Here's the complete find_anagrams() function:

```python
def find_anagrams(word, word_list):

    sorted_word = ''.join(sorted(word.upper()))

    anagrams = [w['Word'] for w in word_list
                if w['Alpha'] == sorted_word
                and w['Word'] != word]

    return anagrams
```

Displaying a welcome message

A well-designed game keeps the user in mind at all times, starting right at the beginning, when the game should welcome the user and provide information they may need to play the game.

Here's the welcome message for Guessagram:

```python
print("\n===============================")
print("    Welcome to Guessagram!")
print("===============================")
print("Your mission, should you choose to accept it, "
      "is to find all the anagrams of a random word.")
print("Some are easy. Some...not so much. Think you're up for the challenge?")
print("Type 'HINT' for a hint, or 'QUIT' to give up (no judgement...maybe).")
print("Let's twist some letters!\n")
```

Setting up the game loop

A common game structure is to set up an endless loop that runs through one iteration of the game and then asks the user if they want to continue. If they want to keep going, the loop runs another iteration of the game; if they're done, the loop ends and the program quits.

Here's some code to implement the endless game loop for Guessagram:

```python
while True:

    # The game code for each iteration will go here
```

```
# Ask the user if they want to play again
again = input("Do you want to play again? (y/n): ").strip().lower()

# If the user doesn't want to play again, exit the game
if again != 'y':
    print("\nOkay, see you. Thanks for playing!")
    break
```

An input() function asks the user if they want to play again and prompts them to press y or n. Then an if statement checks the input: If it was anything other than y, a break statement ends the game's main while loop.

TECHNICAL
STUFF

METHOD CHAINING

Take a closer look at the following statement:

```
again = input("Do you want to play again? (y/n): ").strip().lower()
```

Note that the end of the statement calls two methods: strip() and lower(). When a statement includes one method after another, it's called *method chaining*. In this example, the input() function returns a string object, which is then used as the object for the strip() method (which removes any whitespace characters from the beginning and end of the input text). That method also returns a string object, which is then used as the object for the lower() method (which converts the stripped input to lowercase).

That is, this one statement:

```
again = input("Do you want to play again? (y/n): ").strip().lower()
```

is the same as these three statements:

```
again = input("Do you want to play again? (y/n): ")
again = again.strip()
again = again.lower()
```

Condensing three statements into one concise statement is *very* Pythonic (although method chaining isn't exclusive to Python; you can do it with JavaScript, too, for example).

Getting a random word and its anagrams

The first thing the game needs to do once it enters the main game loop is grab a random word from the list of words. A Python library called random is a perfect choice because it includes a method called choice() that returns a random element from a collection, such as a list. So, at the top of the program, be sure to import that module:

```
import random
```

The code shouldn't just pick out any old word because some words don't have any anagrams or have just a trivial number of them (one or two). So, the code needs to use a list comprehension to filter the word list to include only those words where the AnagramCount column is at least 3:

```
random_word = random.choice([word['Word'] for word in words
                            if int(word['AnagramCount']) >= 3])
```

With the word in hand, the code can determine its anagrams:

```
anagrams = find_anagrams(random_word, words)
```

Finally, we tell the user what the word is and how many anagrams they have to find:

```
print(f"\nFind {len(anagrams)} anagrams of the word "
      f"'{random_word.upper()}':\n")
```

Tracking user data

Any game worthy of the description will track one or more bits of data about the user, such as their current score or current level. For Guessagram, two pieces of user data seem appropriate: the correct anagram guesses and the total number of guesses they've made so far.

The main loop next initializes two variables to store this data:

```
# Initialize an empty list to store the guessed anagrams
guessed = []

# Track the number of guesses
guesses = 0
```

Looping a single round

The main `while` loop is for the overall game, but within that loop the user can play multiple rounds, so the game needs an inner loop to handle a single round. That loop will run until one of the following happens:

>> The user guesses all the anagrams for the random word.

>> The user quits the round.

To determine whether the user has guessed all the anagrams, the code compares the number of items in the user's `guessed` list with the number of items in the `anagrams` list:

```
while len(guessed) < len(anagrams):
    remaining = len(anagrams) - len(guessed)
```

Each time through this loop, the code calculates how many anagrams the user has left to find and stores that value in the `remaining` variable.

Handling user input

Now the code is ready to start handling the user's anagram guesses. This game offers two other input options to the user:

>> Type `hint` to see the first letter of one of the unfound anagrams.

>> Type `quit` to end this round without finding all the anagrams.

Here's the `input()` function with a prompt that also uses the `remaining` value to tell the user how many anagrams they have left to find:

```
guess = input(f"Enter your guess ({remaining} left to find): ").strip().upper()

# Increment the number of guesses
if guess != "HINT" and guess != "QUIT":
    guesses += 1
```

This code also increments the `guesses` value when the input isn't `HINT` or `QUIT`.

Now the code needs to handle all the input possibilities using a series of `if`, `elif`, and `else` statements:

```python
# Has the user already guessed this word?
if guess in guessed:
    print("\nYou already guessed that one!\n")


# Did the user guess an anagram?
elif guess in [a.upper() for a in anagrams]:


    # If so, add it to the list of guessed anagrams
    guessed.append(guess)
    print("\nYes! Good one!\n")


# Does the user want a hint?
elif guess == "HINT":
    # Loop through the anagrams
    for a in anagrams:
        # If the anagram hasn't been guessed yet
        if a.upper() not in guessed:
            # Print the anagram's first letter as a hint
            print(f"\nPsst. One of the remaining anagrams starts with "
                    f"{a[0].upper()}.\n")
            break


# Does the user want to quit?
elif guess.upper() == "QUIT":
    # If so, print a message and break out of the loop
    print("\nOkay, thanks for playing!\n")
    break


# If we get this far, the guess was not an anagram
else:
    print("\nNope, sorry. Please try again.\n")


# Print the user's found anagrams (if any)
if len(guessed) > 0:
    print("So far, you've found:")
    print(", ".join(guessed) + "\n")
```

This inner `while` loop finishes by printing the user's found anagrams (if there are any to print, that is).

Completing a round

Once the user has finished a round (by guessing all the anagrams or by typing `quit` at the prompt), the game needs to offer a summary of the round:

```python
# Check if the user found all the anagrams
if len(guessed) == len(anagrams):
    print(f"Great job! You found all {len(anagrams)} anagrams in "
        f"{guesses} guesses!\n")
    print("You are now officially an Anagram Wizard.\n")
else:
    print("Guessagram wins this round. Better luck next time!\n")

    # Print the list of anagrams
    print("The anagrams were:")
    print(", ".join(anagrams) + "\n")
```

If the user's `guessed` list and the `anagrams` list contain the same number of items, the user found every anagram, so a congratulatory message is displayed. Otherwise, a consolatory message appears and the list of anagrams is printed.

The full code

Here's the full code for Guessagram (chapter09/project01.py):

```python
# Import some libraries
import sys
import csv
import random


# Function to load words from a CSV file.
# It returns a list of dictionaries with the filtered words
def load_words(path):

    # Open the CSV file
    try:
        with open(path, newline='') as csv_file:

            # Read the CSV file into a dictionary
            # The keys are the column names and
            # the values are the cell values
            reader = csv.DictReader(csv_file)
            # Filter the words based on the criteria
            # This list comprehension filters out words that are
```

```
#       * Too short (less than 4 letters)
#       * Too long (more than 10 letters)
#       * Too obscure (Rank = 4)
        words = [row for row in reader
                if len(row['Word']) >= 4
                and len(row['Word']) <= 10
                and row['Rank'] != '4']

        # Return the list of word dictionaries
        return words
    except FileNotFoundError:
        print(f"Whoops! The file {path} wasn't found!")
        print("Make sure it's in the same folder as this script.")
        sys.exit()

# Get the list of words from the CSV file
# The file should be in the same directory as this script
words = load_words('word_list.csv')

# Function to find anagrams of a word from a list of words
def find_anagrams(word, word_list):

    # Sort the letters of the word alphabetically
    sorted_word = ''.join(sorted(word.upper()))

    # The anagrams are all the words in the word list where
    # the Alpha key is the same as the word's sorted letters
    # The list comprehension also filters out the original word
    anagrams = [w['Word'] for w in word_list
                if w['Alpha'] == sorted_word
                and w['Word'] != word]

    # Return the list of anagrams
    return anagrams

# Print the welcome message
print("\n==============================")
print("    Welcome to Guessagram!")
print("==============================")
print("Your mission, should you choose to accept it, "
      "is to find all the anagrams of a random word.")
print("Some are easy. Some...not so much. Think you're up for the challenge?")
print("Type 'HINT' for a hint, or 'QUIT' to give up (no judgement...maybe).")
print("Let's twist some letters!\n")
```

```python
# Run the main game loop
# The game continues until the user decides to quit
while True:
    # Get a random word
    # The word must have at least 3 anagrams
    random_word = random.choice([word['Word'] for word in words
                                 if int(word['AnagramCount']) >= 3])

    # Find the anagrams of the random word
    anagrams = find_anagrams(random_word, words)

    # Print the word and the number of anagrams
    print(f"\nFind {len(anagrams)} anagrams of the word "
          f"'{random_word.upper()}':\n")

    # Initialize an empty list to store the guessed anagrams
    guessed = []

    # Track the number of guesses
    guesses = 0

    # Loop until all anagrams are guessed or the user quits
    while len(guessed) < len(anagrams):

        # Calculate the number of remaining anagrams
        remaining = len(anagrams) - len(guessed)

        # Prompt the user for a guess. The user can
        # enter a word, ask for a hint, or quit the game
        guess = input(f"Enter your guess ({remaining} left to find): ").
                strip().upper()

        # Increment the number of guesses
        if guess != "HINT" and guess != "QUIT":
            guesses += 1

        # Has the user already guessed this word?
        if guess in guessed:
            print("\nYou already guessed that one!\n")

        # Did the user guess an anagram?
        elif guess in [a.upper() for a in anagrams]:
```

```python
        # If so, add it to the list of guessed anagrams
        guessed.append(guess)
        print("\nYes! Good one!\n")

    # Does the user want a hint?
    elif guess == "HINT":
        # Loop through the anagrams
        for a in anagrams:
            # If the anagram hasn't been guessed yet
            if a.upper() not in guessed:
                # Print the anagram's first letter as a hint
                print(f"\nPsst. One of the remaining anagrams starts with "
                      f"{a[0].upper()}.\n")
                break

    # Does the user want to quit?
    elif guess == "QUIT":
        # If so, print a message and break out of the loop
        print("\nOkay, thanks for playing!\n")
        break

    # If we get this far, the guess was not an anagram
    else:
        print("\nNope, sorry. Please try again.\n")

    # Print the user's found anagrams (if any)
    if len(guessed) > 0:
        print("So far, you've found:")
        print(", ".join(guessed) + "\n")

# Check if the user found all the anagrams
if len(guessed) == len(anagrams):
    print(f"Great job! You found all {len(anagrams)} anagrams in "
          f"{guesses} guesses!\n")
    print("You are now officially an Anagram Wizard.\n")
else:
    print("Guessagram wins this round. Better luck next time!\n")

    # Print the list of anagrams
    print("The anagrams were:")
    print(", ".join(anagrams) + "\n")
```

```
# Ask the user if they want to play again.
again = input("Do you want to play again? (y/n): ").strip().lower()

# If the user doesn't want to play again, exit the game
if again != 'y':
    print("\nOkay, see you. Thanks for playing!\n")
    break
```

Project 2: Text Analyzer

One of Python's strong suits is analyzing text, which can mean finding the words in an email or essay that are used most often, finding the longest words used in a document, or determining whether the sentiment of a letter is positive, negative, or neutral.

In this project, you bring all these text analyses to bear on a fairly large text (a public domain copy of *Alice's Adventures in Wonderland*). Which Python skills will you need? More than you might think:

>> Importing libraries

>> Opening and reading a text file and catching any errors that occur

>> Using string methods to clean up the text and prepare it for analysis

>> Splitting the words into a list

>> Using a set to get the unique words from the text

>> Sorting dictionaries and sets

>> Looping through lists, dictionaries, and sets

Okay, word nerds, it's time to get the project started.

Installing and downloading some stuff

You're going to need some elements from Python's Natural Language Toolkit (NLTK) for this project, so first you need to install that library. Crank up a terminal window, exit your Python REPL session if you have one going, and enter the following command:

```
pip install nltk
```

On some Macs, you might need to use pip3, instead:

```
pip3 install nltk
```

With that done, launch a Python session and run the following commands at the REPL prompt:

```
>>> import nltk
>>> nltk.download('stopwords')
>>> nltk.download('punkt')
>>> nltk.download('vader_lexicon')
```

WARNING

At some point while entering these commands, you may get a CERTIFICATE_VERIFY_FAILED error. It's always something! If this error pops up, get yourself to a terminal prompt and run the following command:

```
/Applications/Python\ x.y/Install\ Certificates.command
```

Replace x.y with the version of Python you're using, such as 3.15. Restart your Python session and try the above commands again.

Next, you need to install the Matplotlib library:

```
pip install matplotlib
```

Or:

```
pip3 install matplotlib
```

Now you're ready to code! In a new .py file, specify what you need to import into the project:

```
import sys
import string
import matplotlib.pyplot as plt
from nltk.corpus import stopwords
from nltk.tokenize import sent_tokenize, word_tokenize
from nltk.sentiment import SentimentIntensityAnalyzer
```

Over the next few sections, I explain what these libraries do.

Opening and reading the text file

The text to be analyzed is in a file named alice.txt, so the first order of business is to read that file's data:

```
try:
    with open("alice.txt", encoding="utf-8-sig") as file:
        raw_text = file.read()
except FileNotFoundError:
    print("Whoops! The file wasn't found!")
    print("Make sure it's in the same folder as this script.")
    sys.exit()
```

Within a try/accept block, the open() function opens the file in read mode (not specified here because it's the default mode). The encoding="utf-8-sig" argument is there to make sure the program can read characters such as curly (versus straight) quotes, em dashes, accented letters, and emojis without crashing. The file's data is stored in the raw_text variable.

If the file wasn't found, the FileNotFoundError is raised and the code jumps to the except block, where it displays a message and exits the program using sys. exit() (which comes from the sys module imported at the top of the code).

Cleaning the text

Most of the time, you'll want to clean up your text so that it can be analyzed properly. For this project, cleaning the data means just two things:

>> Converting all the text to lowercase so that, say, "rabbit" and "Rabbit" are treated as the same word. You accomplish this with the lower() method applied to the text:

```
clean_text = raw_text.lower()
```

>> Removing all punctuation from the text so that it doesn't interfere with operations such as counting the words.

In just a second, the code will use a loop to remove every punctuation mark by replacing each punctuation character with an empty string (""). However, using this approach leads to problems with two characters: the hyphen (-) and the em dash(—). Just removing hyphens, for example, would mean turning phrases such as *rabbit-hole* and *tea-party* into *rabbithole* and *teaparty*.

Instead, it's better to replace these characters with spaces:

```
clean_text = clean_text.replace("-", " ")
clean_text = clean_text.replace("—", " ")
```

At the beginning of the project, the `string` module was imported so that the code can take advantage of a predefined list of punctuation marks:

```
string.punctuation
```

However, that list doesn't include a few common punctuation marks, such as single and double curly quotes, so the code specifies them directly:

```
extra_punctuation = '""''...'
```

Now a loop can run through all the punctuation marks to remove them:

```
for mark in string.punctuation + extra_punctuation:
    clean_text = clean_text.replace(mark, "")
```

Finding the most common words

A useful text analysis is to display a list of the words that appear in the text most frequently. This can tell you if you're overusing a particular word, for example, or if a word you want to emphasize in the text appears often enough.

The task of finding the most frequently used words begins by splitting the text into a list of individual words:

```
words = clean_text.split()
```

Now create a dictionary to count the occurrences of each word:

```
word_counts = {}
```

It's important at this point to decide whether you want your analysis to include filler words such as *the, and, to,* and *a.* In the text analysis industry, such words are known as *stop words.* This project assumes you don't want to include those words, which is why earlier in the code we imported the `stopwords` list from the `nltk` library. Your code now needs to store that list in a set:

```
stop_words = set(stopwords.words("english"))
```

Now you're ready to loop through the list of words:

```
for word in words:
    # If the word is a stop word, don't count it
    if word in stop_words:
        continue
    # Has the word already come up?
    if word in word_counts:
        # If so, increment its count
        word_counts[word] += 1
    else:
        # If not, add it to the dictionary with a count of 1
        word_counts[word] = 1
```

This loop first checks to see if the word is a stop word; if it is, a continue statement skips the rest of the loop. If it's not a stop word, the loop checks to see if the word is already in the dictionary. If it is, the word's count is incremented; otherwise, the word is added to the dictionary and its count is set to 1.

With the loop complete, the word_counts dictionary now contains a count for each word, where each key is a word and each value is the count for that word. Here's a sample:

```
{
'alices': 13,
'adventures': 7,
'wonderland': 3,
'rabbit': 49,
'hole': 6,
'pool': 12,
'tears': 12,
...
}
```

Now the code needs to sort the dictionary by descending order of word frequency:

```
sorted_words = sorted(word_counts.items(), key=lambda item: item[1],
    reverse= True)
```

Okay, there's a lot going on here, so let me unpack it for you:

>> sorted(): Sorts iterables such as lists and dictionaries.

>> word_counts.items(): Turns the dictionary into a list of (*word*, *count*) tuples. Here's a taste:

```
[('alices', 13), ('adventures', 7), ('wonderland', 3),...]
```

>> key=lambda item: item[1]: Tells Python what data to use for the sort. Each item is a tuple, such as (alices, 13). The code item[1] grabs the number part (13), so the word count values are used for the sort.

>> reverse=True: Sorts from highest to lowest.

TECHNICAL STUFF

What's up with the lambda keyword in the second sorted() argument? Believe it or not, it's a function! A *lambda function* is a short, one-line, anonymous function. So, this:

```
lambda item: item[1]
```

is basically the same as this:

```
def get_value(item):
    return item[1]
```

But instead of writing a whole def block, Python lets you use lambda when all you need is a quick, simple function, which is particularly useful when sorting or filtering.

Okay, now the code is ready to print the ten most common words:

```
print("The 10 most common words in the text are:")
for word, count in sorted_words[:10]:
    print(f"{word}: {count}")
```

In the for loop, sorted_words[:10] means "everything from the start of the list up to, but not including, the item with index 10."

Here's the output:

```
The 10 most common words in the text are:
said: 462
alice: 386
little: 129
one: 103
know: 87
```

```
like: 85
would: 83
went: 83
could: 77
thought: 74
```

Interesting!

Finding the longest words

The next text analysis trick is to print a list of the longest words in the text. This technique is useful for an essay or a post to let you know if you're using too many (or not enough!) big words.

The analysis begins by getting the set of the unique words in the text:

```
unique_words = set(words)
```

Here you see where converting a dictionary into a set is super helpful. Since a set can contain only unique items, the code simply has to run set(words) and you've got your unique words, just like that.

Next you sort that set based on the length of each word, from largest to smallest:

```
longest_words = sorted(unique_words, key=len, reverse=True)
```

Now all that's left is to print the top ten:

```
print("Top 10 longest words:")
for word in longest_words[:10]:
    print(f"{word} is {len(word)} characters long.")
```

Here's the output:

```
Top 10 longest words:
multiplication is 14 characters long.
contemptuously is 14 characters long.
disappointment is 14 characters long.
affectionately is 14 characters long.
inquisitively is 13 characters long.
straightening is 13 characters long.
circumstances is 13 characters long.
conversations is 13 characters long.
extraordinary is 13 characters long.
uncomfortable is 13 characters long.
```

Analyzing sentence lengths

One of the keys to strong writing is to monitor the lengths of your sentences:

» Too many short sentences may mean your text is pitched at too low a level (depending on your target audience, of course).

» Too many long sentences may mean your text is pitched at too high a level (again, taking into account your typical reader).

» Too many sentences of approximately the same length may mean your text lacks the variety that provides for a good text flow.

Okay, it's time to whip up some code to analyze sentence lengths and even display a graph that shows the distribution of the lengths!

First up, you need to break the text into sentences using NLTK's `sent_tokenize()` function. However, that function doesn't do well with sentences that end with a period followed by a curly quote. So, just in case your text has such a combination, it's best to first clean the raw text to replace curly quotes with straight quotes:

```
raw_text = raw_text.replace(""", '"').replace(""", '"')
raw_text = raw_text.replace("'", "'").replace("'", "'")
```

Okay, now the raw text is ready for the `sent_tokenize()` function:

```
sentences = sent_tokenize(raw_text)
```

REMEMBER

Note that I used `raw_text` for tokenizing sentences. You can't use the cleaned version of the text for the sentence tokenizing because that text has been scrubbed of sentence-ending punctuation such as periods, question marks, and exclamation points.

Now you can use a list comprehension to store the length of each sentence, in words, using NLTK's `word_tokenize()` function:

```
sentence_lengths = [len(word_tokenize(sentence)) for sentence in
    sentences]
```

Alright, it's time to do some honest-to-goodness sentence analysis, specifically the number of sentences, the shortest sentence, the longest sentence, and the average sentence length:

```
total_sentences = len(sentences)
shortest_sentence = min(sentence_lengths)
longest_sentence = max(sentence_lengths)
```

```
average_sentence = sum(sentence_lengths) / total_sentences

# Display the results
print(f"Number of sentences: {total_sentences}")
print(f"Shortest sentence: {shortest_sentence} words")
print(f"Longest sentence: {longest_sentence} words")
print(f"Average length: {average_sentence:.1f} words")
```

Here's a sample output:

```
Number of sentences: 1624
Shortest sentence: 2 words
Longest sentence: 202 words
Average length: 21.00 words
```

Wow: a 202-word sentence!

In general, here, you want to look out for super-long sentences, which might be due either to a mistake (you typed, say, a comma instead of a period) or to your words getting away from you. The average sentence length is useful, as well:

>> **Short sentences (average words: 5–15):** Easier to read and understand, so are best used for casual writing or text aimed at children. Shorter sentences also suggest clarity and conciseness, so they're a good choice for how-to manuals and other teaching materials.

>> **Medium length sentences (average words: 15–25):** Provide a balance between clarity and complexity, so are often found in general non-fiction, journalism, and web writing.

>> **Long sentences (average words: 25 and up):** An indication of complexity, so are typical in academic texts, legal documents, and classic literature. However, long sentences can also be the hallmark of verbosity. They're also harder to parse, which can affect readability.

That's pretty good, but now it's time to raise the text analysis game to a higher level by plotting the sentence lengths on a graph. To do that, the code uses a library called Matplotlib, which offers rich tools for visualizing data in Python.

Recall the following from the top of this project:

```
import matplotlib.pyplot as plt
```

This statement imports Matplotlib's pyplot() function (under the alias plt), which is used for creating static, interactive, and animated visualizations, particularly 2D plots like line graphs, bar charts, and scatter plots.

For this project, a histogram chart will do the job nicely, so let's use `pyplot()` to build a histogram from the `sentence_lengths` list, using 30 bins (in a histogram, a *bin* is a range of values used to group data points):

```
plt.hist(sentence_lengths, bins=30, edgecolor='black')
```

Toss in a title and some axis labels:

```
plt.title("Sentence Lengths in Words")
plt.xlabel("Words per sentence")
plt.ylabel("Number of sentences")
```

Then display the graph:

```
plt.show()
```

Figure 9-1 shows the graphs that appears for this project's sample data.

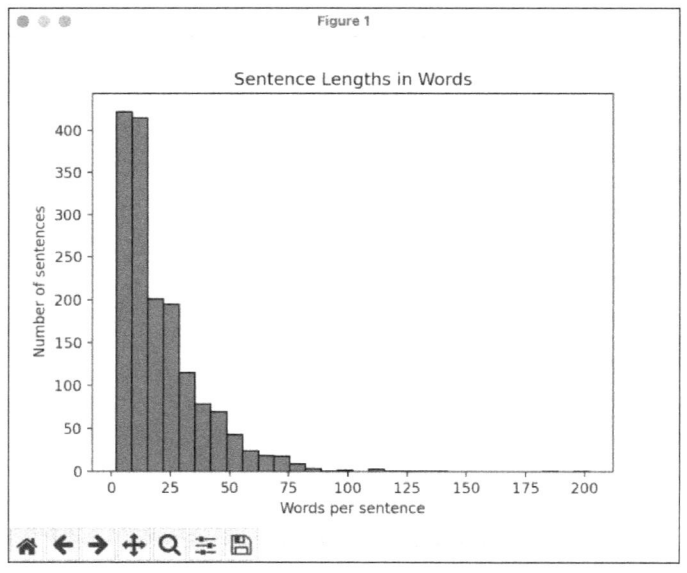

FIGURE 9-1:
A histogram of sentence lengths generated by Matplotlib's `pyplot()` function.

Analyzing text sentiment

One of the most interesting ways you can analyze text is to determine its overall *sentiment*, which refers to the emotional tone or attitude expressed in the text. Sentiment analysis is a way of identifying and categorizing the subjective information embedded in written language.

Most sentiment analysis identifies three common sentiment categories:

» **Positive:** The text shows approval, happiness, or praise (for example, "The movie was amazing!" or "I'm finding this book about coding super helpful!").

» **Negative:** The text indicates disapproval, anger, or criticism (for example, "The service was terrible!" or "Naked handball was the worst experience of my life!").

» **Neutral:** The text is generally factual, objective, or without emotional tone (for example, "The meeting starts at 3 PM." or "That kumquat was only so-so.").

Several approaches to detecting the sentiment of text exist, but perhaps the most straightforward is *lexicon-based*, which uses a predefined dictionary of words (a *lexicon*) in which each word is associated with a sentiment score. If the words in a text are mostly positive, the sentiment is probably positive, and the same goes with negative and neutral words.

NLTK offers a lexicon-based sentiment analysis tool called VADER (Valence Aware Dictionary and sEntiment Reasoner), which you downloaded at the beginning of this project. You import it into your Python code with the following statement:

```
from nltk.sentiment import SentimentIntensityAnalyzer
```

Using VADER for a basic sentiment analysis requires just two statements:

```
analyzer = SentimentIntensityAnalyzer()
scores = analyzer.polarity_scores(raw_text)
```

Then you print the results:

```
print("Sentiment scores:")
print(scores)
```

Here's the output from the sample text:

```
Sentiment scores:
{'neg': 0.086, 'neu': 0.821, 'pos': 0.093, 'compound': 0.9998}
```

Here's what each part means:

» neg: How much of the text is negative in tone

» neu: How much is neutral

>> pos: How much is positive

The three values neg, neu, and pos are proportions of the total, so they add up to 1.0 (or very close to it, depending on rounding errors).

>> compound: The overall sentiment score, squished into a single number from -1 to +1. Here's how you interpret this score:

- \> 0.05: Positive overall sentiment; the higher the value, the more positive the sentiment

- < -0.05: Negative overall sentiment; the lower the value, the more negative the sentiment

- -0.05 to 0.05: Neutral or mixed sentiment

Just for fun, I wrote a short Python script (chapter09/example01.py) where you type some text and the program analyzes the sentiment.

The full code

Here's the full code for the text analysis project (chapter09/project02.py):

```
# Import all the things
import sys
import string
import matplotlib.pyplot as plt
from nltk.corpus import stopwords
from nltk.tokenize import sent_tokenize, word_tokenize
from nltk.sentiment import SentimentIntensityAnalyzer

# Open and read the text file
try:
    with open("alice.txt", encoding="utf-8-sig") as file:
        raw_text = file.read()
except FileNotFoundError:
    print("Whoops! The file wasn't found!")
    print("Make sure it's in the same folder as this script.")
    sys.exit()

# Make everything lowercase
clean_text = raw_text.lower()

# Replace hyphens and em dashes with spaces
clean_text = clean_text.replace("-", " ")
clean_text = clean_text.replace("—", " ")
```

```python
# Define extra punctuation to remove (e.g., curly quotes)
extra_punctuation = '""''...'

# Remove punctuation marks such as commas and periods
for mark in string.punctuation + extra_punctuation:
    clean_text = clean_text.replace(mark, "")

# Split the text into a list of individual words
words = clean_text.split()

# Create a dictionary to count the occurrences of each word
word_counts = {}

# Store all the stop words
stop_words = set(stopwords.words("english"))

# Loop through the list of words
for word in words:
    # If the word is a stop word, don't count it
    if word in stop_words:
        continue
    # Has the word already come up?
    if word in word_counts:
        # If so, increment its count
        word_counts[word] += 1
    else:
        # If not, add it to the dictionary with a count of 1
        word_counts[word] = 1

# Sort the dictionary by word count (highest first)
sorted_words = sorted(word_counts.items(),
                      key=lambda item: item[1],
                      reverse= True)

# Print the 10 most common words
print("The 10 most common words in the text are:")
for word, count in sorted_words[:10]:
    print(f"{word}: {count}")

# Get a list of unique words
unique_words = set(words)

# Sort the unique words by length (longest first)
longest_words = sorted(unique_words, key=len, reverse=True)
```

```
# Print the 10 longest words
print("Top 10 longest words:")
for word in longest_words[:10]:
    print(f"{word} is {len(word)} characters long.")


# Replace curly quotes with regular quotes
raw_text = raw_text.replace(""", '"').replace(""", '"')
raw_text = raw_text.replace("'", "'").replace("'", "'")


# Break the text into sentences
sentences = sent_tokenize(raw_text)


# Determine the length of each sentence, in words
sentence_lengths = [len(word_tokenize(sentence)) for sentence in sentences]


# Now get some basic stats
total_sentences = len(sentences)
shortest_sentence = min(sentence_lengths)
longest_sentence = max(sentence_lengths)
average_sentence = sum(sentence_lengths) / total_sentences


# Display the results
print(f"Number of sentences: {total_sentences}")
print(f"Shortest sentence: {shortest_sentence} words")
print(f"Longest sentence: {longest_sentence} words")
print(f"Average length: {average_sentence:.2f} words")


# Plot the sentence lengths on a graph
plt.hist(sentence_lengths, bins=30, edgecolor='black')
plt.title("Sentence Lengths in Words")
plt.xlabel("Words per sentence")
plt.ylabel("Number of sentences")
plt.show()


# Get a reference to VADER
analyzer = SentimentIntensityAnalyzer()


# Run a sentiment analysis on the raw text
scores = analyzer.polarity_scores(raw_text)


# Print the sentiment scores
print("Sentiment scores:")
print(scores)
```

3

Learning JavaScript: The Language of the Web

Learn the basics of JavaScript.

Master variables, loops, and functions.

Wield strings, dates, and arrays like a pro.

Use JavaScript to make dynamic web pages.

Debug your JavaScript apps.

Code some JavaScript projects.

Chapter **10**

Getting Your Feet Wet with JavaScript

JavaScript is the duct tape of the internet.

— CHARLIE CAMPBELL

When many people hear the word *coding* these days, their thoughts automatically do one of two things: Shut down completely until the threat goes away, or fantasize about building amazing web pages. Web pages? Yep. Even though the technologies that underly all web pages — HTML and CSS — don't technically qualify as programming languages, to many people that's nerdy nitpicking. (Hey, who're you calling a nerd!?) They just want to get a presence on the web without resorting to lame, one-size-fits-no-one templates.

Alas, I don't focus on HTML and CSS in this book (although I do offer a taste of these technologies in Chapter 17). But if you already have a basic web page built and want to do some *real* coding, have I got a language for you! JavaScript is the default coding language of the web and is available in all web browsers, free of charge. Anybody can use HTML and CSS to cobble together a standard-issue page, but if you want to craft dynamic, interactive pages (of course you do!), welcome to JavaScript world.

JavaScript: Controlling the Machine

When a web browser is confronted with an HTML file, it goes through a simple but tedious process: It reads the file one line at a time, starting from (usually) the `<html>` tag at the top and finishing with the `</html>` tag at the bottom. Along the way, it might have to break out of this line-by-line monotony to perform some action based on what it's read. For example, if it comes upon an `<img>` tag, the browser will immediately ask the web server to ship out a copy of the graphics file specified in `src`.

The point here is that, at its core, a web browser is just a page-reading machine that doesn't know how to do much of anything else besides follow the instructions (the markup) in an HTML file. (For convenience, I'm ignoring the browser's other capabilities, such as saving bookmarks.)

One of the reasons that many folks get hooked on creating web pages is that they realize from the beginning that they have control over this page-reading machine. Slap some text between an `<a href="url">` tag and its corresponding `</a>` end tag, replace *url* with an address, and the browser dutifully displays the text as a link. Create a CSS Grid structure and the browser displays your formerly haphazard text in nice, neat rows and columns, no questions asked. These two examples show that, instead of just viewing pages from the outside, you now have a key to get inside the machine and start working its controls. *That* is the hook that grabs people and gets them seriously interested in web page design.

Imagine that you could take this idea of controlling the page-reading machine to the next level. Imagine that, instead of ordering the machine to process mere tags and text, you could issue much more sophisticated commands that could control the inner workings of the page-reading machine. Who wouldn't want that?

Well, that's the premise behind JavaScript. It's essentially just a collection of commands that you can wield to control a web page. Like HTML tags, JavaScript commands are inserted directly in the web page file. When the browser does its line-by-line reading of the file and comes across a JavaScript command, it executes that command, just like that.

However, the key here is that the amount of control JavaScript gives you over the page-reading machine is much greater than what you get with HTML tags. The reason is that JavaScript is a full-fledged programming language. Although the *L* in HTML stands for *language,* there isn't even the tiniest hint of a programming language associated with HTML. JavaScript, though, is the real programming deal.

What You Need to Get Started

One of the nicest things about building web pages with HTML and CSS is that the hurdles you have to leap to get started are not only low but few in number. In fact, you really need only two things, both of which are free: a text editor to enter the text, tags, and properties and a browser to view the results. (You also need access to a web server to host the finished pages, but the server isn't necessary when you're creating the pages.) Yes, there are high-end HTML editors and fancy graphics programs, but these fall into the bells-and-whistles category; you can create perfectly respectable web pages without them.

The basic requirements for JavaScript programming are the same as for HTML: a text editor and a browser. Again, programs are available to help you write and test your scripts, but you don't need them.

Basic Script Construction

Okay, that's more than enough theory. It's time to roll up your sleeves, crack your knuckles, and start coding. This section describes the standard procedure for constructing and testing a script and shows you where to put the script to make it work.

The <script> tag

The basic container for a script is, naturally enough, the HTML `<script>` tag and its associated `</script>` end tag:

```
<script>
    JavaScript statements go here
</script>
```

Where do you put the <script> tag?

With certain exceptions, it doesn't matter a great deal where you put your `<script>` tag. Some people place the tag between the page's `</head>` and `<body>` tags. The HTML standard recommends placing the `<script>` tag in the page header (that is, between `<head>` and `</head>`), so that's the style I use in this book:

```
<!DOCTYPE html>
<html lang="en">
    <head>
```

```
            <meta charset="utf-8">
            <title>Where do you put the script tag?</title>
            <script>
                JavaScript statements go here
            </script>
        </head>
        <body>
        </body>
    </html>
```

Here are the exceptions to the put-your-script-anywhere technique:

>> If your script is designed to write data to the page, the `<script>` tag must be positioned in the page body (that is, between the `<body>` and `</body>` tags) in the exact position where you want the text to appear.

>> If your script refers to an item on the page (such as a form object), the script must be placed *after* that item. In most cases where the script refers to one or more page objects, coders plop the `<script>` tag at the bottom of the page body (that is, just above the `</body>` tag).

>> With many HTML tags, you can add one or more JavaScript statements as attributes directly in the tag.

It's perfectly acceptable to insert multiple `<script>` tags in a single page, as long as each one has a corresponding `</script>` end tag and as long as you don't put one `<script>` block in another one.

Adding Comments to Your Code

As I describe in Chapter 2, to help others decipher your code (or to help you decipher it after you haven't looked at it for a while), it's good programming practice to make liberal use of comments throughout the script. For short, single-line comments, use the double-slash (//). Put the // at the beginning of the line and then type in your comment after it. Here's an example:

```
// Change the background color of the page
document.body.style.backgroundColor = 'antiquewhite';
```

You can also use // comments for two or three lines of text by adding // at the beginning of each line. If you have more lines than that, however, you're better off using multiple-line comments that begin with the /* symbol and end with the */ symbol. Most JavaScript coders put these comment symbols on separate lines, begin each comment line with an asterisk, and align the asterisks for maximum readability. Here's an example:

```
/*
 * This script demonstrates JavaScript's capability
 * to change the background color of the web page
 * by setting the backgroundColor property to a
 * color name, hex code, RGB value, or HSL value.
 * This script is copyrighted 2026 Paul McFedries.
 */
```

Creating External JavaScript Files

Putting a script inside the page header or body isn't a problem if the script is relatively short. However, if your script takes up dozens or hundreds of lines, your HTML code can look cluttered. Another problem you might run into is needing to use the same code on multiple pages. Sure, you can just copy the code to each page that requires it, but if you make changes down the road, you need to update every page that uses the code.

The solution to both problems is to move the code out of the HTML file and into an external JavaScript file. Moving the code reduces the JavaScript presence in the HTML file to a single line (as you learn shortly) and means that you can update the code by editing only the external file.

Here are some things to note about using an external JavaScript file:

» The file must use a plain text format.

» Use the .js extension when you name the file.

» Don't use the <script> tag in the file. Just enter your statements directly.

» The rules for when the browser executes statements in an external file are identical to those used for statements in an HTML file. That is, statements outside functions are executed automatically when the browser comes across your file reference, and statements in a function aren't executed until the function is called.

To let the browser know that an external JavaScript file exists, add the `src` attribute to the `<script>` tag. For example, if the external file is named `myscripts.js`, you set up your `<script>` tag as follows:

```
<script src="myscripts.js">
```

This example assumes that the `myscripts.js` file is in the same directory as the HTML file. If the file resides in a different directory, adjust the `src` value accordingly. For example, if the `myscripts.js` file is in a subdirectory named `scripts`, you use this:

```
<script src="scripts/myscripts.js">
```

You can even specify a file from another site (presumably your own!) by specifying a full URL as the `src` value:

```
<script src="http://www.host.com/myscripts.js">
```

Getting to Know the Console

All major web browsers come with a sophisticated set of debugging tools that can make your life as a web developer much easier and much saner. Most web developers debug their scripts using Google Chrome, so I focus on that browser in this book. But in this section, I give you an overview of the tools available in all the major browsers and how to get at them.

Displaying the developer tools in various browsers

Here's how you open the web development tools (often shorted to just *dev tools* by all the cool kids) in Chrome, Firefox, Microsoft Edge, and Safari:

>> **Chrome for Windows:** Click the Customize and Control Google Chrome icon (three vertical dots to the right of the address bar), and then choose More Tools ⇨ Developer Tools. Shortcut: Ctrl+Shift+I.

>> **Chrome for Mac:** Choose View ⇨ Developer ⇨ Developer Tools. Shortcut: Option+⌘+I.

>> **Firefox for Windows:** Click the open Application menu icon (three horizontal lines on the far right of the toolbar), and then choose More Tools ⇨ Web Developer Tools. Shortcut: Ctrl+Shift+I.

>> **Firefox for Mac:** Choose Tools ⇨ Browser Tools ⇨ Web Developer Tools. Shortcut: Option+⌘+I.

>> **Microsoft Edge for Windows or Mac:** Click the settings and more icon (the three vertical dots to the right of the address bar), and then choose More Tools ⇨ Developer Tools. Shortcuts: Ctrl+Shift+I (Windows) or Option+⌘+I (Mac).

>> **Safari:** Click Develop ⇨ Show Web Inspector. Shortcut: Option+⌘+I. If you don't have the Develop menu, click Safari ⇨ Settings, click the Advanced tab, and then select the Show Features for Web Developers check box.

These development tools vary in the features they offer, but each provides the same set of basic tools, which are the tools you'll use most often. These basic web development tools include the following:

>> **HTML viewer:** This tab (called Inspector in Firefox and Elements in the other browsers) shows the HTML source code used in the web page. When you hover the mouse pointer over a tag, the browser highlights the element in the displayed page and shows its width and height, as shown in Figure 10-1. When you click a tag, the browser shows the CSS styles applied with the tag, as well as the tag's box dimensions (again, refer to Figure 10-1).

>> **Console:** This tab enables you to view error messages, log messages, test expressions, and execute statements. I cover the Console window in more detail in the next section.

>> **Debugging tool:** This tab (called Debugger in Firefox and Sources in the other browsers) enables you to pause code execution, step through your code, watch the values of variables and properties, and much more. This is the most important JavaScript debugging tool, so I cover it in detail later in Chapter 14.

>> **Network:** This tab tells you how long it takes to load each file referenced by your web page. If you find that your page is slow to load, this tab can help you find the bottleneck.

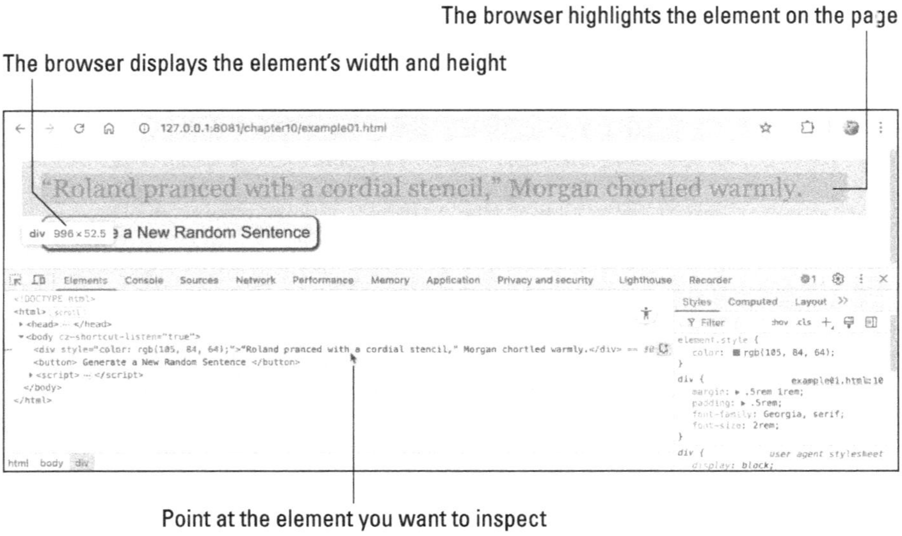

FIGURE 10-1:
The HTML viewer,
such as Chrome's
Elements tab,
enables you to
inspect each
element's styles
and box
dimensions.

Point at the element you want to inspect

Displaying the Console window in various browsers

If your web page is behaving strangely — for example, the page is blank or missing elements — you should first check your HTML code to make sure it's correct. (Common HTML errors are not finishing a tag with a greater than sign — > — not including a closing tag, and missing a closing quotation mark for an attribute value.) If your HTML checks out, there's a good chance that your JavaScript code is wonky. How do you know? A trip to the Console window is your first step.

The Console window is an interactive browser window that shows warnings and errors, displays the output of `console.log()` statements, and enables you to execute expressions and statements without having to run your entire script. The Console window is one of the handiest web browser debugging tools, so you need to know your way around it.

To display the Console window, open your web browser's development tools and then click the Console tab. You can also use the following keyboard shortcuts:

>> **Chrome for Windows:** Press Ctrl+Shift+J.

>> **Chrome for Mac:** Press Option+⌘+J.

>> **Firefox for Windows:** Press Ctrl+Shift+K.

>> **Firefox for Mac:** Press Option+⌘+K.

>> **Microsoft Edge for Windows:** Press Ctrl+Shift+J.

>> **Microsoft Edge for Mac:** Press Option+⌘+J.

>> **Safari:** Press Option+⌘+C.

Example: Logging data to the Console window

The first thing you need to know is that your JavaScript code can use the `console.log()` method to output a message to the console. Displaying messages to the console is one of the most common techniques that developers use when writing and troubleshooting their code. The simplest method for sending a message to the console is to invoke `console.log` with some text:

```
console.log("message")
```

Replace *message* with the text you want to appear in the console. The following example (chapter10/example02.html in this book's example files) sends the message `Hello JavaScript World!` to the console:

```
<!DOCTYPE html>
<html lang="en">
    <head>
        <meta charset="utf-8">
        <title>Sending a Message to the Console</title>
        <script>
            console.log("Hello JavaScript World!");
        </script>
    </head>
    <body>
    </body>
</html>
```

Figure 10-2 shows Chrome's Console tab with the `Hello JavaScript World!` message displayed.

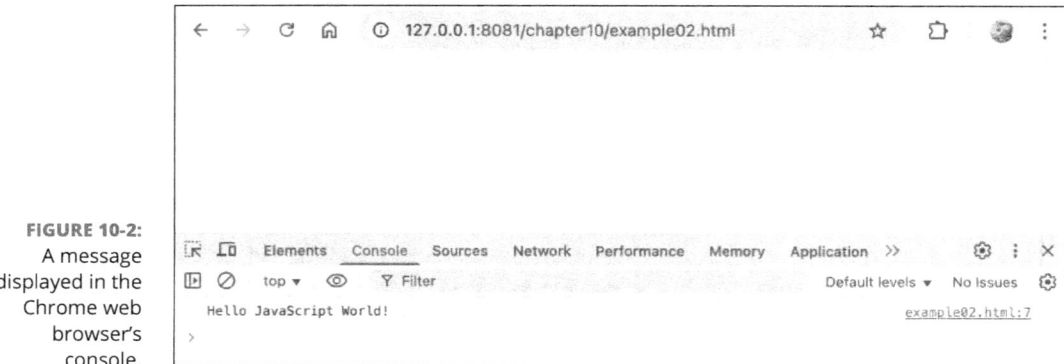

FIGURE 10-2:
A message displayed in the Chrome web browser's console.

Chapter **11**

Getting the Hang of a Few JavaScript Fundamentals

Always bet on JavaScript.

—BRENDAN EICH (CREATOR OF JAVASCRIPT)

JavaScript is a massive and powerful programming language, a full description of which would require ten books this size. I'm pretty sure you'd have no interest in reading all those books even if they did exist, so my challenge here is to condense all the JavaScript fundamentals down to just a few dozen pages in this chapter and the next. I'm not going to lie to you: There's a lot of material to explore, but once you're done, you're going to have such a solid base of JavaScript know-how in your brain that you'll be able to code some pretty amazing web apps even without the slightly more advanced topics that I cover in subsequent chapters. So, pour yourself a coffee, a tea, something pumpkin-spiced, or whatever is your go-to energy drink, and let's get started.

I Do Declare: Variables in JavaScript

To declare a variable in JavaScript, you precede the variable name with either the `let` keyword or the `const` keyword:

```
let variableName1 = value1;
const variableName2 = value2;
```

One difference between the two is that the value of a variable declared with `let` can be changed, but the value of a variable declared with `const` (which is short for *constant*) can't be changed.

REMEMBER

Older versions of JavaScript declared variables using the obsolete `var` keyword, which is still part of the language and is prevalent in many older scripts, so you'll still see it here and there.

Why would you ever want a variable that doesn't change? Sometimes a variable holds a value that, if changed, could cause errors to crop up in your script. For example, if your script converts miles to kilometers, you might include the following declaration:

```
const milesToKilometers = 1.60934;
```

It makes sense to use `const` here because you don't want some later part of your script to change that conversion value.

The other main difference between `const` and `let` is that you must specify a value when declaring `const` variables, but with `let` you can just declare the variable by itself and assign it a value later:

```
let interestRate;
```

JavaScript has only a few rules for variable names:

>> The first character must be a letter or an underscore (_). You can't use a number as the first character.

>> The rest of the variable name can include any letter, any number, or the underscore. You can't use any other characters, including spaces, symbols, and punctuation marks.

>> As with the rest of JavaScript, variable names are case sensitive. That is, a variable named `InterestRate` is treated as a different variable than one named `interestRate`.

>> There's no limit to the length of the variable name.

>> You can't use one of JavaScript's reserved words (such as `let`, `const`, or `var`) as a variable name.

REMEMBER

Right about here is where I'd normally add some coverage of building expressions in JavaScript. But I've already done that! That's right: Everything I wrote about expressions in Chapter 2 applies to JavaScript, so if you need an expressions refresher, that chapter is the place to go.

Code Looping in JavaScript

When you need your JavaScript code to repeat some statements a few times, the language offers a few different loop types you can turn to. First, know that JavaScript supports the `while` loops that I introduced in Chapter 2. But JavaScript also offers two other loop methods, which I talk about in the next couple of sections.

Using for loops

Although `while` is the most straightforward of the JavaScript loops, the most common type by far is the `for` loop. This is slightly surprising when you consider (as you will shortly) that the `for` loop's syntax is a bit more complex than that of the `while` loop. However, the `for` loop excels at one thing: looping when you know exactly how many times you want to repeat a group of statements. This task is common in all types of programming, so it's no wonder `for` is so often used in scripts.

The general syntax used with `for` loops is complicated, so I'm going to simplify things considerably by presenting the version of the syntax that's used in 99 percent of `for` loops:

```
for (let counter = start; counterExpression; counterUpdate) {
    statement(s)
}
```

There's a lot going on here, so I'll take it one bit at a time:

>> *counter*: A numeric variable used as a *loop counter*. The loop counter is a number that counts how many times the procedure has gone through the loop. (Note that you need to include `let` only if this is the first time you've

used the variable in the script.) It's common to use letters such as i and j for the counter variable name.

>> *start*: The initial value of *counter*. This value is usually 1, but you can use whatever value makes sense for your script.

>> *counterExpression*: A comparison or logical expression that determines the number of times through the loop. This expression usually compares the current value of *counter* to some maximum value.

>> *counterUpdate*: An expression that changes the value of *counter*. Most of the time you'll increment the value of counter with the expression *counter++*.

Here's an example (in this book's example files, check out chapter11/example01. html):

```
let sum = 0;
let num;
for (let i = 1; i <= 3; i++) {
    num = prompt("Type a number:", 1);
    sum += Number(num);
}
console.log("The total of your numbers is " + sum);
```

After declaring a couple of variables, this script sets up a for loop. The counter variable is i, which starts at 1, and the code loops until i is 3, so there are three iterations altogether. Within each loop, the code uses JavaScript's prompt() function to ask the user for input (a number, in this case), which is added to the sum variable. The prompt() function returns a string, so the code uses Number() to convert the string to a number. After the loop is done, the sum of the three numbers is displayed in the Console window. (Refer to Chapter 10 to learn how to display the Console window in your browser.)

Using do. . .while loops

Besides while and for, JavaScript has a third and final type of loop that I've left until last because it isn't one you'll use often. It's called a do...while loop, and its general syntax looks like this:

```
do {
    statements
}
while (expression);
```

Here, *statements* represents a block of statements to execute each time through the loop, and *expression* is a comparison or logical expression that, as long as it returns `true`, tells JavaScript to keep executing the *statements* within the loop. This structure ensures that JavaScript executes the loop's statement block at least once.

For example, the following shows you how to use `do...while` to restructure the prompt-and-sum code I presented in the preceding section (chapter11/example02.html):

```
let sum = 0;
let num;
do {
    num = prompt("Type a number; when you're done, click Cancel:", 1);
    sum += Number(num);
}
while (num !== null || sum === 0);
console.log("The total of your numbers is " + sum);
```

This code is similar to a `while` loop. All that's really changed is that the `while` statement and its expression have been moved after the statement block so that the loop must be executed once before the expression is evaluated.

Controlling loop execution

Most loops run their natural course and then the procedure moves on. Sometimes, however, you may want to exit a loop prematurely or skip over some statements and continue with the next pass through the loop. You can handle each situation with, respectively, the `break` and `continue` statements.

You use `break` when your loop comes across some value or condition that would prevent the rest of the statements from executing properly or that satisfies what the loop was trying to accomplish.

Here's an example (chapter11/example03.html):

```
let sum = 0;
let num;
for (let i = 1; i <= 3; i++) {
    num = prompt("Type a number: (or click Cancel to bail out)", 1);
    if (num === null) {
        break;
    }
```

```
        sum += Number(num);
    }
    console.log("The total of your numbers is " + sum);
```

If when prompted to enter a number the user instead clicks Cancel, the `input()` function returns the value `null`. This code checks for that value with `if(num === null)`. If this expression returns `true`, the code runs `break` to bail out of the `for` loop.

The `continue` statement is similar to `break`, but instead of exiting a loop entirely, `continue` tells JavaScript to bypass the rest of the statements in the loop block and begin a new iteration of the loop. Here's an example (chapter11/example04.html):

```
let sum = 0;
let num;
do {
    num = prompt("Type a number; when you're done, click Cancel:", 1);
    if (isNaN(num) && num !== null) {
        continue;
    }
    sum += Number(num);
}
while (num !== null || sum === 0);
console.log("The total of your numbers is " + sum);
```

After getting the user's input, this code uses JavaScript's `isNaN()` function (short for is Not a Number) to determine if the input is a number (in which case `isNaN()` returns `false`) or something else, such as a string (in which case `isNaN()` returns `true`). To handle the case where the user clicks Cancel, the `if` statement also checks `num !== null`).

Harnessing the Power of Functions

The function syntax that I described in Chapter 2 is identical to the syntax used by JavaScript, so here I'll just cover some other JavaScript-specific material related to functions.

For most applications, it doesn't matter where you put your functions, as long as they reside in a `<script>` block. However, one of the most common uses of functions is to handle triggered events (refer to Chapter 13). It's possible that a particular event may fire when the page is loading, and if that happens before the browser has parsed the corresponding function, you could get strange results or an error. To prevent that, it's good practice to place the script containing all your functions in the page's header section (or in an external JavaScript file).

After your function is defined, you'll eventually need to tell the browser to execute — or *call* — the function. You can do this in three main ways:

>> When the browser parses the `<script>` tag

>> After the page is loaded

>> In response to an event, such as the user clicking a button

The next two sections cover the first two scenarios. You'll need to head over to Chapter 13 to learn about event handling in JavaScript.

Calling a function when the `<script>` tag is parsed

The simplest way to call a function is to include in your script a statement consisting of only the function name, followed by parentheses (assuming for the moment that your function uses no arguments). The following code (check out chapter11/example05.html) provides an example. (I listed the entire page to show you the location in the page code of the function and the statement that calls it.)

```
<!DOCTYPE html>
<html lang="en">
<head>
    <meta charset="utf-8">
    <title>Calling a function when the &lt;script&gt; tag is parsed</title>
    <script>
        function displayGreeting() {
            const currentHour = new Date().getHours();
            if (currentHour < 12) {
                console.log("Good morning!");
            } else {
                console.log("Good day!");
            }
        }
        displayGreeting();
    </script>
</head>
```

```
<body>
    <h1> Calling a function when the &lt;script&gt; tag is parsed</h1>
    <p>
        (Please open the browser's console to see
        the result of this page's script.)
    </p>
</body>
</html>
```

The `<script>` tag includes a function named `displayGreeting`, which determines the current hour of the day and then writes a greeting to the console based on whether it's currently morning. The function is called by the `displayGreeting` statement that appears just after the function.

Calling a function after the page is loaded

If your function references a page element, calling the function from the page's head section won't work because when the browser parses the script, the rest of the page hasn't loaded yet, so your element reference will fail.

To work around this problem, place another `<script>` tag at the end of the body section, just before the closing `</body>` tag, as shown here (chapter11/example06.html):

```
<!DOCTYPE html>
<html lang="en">
<head>
    <meta charset="utf-8">
    <title>Calling a function after the page is loaded</title>
    <script>
        function makeBackgroundTomato() {
            document.body.style.backgroundColor = "tomato";
            console.log("The background is now tomato.");
        }
    </script>
</head>
<body>
    <h1>Calling a function after the page is loaded</h1>
    <p>
        (Please open the browser's console to see
        the result of this page's script.)
    </p>

    <script>
```

```
        makeBackgroundTomato();
    </script>
</body>
</html>
```

The `makeBackgroundTomato` function does two things: It uses `document.body.style.backgroundColor` to change the background color of the `body` element to `tomato`, and it uses `console.log` to write a message to that effect on the console.

In the function, `document.body` is a reference to the `body` element, which doesn't exist until the page is fully loaded. If you try to call the function in the `head` section, you'll get an error. To execute the function properly, a second `<script>` tag appears at the bottom of the `body` element, and that script calls the function with the following statement:

```
makeBackgroundTomato();
```

By the time the browser executes that statement, the `body` element exists, so the function runs without an error.

Getting the Hang of Variable Scope

In programming, the *scope* of a variable defines where in the script a variable can be used and where it can't be used. Put another way, a variable's scope determines which statements and functions can access and work with the variable. You need to be concerned with scope for two main reasons:

>> **You may want to use the same variable name in multiple functions.** If these variables are otherwise unrelated, you'll want to make sure that there's no confusion about which variable you're working with. In other words, you'll want to restrict the scope of each variable to the block or function in which it is declared.

>> **You may need to use the same variable in multiple blocks or functions.** For example, a function may use a variable to store the results of a calculation, and other functions may also need to use that result. In this case, you'll want to set up the scope of the variable so that it's accessible to multiple functions.

JavaScript lets you establish three types of scope for your variables:

» Block scope

» Function scope

» Global scope

The next three sections describe each type in detail.

Working with block scope

When a variable has *block scope,* the variable was declared using `let` or `const` inside a statement block — that is, between a set of braces: { and } — and the only statements that can access the variable are the ones in that same block. Statements outside the block and statements in other blocks can't access the variable (chapter11/example07.html):

```
if (true) {
    const myMessage = "I'm in the scope!";
    console.log("Inside the if block: " + myMessage);
}
console.log("Outside the if block: " + myMessage);
```

This code uses an `if` construction to create a statement block. Inside that block, the code declares a variable named `myMessage`, sets its value to a text string, and uses JavaScript's `console.log` method to display the string in the console.

After the `if` block, another `console.log` statement attempts to display the `myMessage` variable. However, JavaScript generates an error that says `myMessage is not defined`:

```
Inside the if block: I'm in the scope!
Uncaught ReferenceError: myMessage is not defined
```

Why? Because the scope of the `myMessage` variable extends only to the `if` block. Any statement outside that block can't "see" the `myMessage` variable, so it has nothing to display. In fact, after the `if` statement finishes executing, JavaScript removes the `myMessage` variable from memory, so that's why the `myMessage` variable referred to in the final line is undefined.

Working with function scope

When a variable has *function scope* (often also known as *local scope*), the variable was declared inside a function and the only statements that can access the variable are the ones that come after that declaration in that same function. Statements outside the function and statements in other functions can't access the variable.

The following code demonstrates function scope (chapter11/example08.html):

```
function A() {
    const myMessage = "I'm in the scope!";
    console.log("Function A: " + myMessage);
}
function B() {
    console.log("Function B: " + myMessage);
}
A();
B();
```

There are two functions here, named A and B. Function A declares a variable named myMessage, sets its value to a text string, and uses JavaScript's console.log method to display the string in the console.

Function B also uses console.log to attempt to display the myMessage variable. As shown next, JavaScript generates an error that says myMessage is not defined.

```
Function A: I'm in the scope!
Uncaught ReferenceError: myMessage is not defined
```

Why? Because the scope of the myMessage variable extends only to function A; function B can't "see" the myMessage variable, which was removed from memory as soon as function A finished executing.

The same result occurs if you attempt to use the myMessage variable outside any function, as in the following code:

```
function A() {
    const myMessage = "I'm in the scope!";
    console.log("Function A: " + myMessage);
}
A();
// The following statement generates an error:
console.log(myMessage);
```

Working with global scope

What if you want to use the same variable in multiple functions or even in multiple script blocks within the same page? In that case, you need to use *global scope,* which makes a variable accessible to any statement or function on a page. (That's why global scope is also called *page-level scope.*) To set up a variable with global scope, declare it outside any block or function. The following code gives this a whirl (chapter11/example09.html):

```
const myMessage = "I've got global scope!";

if (true) {
    console.log("Inside the if block: " + myMessage);
}
function C() {
    console.log("Function C: " + myMessage);
}
C();
console.log("Outside any block or function: " + myMessage);
```

The script begins by declaring the myMessage variable and setting it equal to a string literal. Then an if block uses a console.log statement to attempt to display the myMessage value. Next, a function named C is created and displays a console message that attempts to display the value of myMessage. After the function is called, another console.log statement attempts to display the myMessage value outside any block or function. Here are the results:

```
Inside the if block: I've got global scope!
Function C: I've got global scope!
Outside any block or function: I've got global scope!
```

All three console.log statements display the value of myMessage without a problem.

Chapter **12**

Tackling Some JavaScript Objects

Learning JavaScript used to mean you weren't a serious software developer. Today, not learning JavaScript means the same thing.

—TIM O'REILLY

A lthough your JavaScript code will spend much of its time dealing with web page knickknacks such as HTML tags and CSS properties, it will also perform lots of behind-the-scenes chores that require manipulating strings, dealing with dates and times, and performing mathematical calculations. To help you through these tasks, in this chapter you explore four of JavaScript's built-in objects: the String object, the Date object, the Math object, and the Array object. You investigate the most important properties of each object, master the most frequently used methods, and encounter lots of useful examples along the way.

Pulling Strings

Strings play a major role in all JavaScript programming, and it will be a rare script that doesn't have to deal with strings in some fashion. So, it pays to become proficient at manipulating strings, which includes locating text within a string and extracting text from a string. You learn about all that and more in this section.

Any string you work with — whether it's a string literal or the result of a method or function that returns a string — is a `String` object. So, for example, the following two statements are equivalent:

```
const bookName = new String("Coding For Dummies");
const bookName = "Coding For Dummies";
```

All these different ways of referring to a string means you have quite a bit of flexibility when applying the properties and methods of `String` objects. For example, the `String` object has a `length` property that I describe a bit later (see "Determining the length of a string"). The following are all legal JavaScript expressions that use this property:

```
bookName.length;
"Coding For Dummies".length;
prompt("Enter the book name:").length;
myFunction().length;
```

The last example assumes that `myFunction()` returns a string value.

Working with string templates

Before diving into the properties and methods of the `String` object, take a second to examine a special type of string designed to solve three string-related problems that will come up again and again in your coding career:

>> **Internal quotation marks:** String literals are surrounded by quotation marks, but what do you do when you need the same type of quotation mark inside the string?

One solution is to use a different type of quotation mark to delimit the string. For example, this is illegal:

```
'There's got to be a better way to do this.'
```

But this is fine:

```
"There's got to be a better way to do this."
```

A second solution is to escape the internal quotation mark with a slash, like so:

```
'There\'s got to be a better way to do this.'
```

These solutions work fine, but *remembering* to use them is harder than you may think!

>> **Variable values:** When you need to use the value of a variable inside a string, you usually end up with something ungainly, such as the following:

```
const adjective = "better";
const lament = "There's got to be a " + adjective +
  " way to do this.";
```

>> **Multiline strings:** It's often useful to define a string using multiple lines. However, if you try the following, you'll get a `string literal contains an unescaped line break` error:

```
const myHeader = '
    <nav class="banner">
        <h3 class="nav-heading">Navigation</h3>
        <ul class="nav-links">
            <li>Home</li>
            <li>Away</li>
            <li>In Between</li>
        </ul>
    </nav>'
```

You can solve all three problems by using a *string template* (also called a *template literal*), which is a kind of string literal where the delimiting quotation marks are replaced by back ticks (`` ` ``):

```
`Your string goes here`
```

Here's how you can use a string template to solve each of the three problems just described:

>> **Internal quotation marks:** You're free to plop any number of single or double quotation marks inside a string template:

```
`Ah, here's the better way to do this!`
```

>> **Variable values:** String templates support something called *variable interpolation,* which is a technique for referencing a variable value directly within a string. Here's an example:

```
const adjective = "better";
  const paean = `Ah, here's the ${adjective} way to
    do this!`;
```

Within any string template, using ${*variable*} inserts the value of *variable*, no questions asked. Actually, you don't have to stick to just variables. String templates can also interpolate any JavaScript expression, including function results.

>> **Multiline strings:** String templates are happy to work error-free with strings spread over multiple lines:

```
const myHeader = `
    <nav class="banner">
        <h3 class="nav-heading">Navigation</h3>
        <ul class="nav-links">
            <li>Home</li>
            <li>Away</li>
            <li>In Between</li>
        </ul>
    </nav>`
```

Determining the length of a string

The only inherent property of a String object is its length, which tells you how many characters are in the string:

```
string.length
```

All characters in the string — including spaces and punctuation marks — count towards the length. The only exceptions are escape sequences (such as \n), which count as one character. The following code grabs the length property value for various String object types:

```
function myFunction() {
    return "filename.htm";
}
const bookName = "Coding For Dummies";

length1 = myFunction().length; // Returns 12
length2 = bookName.length; // Returns 18
length3 = "123\n5678".length; // Returns 8
```

What the String object lacks in properties, it more than makes up for in methods. There are dozens, and they enable your code to perform many useful tasks, from converting between uppercase and lowercase letters to finding text in a string to extracting parts of a string.

Searching for substrings

A *substring* is a portion of an existing string. For example, some substrings of the string `"JavaScript"` would be `"Java"`, `"Script"`, `"vaSc"`, and `"v"`. When working with strings in your scripts, you'll often have to determine whether a given string contains a given substring. For example, if you're validating a user's email address, you should check that it contains an @ symbol.

Table 12-1 lists the several `String` object methods that find substrings in a larger string.

TABLE 12-1

String Object Methods for Searching for Substrings

Method	What It Does
string.endsWith(*substring*, *position*)	Tests whether *substring* appears at the end of *string*
string.includes(*substring*, *position*)	Tests whether *substring* appears in *string*
string.indexOf(*substring*, *position*)	Searches *string* for the first instance of *substring*
string.lastIndexOf(*substring*, *position*)	Searches *string* for the last instance of *substring*
string.startsWith(*substring*, *position*)	Tests whether *substring* appears at the beginning of *string*

Methods that extract substrings

Finding a substring is one thing, but you'll often have to extract a substring, as well. For example, if the user enters an email address, you may need to extract just the username (the part to the left of the @ sign) or the domain name (the part to the right of @). For these kinds of operations, JavaScript offers six methods, listed in Table 12-2.

TABLE 12-2

String Object Methods for Extracting Substrings

Method	What It Returns
string.charAt(*index*)	The character in *string* that's at the index position specified by *index*
string.charCodeAt(*index*)	The code of the character in *string* that's at the index position specified by *index*
string.slice(*start*, *end*)	The substring in *string* that starts at the index position specified by *start* and ends immediately before the index position specified by *end*
string.split(*separator*, *limit*)	An array where each item is a substring in *string*, where those substrings are separated by the *separator* character
string.substr(*start*, *length*)	The substring in *string* that starts at the index position specified by *start* and is *length* characters long
string.substring(start, end)	The substring in *string* that starts at the index position specified by *start* and ends immediately before the index position specified by *end*

Dealing with Dates and Times

Dates and times seem like the kind of things that ought to be straightforward programming propositions. After all, there are only 12 months in a year, 28 to 31 days in a month, 7 days in a week, 24 hours in a day, 60 minutes in an hour, and 60 seconds in a minute. Surely something so set in stone couldn't get even the least bit weird, could it?

You'd be surprised. Dates and times *can* get strange, but they are much easier to deal with if you remember three crucial points:

>> JavaScript time is measured in milliseconds, or thousandths of a second. More specifically, JavaScript measures time by counting the number of milliseconds that elapsed between January 1, 1970 and the date and time in question. So, for example, *you* may come across the date January 1, 2001 and think, "Ah, yes, the start of the new millennium." *JavaScript,* however, comes across that date and thinks "978307200000."

>> In the JavaScript world, time began on January 1, 1970, at midnight Greenwich Mean Time. Dates before that have *negative* values in milliseconds.

>> Since your JavaScript programs run inside a user's browser, dates and times are almost always the user's *local* dates and times. That is, the dates and times your scripts will manipulate will *not* be those of the server on which your page resides. This means you can never know what time the user is viewing your page.

Arguments used with the Date object

Before getting to the nitty-gritty of the Date object and its associated methods, I'll take a second to run through the various arguments that JavaScript requires for many date-related features. Doing so will save me from repeating these arguments tediously later. Table 12-3 has the details.

TABLE 12-3 **Arguments Associated with the Date Object**

Argument	What It Represents	Possible Values
date	A variable name	A Date object
yyyy	The year	Four-digit integers
yy	The year	Two-digit integers
month	The month	The full month name from "January" to "December"
mth	The month	Integers from 0 (January) to 11 (December)
dd	The day of the month	Integers from 1 to 31
hh	The hour of the day	Integers from 0 (midnight) to 23 (11:00 PM)
mm	The minute of the hour	Integers from 0 to 59
ss	The second of the minute	Integers from 0 to 59
ms	The milliseconds of the second	Integers from 0 to 999

Working with the Date object

Whenever you work with dates and times in JavaScript, you work with an instance of the Date object. More to the point, when you deal with a Date object in JavaScript, you deal with a specific moment in time, down to the millisecond. A Date object can never be a block of time, and it's not a kind of clock that ticks along while your script runs. Instead, the Date object is a temporal snapshot that you use to extract the specifics of the time it was taken: the year, month, date, hour, and so on.

Specifying the current date and time

The most common use of the Date object is to store the current date and time. You do that by invoking the Date() function, which is the constructor function for creating a new Date object. Here's how you use the Date() function:

```
const dateToday = new Date();
```

Specifying any date and time

If you need to work with a specific date or time, you need to use the Date() function's arguments. There are five versions of the Date() function syntax (refer to the list of arguments near the beginning of this section):

```
const date = new Date("month dd, yyyy hh:mm:ss");
const date = new Date("month dd, yyyy");
const date = new Date(yyyy, mth, dd, hh, mm, ss);
const date = new Date(yyyy, mth, dd);
const date = new Date(ms);
```

The following statements give you an example for each syntax:

```
const myDate = new Date("August 23, 2026 3:02:01");
const myDate = new Date("August 23, 2026");
const myDate = new Date(2026, 8, 23, 3, 2, 1);
const myDate = new Date(2026, 8, 23);
const myDate = new Date(1790136000000);
```

Extracting information about a date

When your script just coughs up whatever Date object value you stored in the variable, the results aren't particularly appealing. If you want to display dates in a more attractive format or if you want to perform arithmetic operations on a date, you need to dig a little deeper into the Date object to extract specific information such as the month, year, and hour. You do that by using the Date object methods listed in Table 12-4.

TABLE 12-4

Date Object Methods That Extract Date Values

Method Syntax	What It Returns
date.getFullYear()	The year as a four-digit number (1999, 2000, and so on)
date.getMonth()	The month of the year from 0 (January) to 11 (December)
date.getDate()	The date in the month from 1 to 31
date.getDay()	The day of the week from 0 (Sunday) to 6 (Saturday)
date.getHours()	The hour of the day from 0 (midnight) to 23 (11:00 PM)
date.getMinutes()	The minute of the hour from 0 to 59
date.getSeconds()	The second of the minute from 0 to 59
date.getMilliseconds()	The milliseconds of the second from 0 to 999
date.getTime()	The milliseconds since January 1, 1970 GMT

Setting the date

When you perform date arithmetic, you often have to change the value of an existing Date object. For example, an e-commerce script may have to calculate a date that is 90 days from the date that a sale occurs. It's usually easiest to create a Date object and then use an expression or a literal value to change the year, month, or some other component of the date. You do that by using the Date object methods listed in Table 12-5.

TABLE 12-5

Date Object Methods That Set Date Values

Method Syntax	What It Sets
date.setFullYear(*yyyy*)	The year as a four-digit number (1999, 2000, and so on)
date.setMonth(*mth*)	The month of the year from 0 (January) to 11 (December)
date.setDate(*dd*)	The date in the month from 1 to 31
date.setHours(*hh*)	The hour of the day from 0 (midnight) to 23 (11:00 PM)
date.setMinutes(*mm*)	The minute of the hour from 0 to 59
date.setSeconds(*ss*)	The second of the minute from 0 to 59
date.setMilliseconds(*ms*)	The milliseconds of the second from 0 to 999
date.setTime(*ms*)	The milliseconds since January 1, 1970 GMT

For example, here's some code that creates a new Date object (orderDate) based on today's date, creates a second Date object (paymentDueDate) from the first one, and then sets that second date to 90 days in the future:

```
const orderDate = new Date();
const paymentDueDate = new Date(orderDate);
paymentDueDate.setDate(paymentDueDate.getDate() + 90);
```

Working with Numbers: The Math Object

It's a rare JavaScript programmer who never has to deal with numbers. Most of us have to cobble together scripts that process order totals, generate sales taxes and shipping charges, calculate mortgage payments, and perform other number-crunching duties. JavaScript's numeric tools aren't the greatest in the programming world, but they have plenty of features to keep most scripters happy. This section tells you about those features, with special emphasis on the Math object.

The first thing to know is that JavaScript likes to keep things simple, particularly when it comes to numbers. For example, JavaScript is limited to dealing with just two types of numeric data: *integers* — numbers without a fractional or decimal part, such as 1, 759, and –50 — and *floating-point numbers* — values that have a fractional or decimal part, such as 2.14, 0.01, and –25.3333.

Converting between strings and numbers

When you're working with numeric expressions in JavaScript, it's important to make sure that all your operands are numeric values. For example, if you prompt the user for a value, you need to check the result to make sure it's not a letter or undefined (the default prompt() value). If you try to use the latter, for example, JavaScript will report that its value is NaN (not a number).

Similarly, if you have a value that you know is a string representation of a number, you need some way of converting that string into its numerical equivalent.

For these situations, JavaScript offers several techniques to ensure that your operands are numeric.

The parseInt() function

I begin with the parseInt() function, which you use to convert a string into an integer:

```
parseInt(string[,base]);
```

where:

- *string* is the string value you want to convert.

- *base* is an optional base used by the number in *string*. If you omit this value, JavaScript uses base 10.

Note that if the *string* argument contains a string representation of a floating-point value, parseInt() returns only the integer portion. Also, if the string begins with a number followed by some text, parseInt() returns the number (or, at least, its integer portion). The following table shows you the parseInt() results for various *string* values.

string	parseInt(string)
"5"	5
"5.1"	5
"5.9"	5
"5 feet"	5
"take 5"	NaN
"five"	NaN

The parseFloat() function

The parseFloat() function is similar to parseInt(), but you use it to convert a string into a floating-point value:

```
parseFloat(string);
```

Note that if the *string* argument contains a string representation of an integer value, parseFloat() returns just an integer. Also, like parseInt(), if the string begins with a number followed by some text, parseFloat() returns the number. The following table shows you the parseFloat() results for some *string* values.

string	parseFloat(string)
"5"	5
"5.1"	5.1

string	parseFloat(string)
"5.9"	5.9
"5.2 feet"	5.2
"take 5.0"	NaN
"five-point-one"	NaN

The + operator

For quick conversions from a string to a number, I most often use the + operator, which tells JavaScript to treat a string that contains a number as a true numeric value. For example, consider the following code:

```
const numOfShoes = '2';
const numOfSocks = 4;
const totalItems = +numOfShoes + numOfSocks;
```

By adding + in front of the numOfShoes variable, I force JavaScript to set that variable's value to the number 2, and the result of the addition will be 6.

The Math object's properties and methods

The Math object is a bit different than most of the other objects you come across in your JavaScript work because you never create an instance of the Math object that gets stored in a variable. Instead, the Math object is a built-in JavaScript object that you use as is. This section explores some properties and methods associated with the Math object.

Properties of the Math object

The Math object's properties are all constants that are commonly used in mathematical operations. Table 12-6 lists some of the available Math object properties.

Methods of the Math object

The Math object's methods enable you to perform mathematical operations such as square roots, powers, rounding, and trigonometry. Many of the Math object's methods are summarized in Table 12-7.

TABLE 12-6 ## Some Properties of the Math Object

Property Syntax	What It Represents	Approximate Value
Math.E	Euler's constant	2.718281828459045
Math.LN10	The natural logarithm of 10	2.302585092994046
Math.LN2	The natural logarithm of 2	0.6931471805599453
Math.LOG2E	Base 2 logarithm of E	1.4426950408889633
Math.LOG10E	Base 10 logarithm of E	0.4342944819032518
Math.PI	The constant pi	3.141592653589793
Math.SQRT1_2	The square root of 1/2	0.7071067811865476
Math.SQRT2	The square root of 2	1.4142135623730951

TABLE 12-7 ## Some Methods of the Math Object

Method Syntax	What It Returns
Math.abs(*number*)	The absolute value of *number* (that is, the number without any sign)
Math.cbrt(*number*)	The cube root of *number*
Math.ceil(*number*)	The smallest integer greater than or equal to *number* (ceil is short for *ceiling*)
Math.cos(*number*)	The cosine of *number*; returned values range from –1 to 1 radians
Math.exp(*number*)	E raised to the power of *number*
Math.floor(*number*)	The largest integer that is less than or equal to *number*
Math.log(*number*)	The natural logarithm (base E) of *number*
Math.max(*number1*, *number2*)	The larger of *number1* and *number2*
Math.min(*number1*, *number2*)	The smaller of *number1* and *number2*
Math.pow(*number1*, *number2*)	*number1* raised to the power of *number2*
Math.random()	A random number between 0 and 1
Math.round(*number*)	The integer closest to *number*
Math.sin(*number*)	The sine of *number*; returned values range from –1 to 1 radians
Math.sqrt(*number*)	The square root of *number* (which must be greater than or equal to 0)
Math.tan(*number*)	The tangent of *number*, in radians
Math.trunc(*number*)	The integer portion of *number*

For example, to calculate the area of a circle, you use the formula πr^2, where π (pi) is the ratio of the circumference of a circle to its diameter and r is the radius of the circle. Here's a function that takes a radius value and returns the area of the circle (chapter12/example01.html):

```
function areaOfCircle(radius) {
    return Math.PI * Math.pow(radius, 2);
}
```

The code uses `Math.PI` to represent pi and `Math.pow(radius, 2)` to raise the `radius` value to the power of 2.

Working with Arrays

JavaScript is an array powerhouse that boasts not only multiple ways to declare and populate arrays but also an impressive collection of methods for looping through and manipulating arrays. If that sounds like it's going to be complicated, you're right: It certainly would be. Which is why I'm going to spare you most of JavaScript's array complexity and focus on the essentials.

Declaring an array

I mention in the opening paragraph that JavaScript offers multiple ways to declare arrays, but here's a tip: Almost nobody uses most of them! The only way to declare an array in JavaScript that you really need to know about is called creating an *array literal.* In the same way that you create, say, a string literal by enclosing a value in quotation marks, you create an array literal by enclosing one or more values in square brackets. Here's the general format:

```
const arrayName = [value1, value2, ...];
```

where:

>> *arrayName* is the name you want to use for the array variable.

>> *value1*, *value2*, . . . are the initial values with which you want to populate the array.

An example:

```
const fruits = ["aprium", "limequat", "pluot"];
```

REMEMBER

Including values in the declaration of an array literal is optional, which means that you can declare an empty array using the following statement:

```
const arrayName = [];
```

Iterating an array: forEach()

One of the most common array techniques is to loop — or *iterate,* in coding lingo — through each element in an array so that your code can perform some kind of operation on each element. Probably the most common method for iterating an array in JavaScript is the Array object's forEach() method, which runs a function (it's known as a *callback function*) for each element in the array. That function takes up to three arguments:

>> *value*: The value of the element

>> *index*: (Optional) The array index of the element

>> *array*: (Optional) The array being iterated

If the callback function exists elsewhere in your code, you use the following syntax:

```
array.forEach(namedFunction);
```

where:

>> *array* is the Array object you want to iterate.

>> *namedFunction* is the name of an existing function. This function should accept the *value* argument and can accept the optional *index* and *array* arguments.

Alternatively, you can define a function right inside the forEach() method:

```
array.forEach(function (value[, index][, array]) {
    code
});
```

where:

>> *array* is the Array object you want to iterate.

>> *value*, *index*, and *array* are the arguments.

>> *code* is the collection of statements to run during each iteration.

"Hey, wait a minute! When you declare a function, aren't you supposed to give it a name?" Hah, nice catch! Yes, most JavaScript functions have a name, but JavaScript also supports a special class called anonymous functions that don't have names.

Here's an example (chapter12/example02.html):

```
// Declare the array
const fruits = ["aprium", "limequat", "pluot"];

// Iterate the array
fruits.forEach(function(value, index) {
    console.log(`Element ${index} has the value ${value}`);
});
```

After declaring the array, the code uses forEach() to iterate the array. During each iteration, console.log() (refer to Chapter 10) displays a string that includes the index and value parameters. Here's what gets displayed in the browser's Console window:

```
Element 0 has the value aprium
Element 1 has the value limequat
Element 2 has the value pluot
```

Here's another example, this time using a separate callback function (chapter12/example03.html):

```
// Declare the array
const fruits = ["aprium", "limequat", "pluot"];

// Declare the callback function
function capitalizeIt(value, index) {
    console.log(`${index}: ${value.toUpperCase()}`);
}

// Iterate the array
fruits.forEach(capitalizeIt);
```

This code declares the same array, and then declares a function named capitalizeIt(), which takes the value argument. For each element in the array, the forEach() loop calls capitalizeIt() (without the parentheses) and (behind the scenes) passes along the value and index arguments. Here's the output that appears in the Console window:

```
0: APRIUM
1: LIMEQUAT
2: PLUOT
```

Iterating an array: for . . . of

Although you'll usually iterate an array with the `forEach()` method, you'll sometimes need to use a more traditional loop to run through each array element. That
loop type is the `for . . .of` loop:

```
for (element of array) {
    code
}
```

where:

> » *array* is the Array object you want to iterate.

> » *element* it the current array element during each pass through the loop.

> » *code* is the collection of statements to run during each iteration.

Here's an example (chapter12/example04.html):

```
// Declare the array
const fruits = ["aprium", "limequat", "pluot"];

// Iterate the array
for (const fruit of fruits) {
    console.log(`${fruit} is a fruit of ${fruit.length} letters`);
}
```

After declaring the array, the code uses a `for...of` loop to iterate the array.
During each iteration, `console.log()` displays a string that includes the value of
the current element and the length of the value:

```
aprium is a fruit of 6 letters.
limequat is a fruit of 8 letters.
pluot is a fruit of 5 letters.
```

Working with the length property

The `Array` object has just a couple of properties, but the only one of these that you'll use frequently is the `length` property:

```
array.length
```

The `length` property returns the number of elements in the specified array. This is useful whenever you need to reference the number of elements in the array.

Here's an example (chapter12/example05.html):

```
// Declare the array
const fruits = ["aprium", "limequat", "pluot"];

// Iterate the array
fruits.forEach(function(value, index, array) {
    console.log(`${value} is fruit ${index + 1} of ${array.length}`);
});
```

This code iterates through the `fruits` array using a `forEach()` loop where the function takes all three arguments: `value`, `index`, and `array`. For each element, the function displays a console message that outputs the `value`, `index + 1`, and `array.length`:

```
aprium is fruit 1 of 3
limequat is fruit 2 of 3
pluot is fruit 3 of 3
```

More array methods

Arrays are one of JavaScript's most powerful features, but I'm out of space to talk about them! To give you a taste of what's available, Table 12-8 lists a few of the most useful `Array` object methods.

TABLE 12-8   Some Methods of the Array Object

Method Syntax	What It Returns
array.concat(*array1*, *array2*, . . .)	A new array that contains the elements of *array* concatenated with the elements of *array1*, *array2*, and so on.
array.join([*separator*])	A string formed by concatenating the elements of *array*, with each element separated by the optional *separator* character (the default separator is a comma).
array.pop()	The value of the last element in *array*; that element is then removed from *array*.
array.push(*value1*, *value2*, . . .)	A new version of *array* that has *value1*, *value2*, and so on added to the end.
array.reverse()	A new version of *array* with its elements in reverse order.
array.shift()	The value of the first element in *array*; that element is then removed from *array*.
array.slice(*start* [, *end*])	A new array that contains a subset of the elements in *array*, defined by *start*, the index of the first element in *array* that you want to include in the subset, and optionally *end*, the index of the element in array before which you want the subset to end. (If you omit *end*, the last element is used.)
array.sort()	A new version of *array* with its elements sorted in ascending alphabetical or numerical order.
array.unshift(*value1*, *value2*, . . .)	A new version of *array* that has *value1*, *value2*, and so on added to the beginning.

Chapter **13**

Unleashing JavaScript in the Browser

The programmer, like the poet, works only slightly removed from pure thought-stuff. He builds his castles in the air, from air, creating by exertion of the imagination.

—FRED BROOKS

JavaScript was born and raised inside the web browser and that's where JavaScript's tremendous power and flexibility really shine. With JavaScript, you can take control over every aspect of the web page. Want to change some web page text on the fly? JavaScript can do that. Want to add an element to the page? JavaScript's up to the task. Want to modify an element's CSS? JavaScript's all over that. Want to perform some action based on the user clicking something or pressing a key combination? JavaScript raises its hand and says, "Ooh, ooh, pick me, pick me!"

In this chapter, you explore the fascinating world of the Document Object Model. You learn lots of powerful coding techniques that enable you to make your web pages do almost anything you want them to do. You learn, too, that this is where web coding becomes fun and maybe just a little addictive (in a good way, I promise).

Getting to Know the Document Object Model

Here's some source code for a simple web page:

```
<html lang="en">
    <head>
        <title>So Many Kale Recipes</title>
    </head>
    <body>
        <header>
            <h1>Above and Beyond the Kale of Duty</h1>
        </header>
        <main>
            <p>
                Do you love to cook with <a href="kale.html">kale</a>?
            </p>
        </main>
    </body>
</html>
```

One way to examine this code is hierarchically. That is, the html element is the topmost element because every other element is contained in it. The next level down in the hierarchy contains the head and body elements. The head element contains a title element, which contains the text So Many Kale Recipes. Similarly, the body element contains a header element and a main element. The header element contains an h1 element with the text Above and Beyond the Kale of Duty, while the main element contains a p element with the text Do you love to cook with kale?.

Hierarchies are almost always more readily grasped in visual form, so Figure 13-1 graphs the page elements hierarchically.

When speaking of object hierarchies, if object P contains object C, object P is said to be the *parent* of object C, and object C is said to be the *child* of object P. In Figure 13-1, the arrows represent parent-to-child relationships. Also, elements on the same level — such as the header and main elements — are known as *siblings*.

The page as a whole is represented by the document object. Therefore, this hierarchical object representation is known as the *Document Object Model*, or the *DOM* as it's usually called. The DOM enables your JavaScript code to access the complete structure of an HTML document. This access is the source of one of JavaScript's most fundamental features: The capability it offers you as a web developer to read and change the elements of a web page, even after the page is loaded.

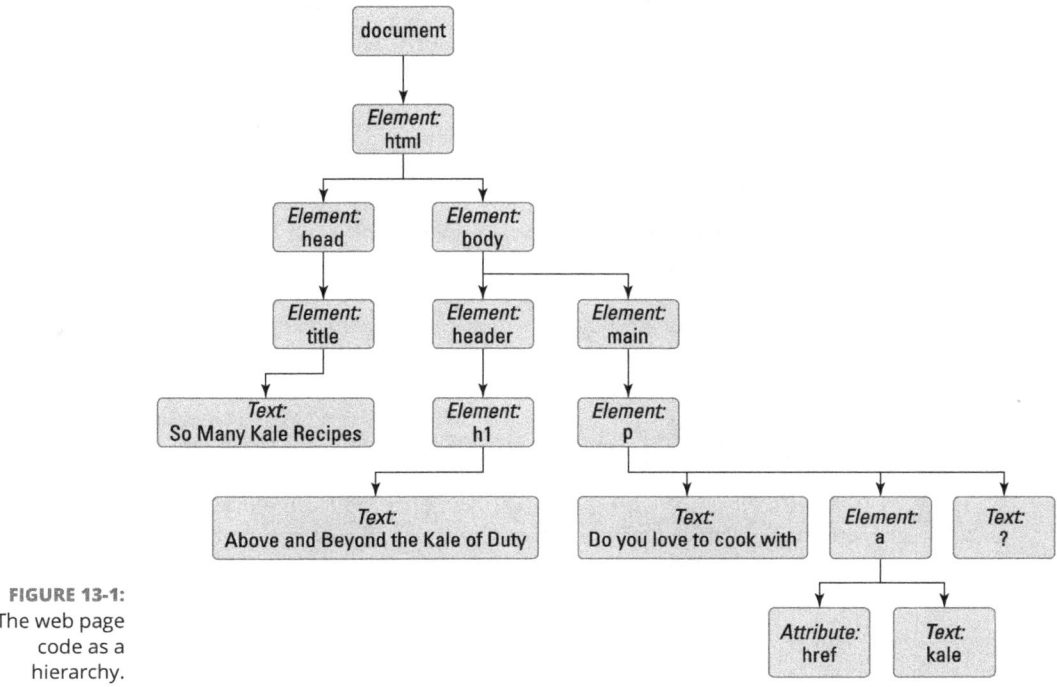

FIGURE 13-1:
The web page
code as a
hierarchy.

Specifying Elements

Elements in the DOM represent the tags in a document, so you'll be using them constantly in your code. This section shows you several methods for referencing one or more elements.

Specifying an element by ID

If you want to work with a specific element in your script, you can reference the element directly by first assigning it an identifier using the id attribute:

```
<header id="page-banner">
```

With that done, you can then refer to the element in your code by using the document object's getElementById() method:

```
document.getElementById(id)
```

where *id* is a string representing the id attribute of the element you want to work with.

For example, the following statement (refer to chapter13/example01.html in this book's example files) returns a reference to the above <header> tag (the one that has id="page-banner"):

```
const pageBanner = document.getElementById("page-banner");
```

WARNING

When you're coding the document object, don't put your <script> tag in the web page's head section (that is, between the <head> and </head> tags). If you place your code there, the web browser will run the code before it has had a chance to create the document object, which means your code will fail, big time. Instead, place your <script> tag at the bottom of the web page, just before the </body> tag.

Specifying elements by tag name

Besides working with individual elements, you can work also with collections of elements. One such collection is the set of all elements in a page that use the same tag name. For example, you could reference all the <a> tags or all the <div> tags. Using a collection is a handy way to make large-scale changes to these tags (such as by changing all the target attributes in your links).

The mechanism for returning a collection of elements that have the same tag is the getElementsByTagName() method:

```
document.getElementsByTagName(tag)
```

where *tag* is a string representing the HTML element name used by the tags you want to work with.

This method returns an array-like collection that contains all the elements in the document that use the specified tag. (Refer to Chapter 12 to find out how arrays work. Also check out "Working with collections of elements," later in this chapter.) For example, to return a collection that includes all the p elements in the current page, you'd use the following statement (chapter13/example02.html):

```
const paragraphs = document.getElementsByTagName("p");
```

Specifying elements by class name

Another collection you can work with is the set of all elements in a page that use the same class. The JavaScript tool for returning all the elements that share a specific class name is the getElementsByClassName() method:

```
document.getElementsByClassName(class)
```

where *class* is a string representing the class name used by the elements you want to work with.

This method returns an array-like collection that contains all the elements in the document that use the specified class name. The collection order is the same as the order in which the elements appear in the document. Here's an example (chapter13/example03.html):

```
const keywords = document.getElementsByClassName("keyword");
```

Specifying elements by selector

CSS offers several selectors that you can use to specify what you want to style (refer to Chapter 17), including the ID, tag, and class selectors, the descendant, child, and subsequent-sibling combinators, pseudo-classes, and pseudo-elements. You can use those same selectors in your JavaScript code to reference page elements by using the document object's querySelector() and querySelectorAll() methods:

```
document.querySelector(selector)
document.querySelectorAll(selector)
```

where *selector* is a string representing the selector for the element or elements you want to work with.

The difference between these methods is that querySelectorAll() returns a collection of all the elements that match your selector but querySelector() returns only the first element that matches your selector.

For example, the following statement returns the collection of all p elements that are direct children of a main element (chapter13/example04.html):

```
const main_paragraphs = document.querySelectorAll("main > p");
```

Rather than use three distinct document object methods to reference page elements by id, tag, and class — that is, getElementById(), getElementsBy TagName(), and getElementsByClassName() — many web developers prefer the more generic approach offered by querySelector() and querySelectorAll().

Working with collections of elements

The getElementsByTagName(), getElementsByClassName(), and querySelector All() methods each return an array-like collection that contains all the elements in the document that use the specified tag, class, or selector, respectively. The collection order is the same as the order in which the elements appear in the document. For example, consider the following HTML code (chapter13/example05.html):

```
<div id="div1">
    This, of course, is div 1.
</div>
<div id="div2">
    Yeah, well <em>this</em> is div 2!
</div>
<div id="div3">
    Ignore those dudes. Welcome to div 3!
</div>
```

Now consider the following statement:

```
divs = document.getElementsByTagName("div");
```

In the resulting collection, the first item (divs[0]) will be the <div> element with id equal to div1; the second item (divs[1]) will be the <div> element with id equal to div2; and the third item (divs[2]) will be the <div> element with id equal to div3.

You can also refer to elements directly by using their id values. For example, the following statements are equivalent:

```
const firstDiv = divs[0];
const firstDiv = divs.div1;
```

To learn how many items are in a collection, use the length property:

```
const totalDivs = divs.length;
```

To perform one or more operations on each item in the collection, you can use a for. . .of loop to run through the collection one item at a time. In the JavaScript trade, this is known as *iterating* over the collection. Here's the syntax to use:

```
for (const item of collection) {
    statements
}
```

where:

>> *item* is a variable that holds an item in the collection. The first time through the loop, *item* is set to the first element in the collection; the second time through the loop, *item* is set to the second element; and so on.

>> *collection* is the collection of elements you want to iterate over.

>> *statements* is the JavaScript code you want to use to manipulate (or view, or whatever) *item*.

For example, here's some code that iterates over the preceding `div` elements and displays each item's `id` value in the console (chapter13/example05.html):

```
divs = document.getElementsByTagName("div");
for (const d of divs) {
    console.log(d.id);
}
```

Traversing the DOM

One common task in JavaScript code is working with the children, parent, or siblings of some element in the page. This is known as *traversing the DOM* because you're using these techniques to move up, down, and across the DOM hierarchy.

In this section, I use the following HTML code for each example technique (chapter13/example06.html):

```
<html lang="en">
    <head>
        <title>So Many Kale Recipes</title>
    </head>
    <body>
        <header id="page-banner">
            <h1>Above and Beyond the Kale of Duty</h1>
        </header>
        <main id="page-content">
            <p>
                Do you love to cook with <a href="kale.html">kale</a>?
            </p>
        </main>
    </body>
</html>
```

Getting the children of a parent element

When you're working with a particular element, it's common to want to perform one or more operations on that element's children. Every parent element offers several properties that enable you to work with all or just some of its child nodes:

>> All the child nodes

>> The first child node

>> The last child node

Getting all the child nodes

To return a collection of all the child element nodes of a parent element, use the `children` property:

```
parent.children
```

where *parent* is the parent element.

For example, the following statement stores all the child element nodes of the `body` element in a variable:

```
const bodyChildren = document.body.children;
```

The result is an HTMLCollection object, which is an array-like collection of element nodes. If you were to use the console to display the value of `bodyChildren` (say, by including the statement `console.log(bodyChildren)` in your code), you'd get the output shown here:

```
HTMLCollection(2) [header#page-banner, main#page-content, page-
    banner: header#page-banner, page-content: main#page-content]
```

Hmm. Click the arrow to the left of this output and you get the following:

```
0: header#page-banner
1: main#page-content
page-banner: header#page-banner
page-content: main#page-content
length: 2
```

Yep, still confusing. Okay, 0 and 1 are the index numbers of each child. For example, you could use `bodyChildren[0]` to refer to the first element in the collection, which in this example is the `header` element. However, because both the `header` element and the `main` element have `id` attributes, the browser is telling you that another way to refer to these nodes is via their `id` values. So, for the `header` element, the following are equivalent:

```
bodyChildren[0]
bodyChildren["page-banner"];
```

Similarly, for the main element, the following are equivalent:

```
bodyChildren[1]
bodyChildren["page-content"];
```

Getting the first child node

If you use a parent element's children property to return the parent's child nodes, as I describe in the preceding section, you can refer to the first item in the resulting collection by tacking [0] onto the collection's variable name. For example:

```
bodyChildren[0]
```

However, the DOM offers a more direct route to the first child node:

```
parent.firstElementChild
```

where *parent* is the parent element.

To get the first child element node of the main element from the code at the beginning of this section, you'd do something like this (chapter13/example07.html):

```
const content = document.getElementById("page-content");
const firstContentChildElement = content.firstElementChild;
```

This code returns the p element.

Getting the last child node

If your code needs to work with the last child element node, use the lastElementChild property:

```
parent.lastElementChild
```

where *parent* is the parent element.

To get the last child element node of the p element from the code at the beginning of this section, you could do this (chapter13/example08.html):

```
const para = document.querySelector("main > p");
const lastParaChildElement = para.lastElementChild;
```

This code returns the a element.

Getting the parent of a child element

If your code needs to work with the parent of a child element, use the child element's `parentNode` property:

```
child.parentNode
```

where `child` is the child element.

For example, suppose you want to work with the parent element of the h1 element from the HTML example at the beginning of this section. This code does the job (chapter13/example09.html):

```
const childElement = document.querySelector("h1");
const parentElement = childElement.parentNode;
```

Manipulating Elements

Once you have a reference to one or more elements, you can use code to manipulate those elements in various ways, as shown in this section.

Adding an element to the page

One of the most common web development chores is to add elements to a web page on the fly. When you add an element, you always specify the parent element to which it will be added, and then you decide whether you want the new element added to the end or the beginning of the parent's collection of children.

To add an element to the page, you follow three steps:

1. **Create an object for the type of element you want to add.**
2. **Add the new object as a child element of an existing element.**
3. **Insert some text and tags into the new object.**

Step 1: Creating the element

For Step 1, you use the `document` object's `createElement()` method:

```
document.createElement(elementName)
```

where `elementName` is a string containing the HTML element name for the type of the element you want to create.

This method creates the element and then returns it, which means you can store the new element in a variable. Here's an example:

```
const newArticle = document.createElement("article");
```

Step 2: Adding the new element as a child

With your element created, Step 2 is to add it to an existing parent element. You have four choices:

» **Add the new element to the end of the parent's collection of child elements:** Use the append( ) method:

```
parent.append(child)
```

where:

- *parent* is a reference to the parent element to which the new element will be appended.
- *child* is a reference to the child element you're appending. Note that you can append multiple elements at the same time by separating each element with a comma. The *child* parameter can also be a text string.

» **Add the new element to the beginning of the parent's collection of child elements:** Use the prepend( ) method:

```
parent.prepend(child)
```

where:

- *parent* is a reference to the parent element to which the new element will be prepended.
- *child* is a reference to the child element you're prepending. Note that you can prepend multiple elements at the same time by separating each element with a comma. The *child* parameter can also be a text string.

» **Insert the new element just after an existing child element of the parent:** Use the after( ) method:

```
child.after(sibling)
```

where:

- *child* is a reference to the child element after which the new element will be inserted.
- *sibling* is a reference to the new element you're inserting. Note that you can insert multiple elements at the same time by separating each element with a comma. The *sibling* parameter can also be a text string.

» Insert the new element just before an existing child element of the parent: Use the before( ) method:

```
child.before(sibling)
```

where:

- *child* is a reference to the child element before which the new element will be inserted.

- *sibling* is a reference to the new element you're inserting. Note that you can insert multiple elements at the same time by separating each element with a comma. The *sibling* parameter can also be a text string.

Here's an example that creates a new article element and then appends it to the main element (chapter13/example10.html):

```
const newArticle = document.createElement("article");
document.querySelector("main").append(newArticle);
```

Here's an example that creates a new nav element and then prepends it to the main element:

```
const newNav = document.createElement("nav");
document.querySelector("main").prepend(newNav);
```

Step 3: Adding text and tags to the new element

With your element created and appended or prepended to a parent, the final step is to add some text and tags using the innerHTML property:

```
element.innerHTML = text
```

where:

» *element* is a reference to the new element within which you want to add the text and tags.

» *text* is a string containing the text and HTML tags you want to insert.

In this example, the code creates a new nav element, prepends it to the main element, and then adds a heading (chapter13/example10.html):

```
const newNav = document.createElement("nav");
document.querySelector("main").prepend(newNav);
newNav.innerHTML = "<h2>Navigation</h2>";
```

If you only want to add text to an element, use the textContent property, instead:

```
element.textContent = text
```

where:

➤ *element* is a reference to the new element within which you want to add the text.

➤ *text* is a string containing the text you want to insert.

For example, suppose your page has an empty p element:

```
<p id="output">

</p>
```

Here's some code that populates this element with text (chapter13/example11. html):

```
const output = document.getElementById("output");
output.textContent = "Hello, kale world!"
```

Whatever value you assign to the innerHTML or textContent property over-writes the element's existing text and tags, so use caution when wielding these properties.

Removing an element

If you no longer require an element on your page, you can use the element's remove() method to delete it from the DOM:

```
element.remove()
```

For example, the following statement removes the element with an id value of temp-div from the page:

```
document.getElementById("temp-div").remove();
```

Modifying CSS with JavaScript

Although you specify your CSS rules in a static stylesheet (`.css`) file, that doesn't mean the rules themselves have to be static. With JavaScript on the job, you can work with and modify an element's CSS in a number of ways. You can

>> Read the current value of a CSS property.

>> Change the value of a CSS property.

>> Add or remove a class.

>> Toggle a class on or off.

This section lets you in on the details.

Changing an element's styles

Most HTML tags can have a `style` attribute that you use to set inline styles. Because standard attributes all have corresponding element object properties, you won't be surprised to learn that most elements also have a `style` property that enables you to get and modify a tag's styles. It works like this: The `style` property returns a `style` object that has properties for every CSS style. When referencing these style properties, you need to keep two things in mind:

>> For single-word CSS properties (such as `color` and `visibility`), use all-lowercase letters.

>> For multiple-word CSS properties, drop the hyphen and use uppercase for the first letter of each subsequent word if the property has more than two. For example, the `font-size` and `border-left-width` CSS properties become the `fontSize` and `borderLeftWidth` `style` object properties, respectively.

Here's an example (chapter13/example12.html):

```
const pageTitle = document.querySelector("h1");
pageTitle.style.fontSize = "64px";
pageTitle.style.color = "maroon";
pageTitle.style.textAlign = "center";
pageTitle.style.border = "1px solid black";
```

This code gets a reference to the page's first `<h1>` element. With that reference in hand, the code then uses the `style` object to style four CSS properties of the heading: `font-size`, `color`, `text-align`, and `border`.

Adding a class to an element

If you have a class rule defined in your CSS, you can apply that rule to an element by adding the `class` attribute to the element's tag and setting the value of the `class` attribute equal to the name of your class rule. You can manipulate these classes using JavaScript.

First, you can get a list of an element's assigned classes by using the `classList` property:

```
element.classList
```

where *element* is the element you're working with.

The returned list of classes is an array-like object that includes an `add()` method that you can use to add a new class to the element's existing classes:

```
element.classList.add(class)
```

where:

>> *element* is the element you're working with.

>> *class* is a string representing the name of the class you want to add to *element*. You can add multiple classes by separating each class name with a comma.

Here's an example (chapter13/example13.html), and Figure 13-2 shows the result.

HTML:

```
<div id="my-div">
    Hello World!
</div>
```

CSS:

```css
.my-class {
    display: flex;
    justify-content: center;
    align-items: center;
    border: 6px dotted black;
    font-family: Verdana, serif;
    font-size: 2rem;
    background-color: lightgray;
}
```

JavaScript:

```javascript
document.getElementById('my-div').classList.add('my-class');
```

If the `class` attribute doesn't exist in the element, the `addClass()` method inserts it in the tag. So, in the preceding example, after the code executes, the `<div>` tag would appear like this:

```html
<div id="my-div" class="my-class">
```

Removing a class

To remove a class from an element's `class` attribute, the `classList` object offers the `remove()` method:

```javascript
element.classList.remove(class)
```

where:

>> *element* is the element you're working with.

>> *class* is a string representing the name of the class you want to remove from *element*. You can remove multiple classes by separating each class name with a comma.

Here's an example:

```javascript
document.getElementById('my-div').classList.remove('my-class');
```

Toggling a class

One common web development scenario is switching a web page element between two different states. For example, you may want to change an element's styles depending on whether a check box is selected or deselected, or you may want to alternate between showing and hiding an element's text when the user clicks the element's heading.

The easiest way to handle switching between two states is to use the `classList` object's `toggle()` method, which does all the hard work for you. That is, it checks the element for the specified class. If the class is there, JavaScript removes it; if the class isn't there, JavaScript adds it. Sweet! Here's the syntax:

```
element.classList.toggle(class)
```

where:

>> *element* is the element you're working with.

>> *class* is a string representing the name of the class you want to toggle for *element*.

Here's an example:

```
document.getElementById('my-div').classList.toggle('my-class');
```

Building Reactive Pages with Events

In web development, an *event* is an action that occurs in response to some external stimulus. A common type of external stimulus is when a user interacts with a web page. Here are some examples:

>> Surfing to or reloading the page

>> Clicking a button

>> Pressing a key

>> Scrolling the page

How can your web page possibly know when any of these actions occur? The secret is that JavaScript was built with events in mind. As the computer science professors would say, JavaScript is an *event-driven* language. This means that you can make your web pages "listen" for particular events to occur. You do that by setting up special chunks of code called *event handlers* that say, in effect, "Be a dear and watch out for event X to occur, will you? When it does, be so kind as to execute the code I've placed here for you. Thanks so much." An event handler consists of two parts:

>> **Event listener:** An instruction to the web browser to watch out ("listen") for a particular event occurring on a particular element

>> **Callback function:** The code that the web browser executes when it detects that the event has occurred

In the rest of this chapter, I talk about how to use JavaScript to build your own event handlers and take your scripts to a more interactive level.

Listening for an event

You configure your code to listen for and react to an event by setting up an event handler using the element object's `addEventListener()` method. Here's the syntax:

```
element.addEventListener(event, callback)
```

where:

>> *element* is the web page element to be monitored for the event. The event is said to be *bound* to the element.

>> *event* is a string specifying the name of the event you want the browser to listen for. For the main events I mention in the preceding section, use one of the following, enclosed in quotation marks: `DOMContentLoaded`, `click`, `dblclick`, `mouseover`, `keypress`, `focus`, `blur`, `change`, `submit`, `scroll`, or `resize`.

>> *callback* is the callback function that JavaScript executes when the event occurs.

Here's an example (chapter13/example14.html):

HTML:

```
<div id="my-div"></div>
<button id="my-button">Click to add some text, above</button>
```

where e is a name for the Event object that the DOM generates when the event fires. You can use whatever name you want, but most coders use e (although evt and event are also common).

For example, when handling the keydown event, you need access to the Event object's which property to find out the code for the key the user is pressing. Here's an example page that can help you determine which code value to check for (chapter13/example15.html):

HTML:

```
<div>
    Type a key:
</div>
<input id="key-input" type="text">
<div>
    Here's the code of the key you pressed:
</div>
<div id="key-output">
</div>
```

JavaScript:

```
const keyInput = document.getElementById('key-input');
keyInput.focus();
keyInput.addEventListener('keydown', function(e) {
    const keyOutput = document.getElementById('key-output');
    keyOutput.textContent = e.which;
});
```

The HTML code sets up an <input> tag to accept a keystroke and a <div> tag with id="key-output" to use for the output. The JavaScript code adds a keydown event listener to the input element, and when the event fires, the callback function writes e.which to the output div. Figure 13-4 shows the page in action.

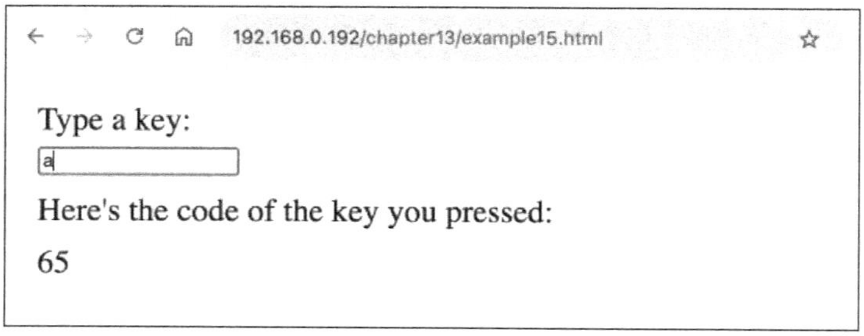

FIGURE 13-4:
Type a key in the input box, and JavaScript displays the numeric code of the pressed key.

Chapter **14**

Debugging JavaScript

Testing proves a programmer's failure. Debugging is the programmer's vindication.

—BORIS BEIZER

t usually doesn't take too long to get short scripts and functions up and running. As your code grows larger and more complex, however, errors inevitably creep in. In fact, it has been proven mathematically that any code beyond a minimum level of complexity will contain at least one error and probably quite a lot more.

Many of the bugs that crawl into your code will be simple syntax problems that you can fix quickly, but others will be more subtle and harder to find. For the latter — whether the errors are incorrect values returned by functions or problems with the overall logic of a script — you need to be able to get inside your code to scope out what's wrong.

The good news is that JavaScript and modern web browsers offer a ton of top-notch debugging tools that can remove some of the burden of program problem solving. In this chapter, you delve into these tools to explore how they can help you find and fix most programming errors.

Examining Your Debugging Tools

All major web browsers come with a sophisticated set of debugging tools that can make your life as a web developer much easier and much saner. Most web developers debug their scripts using Google Chrome, so I focus on that browser in this chapter. But in this section, I give you an overview of the tools available in all the major browsers and how to get at them.

Here's how you open the web development tools in Chrome, Firefox, Microsoft Edge, and Safari:

- » **Chrome for Windows:** Click the Customize and Control Google Chrome icon (shown in the margin), and then choose More Tools ⇨ Developer Tools. Shortcut: Ctrl+Shift+I.

- » **Chrome for Mac:** Choose View ⇨ Developer ⇨ Developer Tools. Shortcut: Option+⌘+I.

- » **Firefox for Windows:** Click the open Application menu icon (shown in the margin), and then choose More Tools ⇨ Web Developer Tools. Shortcut: Ctrl+Shift+I.

- » **Firefox for Mac:** Choose Tools ⇨ Browser Tools ⇨ Web Developer Tools. Shortcut: Option+⌘+I.

- » **Microsoft Edge for Windows:** Click the Settings and More icon (shown in the margin), and then choose More Tools ⇨ Developer Tools. Shortcut: Ctrl+Shift+I.

- » **Microsoft Edge for Mac:** Choose View ⇨ Developer ⇨ Developer Tools. Shortcut: Option+⌘+I.

- » **Safari:** Click Develop ⇨ Show Web Inspector. Shortcut: Option+⌘+I. If you don't have the Develop menu, click Safari ⇨ Settings, click the Advanced tab, and then select the Show Features for Web Developers check box.

These development tools vary in the features they offer, but each provides the same set of basic tools, which are the tools you'll use most often. These basic web development tools include the following:

- » **HTML viewer:** This tab (called Inspector in Firefox and Elements in the other browsers) shows the HTML source code used in the web page. When you hover the mouse pointer over a tag, the browser highlights the element in the displayed page and shows its width and height, as shown in Figure 14-1. When you click a tag, the browser shows the CSS styles applied with the tag, as well as the tag's box dimensions (again, refer to Figure 14-1).

>> **Console:** This tab enables you to view error messages, log messages, test expressions, and execute statements. I cover the Console window in more detail in the next section.

>> **Debugging tool:** This tab (called Debugger in Firefox and Sources in the other browsers) enables you to pause code execution, step through your code, watch the values of variables and properties, and much more. This is the most important JavaScript debugging tool, so I cover it in detail later in this chapter (starting with the "Pausing Your Code" section).

...and the browser highlights the element on the page...

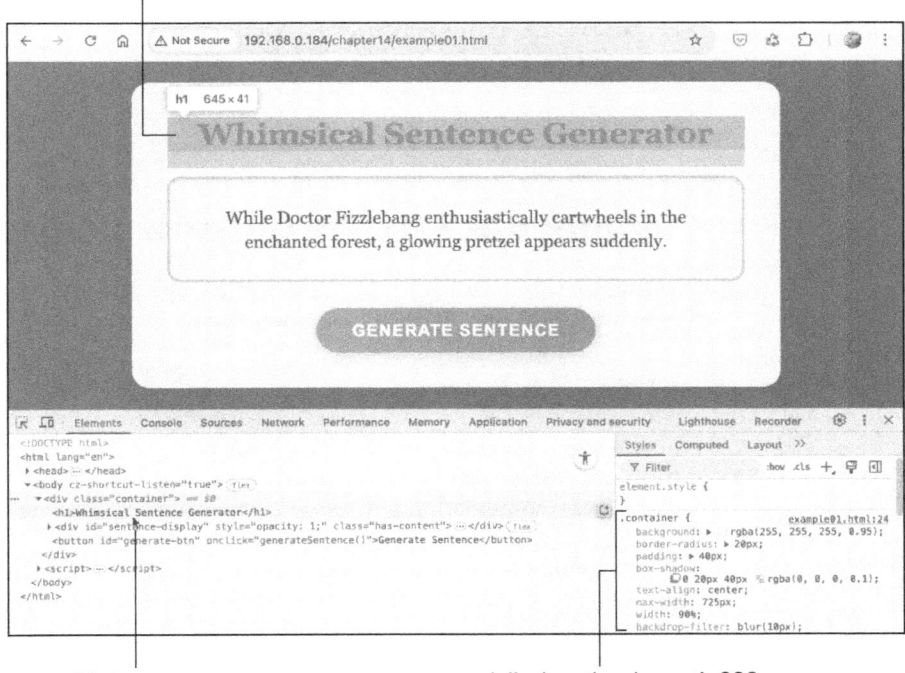

FIGURE 14-1: The HTML viewer, such as Chrome's Elements tab, enables you to inspect each element's styles and box dimensions.

Click a tag... ...and displays the element's CSS.

Debugging with the Console Window

The Console window is an interactive browser window that shows warnings and errors, displays the output of `console.log()` statements, and enables you to execute expressions and statements without having to run your entire script. The Console window is one of the handiest web browser debugging tools, so you need to know your way around it.

Displaying the Console window in various browsers

To display the Console window, open your web browser's development tools and then click the Console tab. You can also use the following keyboard shortcuts:

» **Chrome for Windows:** Press Ctrl+Shift+J.

» **Chrome for Mac:** Press Option+⌘+J.

» **Firefox for Windows:** Press Ctrl+Shift+K.

» **Firefox for Mac:** Press Option+⌘+K.

» **Microsoft Edge for Windows:** Press Ctrl+Shift+J.

» **Microsoft Edge for Mac:** Press Option+⌘+J.

» **Safari:** Press Option+⌘+C.

Logging data to the Console window

You can use the `console.log()` method of the special `Console` object to print text and expression values in the Console window:

```
console.log(output)
```

where *output* is the expression you want to print in the Console window. The *output* expression can be a text string, a variable, an object property, a function result, or any combination of these.

For debugging purposes, you most often use the Console window to keep an eye on the values of variables, object properties, and expressions. That is, when your code sets or changes the value of something, you insert a `console.log()` statement that outputs the new value. When the script execution is complete, you can open the Console window and check out the logged value or values.

Executing code in the Console window

One of the great features of the Console window is that it's interactive, which means that you can not only read messages generated by the browser or by your `console.log()` statements but also type code directly in the Console window. That is, you can use the Console window to execute expressions and statements. There are many uses for this feature:

» You can try some experimental expressions or statements to determine their effect on the script.

» When the script is paused, you can output the current value of a variable or property.

» When the script is paused, you can change the value of a variable or property. For example, if you notice that a variable with a value of zero is about to be used as a divisor, you can change that variable to a nonzero value to avoid crashing the script.

» When the script is paused, you can run a function or method to determine whether it operates as expected under the current conditions.

Each browser's Console tab includes a text box (usually marked by the > prompt) that you can use to enter your expressions or statements.

TIP

If you want to repeat an earlier code execution in the Console window, or if you want to run some code that's very similar to code you ran earlier, you can recall statements and expressions that you used in the current browser session. Press the up arrow key to scroll back through your previously executed code; press the down arrow key to scroll forward through your code.

Pausing Your Code

Pausing your code midstream lets you examine certain elements, such as the current values of variables and properties. It also lets you execute program code one statement at a time so that you can monitor the flow of the script.

When you pause your code, JavaScript enters *break mode,* which means that the browser displays its debugging tool and highlights the current statement (the one that JavaScript will execute next). Figure 14-2 shows a script in break mode in Chrome's debugger (the Sources tab).

Entering break mode

JavaScript gives you two ways to enter break mode:

» By setting breakpoints

» By using a debugger statement

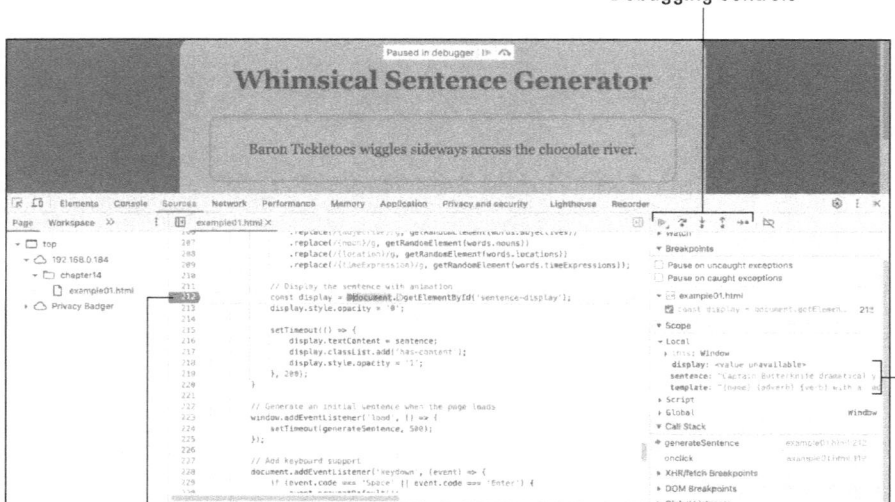

Debugging controls

FIGURE 14-2:
In break mode,
the web browser
displays its
debugging tool
and highlights the
statement that it
will execute next.

The browser pauses on the current statement   The current values of the script's variables

Setting a breakpoint

If you know approximately where an error or a logic flaw is occurring, you can enter break mode at a specific statement in the script by setting a *breakpoint.* Here are the steps to set a breakpoint:

1. **Display your web browser's developer tools and switch to the debugging tool (such as the Sources tab in Chrome).**

2. **Open the file that contains the JavaScript code you want to debug.**

    How you do this depends on the browser: In Chrome (and most browsers), you have two choices:

    - In the left pane, click the HTML file (if your JavaScript code is in a `script` element in your HTML file) or the JavaScript (`.js`) file (if your code resides in an external JavaScript file).

    - Press Ctrl+P (Windows) or ⌘+P (macOS) and then click the file in the list that appears.

3. **Locate the statement where you want to enter break mode.**

    JavaScript will run every line of code up to but not including this statement.

4. **Click the line number to the left of the statement to set the breakpoint, as shown in Figure 14-3.**

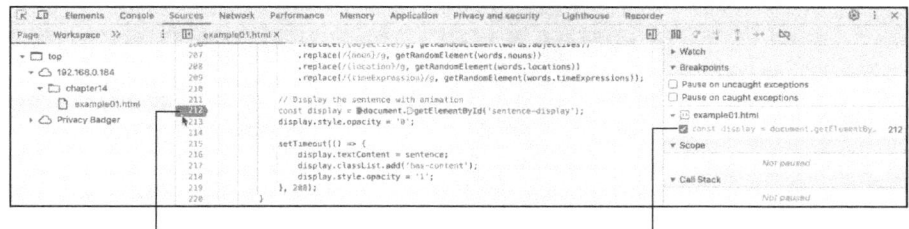

FIGURE 14-3:
In the browser's debugging tool, click a line number to set a breakpoint on that statement.

Click a line number to set a breakpoint   Deselect to disable the breakpoint

To remove a breakpoint, most browsers give you three choices:

>> To disable a breakpoint temporarily, deselect the breakpoint's check box in the Breakpoints list.

>> To disable all your breakpoints temporarily, click the Deactivate Breakpoints icon (shown in the margin). Click this icon again to reactivate all breakpoints.

>> To remove a breakpoint completely, click the statement's line number.

Entering break mode by using a debugger statement

When developing your web pages, you'll often test the robustness of a script by sending it various test values or by trying it out under different conditions. In many cases, you'll want to enter break mode to make sure things appear okay. You could set breakpoints at specific statements, but you'll lose them if you close the file. For something a little more permanent, you can include a debugger statement in a script. JavaScript automatically enters break mode whenever it encounters a debugger statement.

Here's a bit of code that includes a debugger statement (chapter14/example01. html):

```
// Display the sentence with animation
debugger;
const display = document.getElementById('sentence-display');
display.style.opacity = '0';
```

Viewing a variable value in break mode

If you want to just eyeball the current value of a variable, the developer tools in Chrome (and all major browsers) make this straightforward:

1. **Enter break mode in the code that contains the variable you want to check.**

2. **If the script hasn't yet set the value of the variable, step through the code until you're past the statement that supplies the variable with a value.**

   If you're interested in how the variable's value changes during the script, step through the script until you're past any statement that changes the value. Refer to the section "Stepping Through Your Code" to learn how to do just that.

3. **Hover the mouse pointer over the variable name.**

   The browser pops up a tooltip that displays the variable's current value. Figure 14-4 shows an example. Also note in Figure 14-4 that the dev tools display the current value of any variable immediately after any statement that sets or changes the variable value.

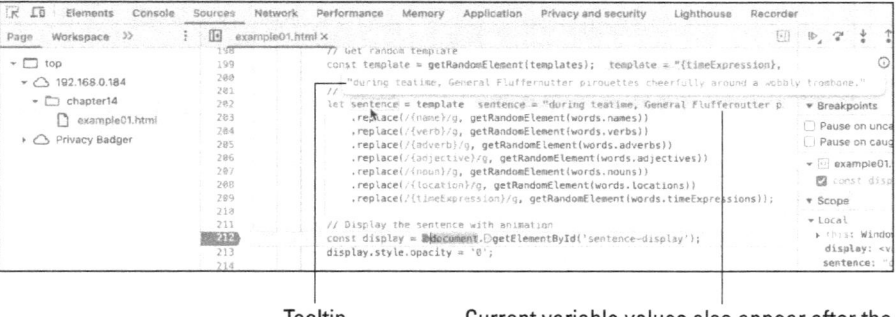

FIGURE 14-4: In break mode, hover the mouse pointer over a variable name to display the variable's current value.

Tooltip

Current variable values also appear after the statement that sets or changes the value

Exiting break mode

To exit break mode, you can use either of the following methods in the browser's debugging tool:

» Click the resume icon. Chrome's version of this icon is shown in the margin.

» Press the browser's Resume keyboard shortcut. In Chrome (and most browsers), either press F8 or press Ctrl+\ (Windows) or ⌘+\ (macOS).

Stepping Through Your Code

One of the most common (and most useful) debugging techniques is to step through the code one statement at a time. Doing so lets you get a feel for the program flow to make sure that things such as loops and function calls are executing properly. You can use four techniques:

>> Step one statement at a time.

>> Step into some code.

>> Step over some code.

>> Step out of some code.

Stepping one statement at a time

The most common way of stepping through your code is to step one statement at a time. In break mode, *stepping one statement at a time* means two things:

>> You execute the current statement and then pause on the next statement.

>> If the current statement to run is a function call, stepping takes you into the function and pauses at the function's first statement. You can then continue to step through the function until you execute the last statement, at which point the browser returns you to the statement after the function call.

To step through your code one statement at a time, set a breakpoint and then, after your code is in break mode, do one of the following to step through a single statement:

>> Click the step icon (the Chrome version is shown in the margin).

>> Press the browser's step keyboard shortcut. In Chrome and most browsers (except Firefox, which doesn't support step as of this writing; use the step into icon instead), press F9.

Keep stepping through until the script ends or until you're ready to resume normal execution (by clicking the resume icon, shown in the margin).

Stepping into some code

In all the major browsers (except Firefox), *stepping into some code* is the same as stepping through the code one statement at a time. The difference comes when a statement executes asynchronously (that is, it performs its operation after some delay rather than right away).

To understand the difference, consider the following code (I added line numbers to the left; they're not part of the code; check out chapter14/example02.html):

```
1    setTimeout(() => {
2        console.log('Inside the setTimeout() block!');
3    }, 5000);
4    console.log('Outside the setTimeout) block!');
```

This code uses `setTimeout()` to execute some code after five seconds (5000 milliseconds). Suppose you enter break mode at the `setTimeout()` statement (line 1). What happens if you use step versus step into here? Check it out:

>> **Step:** Clicking the step icon doesn't take you to line 2, as you might expect. Instead, because `setTimeout()` is asynchronous, step essentially ignores the anonymous function and takes you directly to line 4.

>> **Step into:** Clicking the step into icon *does* take you to line 2 but only after the specified delay (five seconds, in this case). You can then step through the anonymous function as needed.

To step into your code, set a breakpoint and then do one of the following after your code is in break mode:

>> Click the step into icon (Chrome's version of this icon is shown in the margin).

>> Press the browser's step into keyboard shortcut. In Chrome (and most browsers), press F11 or press Ctrl+; (Windows) or ⌘+; (macOS).

REMEMBER

My description of step into here doesn't apply (at least as I write this) to Firefox. Instead, the Firefox step into feature works like the step feature I describe in the preceding section.

Stepping over some code

Some statements call other functions. If you're not interested in stepping through a called function, you can step over it. *Stepping over a function* means that JavaScript executes the function normally and then resumes break mode at the next statement *after* the function call.

To step over a function, first either step through your code until you come to the function call you want to step over, or set a breakpoint on the function call and refresh the web page. When you're in break mode, you can step over the function using either of the following techniques:

>> Click the step over icon (Chrome's version of this icon is shown in ther margin).

>> Press the browser's step over keyboard shortcut. In Chrome (and most browsers), press F10 or press Ctrl+' (Windows) or ⌘+' (macOS).

Stepping out of some code

I'm always accidentally stepping into functions I'd rather step over. If the function is short, I just step through it until I'm back in the original code. If the function is long, however, I don't want to waste time stepping through every statement. Instead, I invoke the *step out feature* using either of these methods:

>> Click the step out icon (Chrome's version of this icon is shown in the margin).

>> Press the browser's step out keyboard shortcut. In Chrome (and most browsers), press Shift+F11 or press Ctrl+Shift+; (Windows) or ⌘+Shift+; (macOS).

JavaScript executes the rest of the function and then reenters break mode at the first line after the function call.

IN THIS CHAPTER

» **Creating a JavaScript-driven photo gallery**

» **Getting data from an API**

» **Understanding asynchronous operations**

» **Fetching data from an API**

» **Populating a page with API data**

Chapter **15**

Putting JavaScript to Work

The only way to learn a new programming language is by writing programs in it.

—DENNIS RITCHIE

his chapter puts your newfound JavaScript know-how to work by building a couple of projects. The first project is a simple photo gallery that shows thumbnails of each photo. The magic happens when you use JavaScript to display the full version of any photo just by double-clicking it.

The second project is more ambitious: fetching data remotely from an API (refer to Chapter 7 is you're not sure what an API is all about) and populating a web page with the returned data. To make this happen, you learn several powerful JavaScript techniques that enable you to get data from any online source, whether it's a public API or a server to which you have access.

Project 1: A Photo Gallery

It's not hard to set up a simple photo gallery page, especially if you lay out the page using Flexbox. But most photo galleries show just thumbnail versions of the images, and the user must perform some action to see the full version. You could go to the trouble of linking each thumbnail to a separate page that contains the full image, but that sounds like a lot of work to me. Instead, why not let JavaScript do the heavy lifting? Specifically, in this project you learn how to display the full version of any image by double-clicking (or double-tapping) it. Double-clicking (or -tapping) the full image again hides it, and the user sees the image gallery once again.

The dblclick event fires when the user double-clicks the primary button of a mouse or double-taps a pointing device such as a trackpad or a touchscreen. (To make the rest of this section less repetitive, from here on when I write *double-click*, I also mean *double-tap*. You're welcome.) So, given an object named image, your app would use the following code to listen for double-clicks. (For the full project code, check out chapter15/project01.html in this book's example files.)

```
image.addEventListener('dblclick', function(e) {
    // Code you want to run goes here
});
```

To style the two versions of each image — that is, the thumbnail version and the full-size version — this project uses two CSS classes:

```
.thumbnail {
    width: 100px;
    height: auto;
}
.full-size {
    position: absolute;
    top: 50px;
    left: 0;
    width: 100%;
}
```

With these two class rules defined, your dblclick event handler just needs to toggle the full-size class on (to show the full image) and off (to return to the regular thumbnail view):

```
// Toggle the full-size class on the image
image.classList.toggle('full-size');
```

JavaScript:

```
const myButton = document.getElementById('my-button');
myButton.addEventListener('click', function() {
    const myDiv = document.getElementById('my-div');
    myDiv.innerHTML = '<h1>Hello Click World!</h1>';
});
```

The HTML code sets up an empty div element and a button element. The JavaScript code attaches a click event listener to the button, and the callback function adds the HTML string <h1>Hello Click World!</h1> to div. Figure 13-3 shows the resulting page after the button has been clicked.

FIGURE 13-3:
The click event callback function adds some HTML and text to the div element.

Getting data about the event

When an event fires, the DOM creates an Event object, the properties of which contain info about the event, including the following:

>> target: The web page element to which the event occurred. For example, if you set up a click handler for a div element, that div is the target of the click.

>> which: A numeric code that specifies the key that was pressed during a keypress event.

>> metaKey: A Boolean value that equals true if the user had the Windows key (⊞) or the Mac Command key (⌘) held down when the event fired.

>> shiftKey: A Boolean value that equals true if the user had the Shift key held down when the event fired.

To access these properties, you insert a name for the Event object as an argument in your event handler's callback function:

```
element.addEventListener(event, function(e) {
    This code runs when the event fires
});
```

Here's a portion of the gallery HTML:

```html
<p>Double-click an image to expand/shrink it</p>
<section class="gallery">
    <div>
        <img src="image01.jpg" class="thumbnail" alt="Thumbnail 1">
    </div>
    <div>
        <img src="image02.jpg" class="thumbnail" alt="Thumbnail 2">
    </div>
    <div>
        <img src="image03.jpg" class="thumbnail" alt="Thumbnail 3">
    </div>
    ...
</section>
```

Now here's the full JavaScript:

```javascript
// Get all the img elements
const images = document.querySelectorAll('.thumbnail');

// Loop through the images
for (const image of images) {

    // Listen for the dblclick event on each image
    image.addEventListener('dblclick', function(e) {

        // Prevent the default action
        e.preventDefault();

        // Toggle the full-size class on the image
        image.classList.toggle('full-size');
    });
}
```

The JavaScript first returns the collection of img elements on the page (each of which is assigned the class thumbnail) and then loops through that collection to add a listener for the dblclick event to each image. The callback function prevents the default action and then toggles the full-size class. Toggling that class means that double-clicking an image expands it to the width of the browser window, and double-clicking the same image shrinks the image back to its thumbnail size.

Project 2: Get a Random Quotation from an API

JavaScript gets super-powerful — and super-useful — when you connect it to an online API to display data, weather, or, as in this project, an inspirational quotation. The source for this project's quotations is called Echoes (`https://echoes.soferity.com/`), which doesn't require you to create an API key or register to use the API.

I begin with the project's HTML code:

```
<h1>Inspiration Station</h1>
<div id="quote-box">
    <div id="quote-text"></div>
    <div id="quote-author"></div>
</div>
<button id="new-quote-button">Get a New Quote</button>
```

Yep, it's pretty simple: a title; a box to display the quotation, which is itself divided into two boxes, one for the quotation and one for the author; and a button to click to get a fresh quotation. A pile of CSS styling makes everything look nice (check out Figure 15-1), but to preserve space I leave it up to you to check it out. (All the code is in chapter15/project02.html.)

FIGURE 15-1:
The interface for this project.

Okay, now it's time to tackle the good stuff: the JavaScript code that makes this project go. The code begins by storing references to the three main page elements (the quote, the author, and the button):

```
const quoteText = document.getElementById('quote-text');
const quoteAuthor = document.getElementById('quote-author');
const button = document.getElementById('new-quote-button');
```

Now the code adds a `click` event listener to the `button` object:

```
button.addEventListener('click', getQuote);
```

The `getQuote()` function that runs when the user clicks the button is the heart of this project, so I'll run through it carefully. First, here's the complete function:

```
async function getQuote() {
    const apiUrl = 'https://echoes.soferity.com/api/quotes/random?lang=en';

    try {
        const response = await fetch(apiUrl);

        if (!response.ok) {
            throw new Error('Could not fetch quote');
        }

        const data = await response.json();

        quoteText.textContent = `"${data.quote}"`;
        quoteAuthor.textContent = `- ${data.author || 'Unknown'}`;

        updateColors();

    } catch (error) {
        quoteText.textContent = 'Oops! Something went wrong.';
        quoteAuthor.textContent = '';
        document.body.style.backgroundColor = '#ffcccc';
    }
}
```

Getting your head around asynchronous operations

When your code deals with only page-related operations, the web browser executes that code one statement after the other, in each case waiting for the current statement to complete before moving on to the next one. In programming parlance, this wait-for-a-task-to-complete-before-moving-to-the-next-task mode is described as *synchronous.*

However, synchronous operations become a problem when you start dealing with back-end tasks (tasks that run on a web server, as opposed to front-end tasks, which run in the web browser), such as asking a remote API to send some data. Why is that a problem? Because you don't know in advance how long a back-end task might take. Typically, front-end statements execute in milliseconds, but it might take a remote server multiple seconds to respond to a request for data. Performing such tasks synchronously means that your code must wait for the server operation to complete before continuing; the remainder of your code is said to be *blocked* by the server request. Blocked code will almost certainly lead to thumb-twiddling frustration on the part of your users.

Fortunately, you can keep your users happy and their thumbs constructively occupied by implementing some powerful techniques that prevent code blocking. The way modern JavaScript prevents such code blocking is by using asynchronous operations, where *asynchronous* describes an operation that runs separately in the background and therefore doesn't prevent the rest of the code from executing.

JavaScript has several techniques for making operations asynchronous. The method I use in this project is the *async function,* which is a function declaration preceded by the keyword `async`:

```
async function functionName() {
    // Asynchronous function code goes here
}
```

where *functionName* is the name of the asynchronous function. Here's how this project sets up its async function:

```
async function getQuote() {
    const apiUrl = 'https://echoes.soferity.com/api/quotes/random?lang=en';
    // The rest of the asynchronous function code goes here
}
```

The function leads off by storing the API's address in the `apiURL` variable for later use.

Using await to wait for an asynchronous operation to complete

Asynchronous operations are awesome, but they create a new problem that's sort of the opposite of the blocking problem described previously. When you eventually get the data from the server, you almost always have to process that data in some way: perform data conversions, write the data to existing HTML elements on the page, create elements for the data, and so on. In other words, in this case you *don't* want the browser to process these statements right away. What's needed here is a way to say something like, "Yo, wait until you get all the data from the server, and then perform the following tasks to process that data."

The way you convince the browser to hold off until an asynchronous operation is complete before processing the code that follows is by using the `await` operator:

```
const resultVar = await expression
```

where:

>> *resultVar* is the name of the variable that stores the result of the asynchronous operation.

>> *expression* is a reference to an object that runs an asynchronous operation.

You always use the `await` operator in an async function. Here's how it's done in this project:

```
const response = await fetch(apiUrl);
```

What's up with the `fetch()` method? The next section explains all.

Fetching data with the fetch() method

Asynchronous operations shine when you use them to fetch data from a server and display that data on a web page. In JavaScript, you fetch remote data by using the aptly named `fetch()` method. Here's the simplified version of the `fetch()` syntax:

```
const responseVar = await fetch(resource);
```

where:

» *responseVar* is the name of the variable that stores the response returned by the asynchronous fetch() operation.

» *resource* is the URL of the resource you want to fetch.

Here's how this is done in this project:

```
const response = await fetch(apiUrl);
```

The code uses fetch() to get data from the API, and then the await operator tells the code to wait until that response is received.

Handling JSON data returned by the server

Most APIs send back a response in JSON format (which I introduce in Chapter 8). To process JSON data returned by an API, you use the response object's json() method to parse the returned data. Here's the syntax:

```
const data = await response.json();
```

where:

» *data* is the variable that will store the parsed data.

» *response* is the variable that contains the response returned by the fetch() call to the API.

Here's how it's done in this project:

```
const data = await response.json();
```

Note that since the conversion of the response to JSON format is also an asynchronous operation, the code again uses await to stand by for the conversion operation to finish before moving on.

Now, with the JSON data in hand, your code can use that data. Most often, you use the JSON data to modify or populate HTML elements on the page. In this project, the code populates the quotation text and author fields:

```
quoteText.textContent = `"${data.quote}"`;
quoteAuthor.textContent = `— ${data.author || 'Unknown'}`;
```

In the final line, if data.author comes back as null or undefined or some other non-response, the code will display the text Unknown, instead.

Handling errors

When working with an API, your code needs to handle any errors that might crop up. The basic error-handling procedure is a try/catch structure, which in JavaScript is similar to the Python try and except blocks, which I talk about in Chapter 8:

```
try {
    const response = await fetch(apiUrl);
    if (!response.ok) {
        throw new Error('Could not fetch quote');
    }
    const data = await response.json();
    quoteText.textContent = `"${data.quote}"`;
    quoteAuthor.textContent = `- ${data.author || 'Unknown'}`;
    updateColors();

} catch (error) {
    quoteText.textContent = 'Oops! Something went wrong.';
    quoteAuthor.textContent = '';
    document.body.style.backgroundColor = '#ffcccc';
}
```

This code says, "Go ahead and try to run all the statements in the try block. If an error comes up, bail out and run the code in the catch block, instead."

Finally, note that the final statement in the try block is a call to the update Colors() function:

```
function updateColors() {
    const randomHue = Math.floor(Math.random() * 360);
    const newBGColor = `hsl(${randomHue} 50% 75%)`;
    const newTextColor = `hsl(${randomHue} 50% 25%)`;
    document.body.style.backgroundColor = newBGColor;

    document.getElementById('new-quote-button').style.backgroundColor =
    newTextColor;
    document.getElementById('quote-text').style.color = newTextColor;
    document.getElementById('quote-author').style.color = newTextColor;
}
```

This function gets a random number between 0 and 359 and uses that value as the hue value of the CSS hsl() function. This color is then applied to the page background and a darker version of the same color is applied to the button background and to the quotation and author text.

At the very bottom of the JavaScript code is the final statement:

```
getQuote();
```

This calls the getQuote() function so that a quotation appears when you first load the page.

4

The Part of Tens

Discover ten not-to-be-missed tidbits about coding with AI.

Get the lowdown on ten HTML tags, CSS properties, and CSS selectors you need to know.

Chapter **16**

Ten Things to Know about AI and Coding

What's in your hands, I think and hope, is intelligence: the ability to see the machine as more than when you were first led up to it, that you can make it more.

—ALAN PERLIS

There has been a proverbial elephant in the room through the first 15 chapters of this book: AI. These days, you can't have a chinwag with anyone even remotely connected to programming without the conversation eventually turning to the connection between AI and coding. Why? For the simple reason that modern AI models such as GitHub Copilot and ChatGPT are scarily good at generating any type of code with a simple text prompt.

So, is it any surprise when surveys show that more than three quarters of pro developers now use AI tools to help them get their work done? At the same time, though, research has shown that almost half of all AI-generated code contains bugs or vulnerabilities. Therefore, before you dive into AI coding, it's vital that you understand both the tremendous opportunities and the serious risks involved. That's what this chapter is all about.

Understanding How You Can Use AI

Today's code-focused AI tools are powerful assistants that can perform a wide variety of tasks. Many of these tasks are suitable only for professional developers, but folks relatively new to coding can leverage AI, too. There are five main ways to use AI to help you code:

>> **Autocompleting:** Automatically entering one or more lines of code based on the context. Integrating a tool such as GitHub Copilot into an editor such as Visual Studio Code for autocompletion can be a huge timesaver.

>> **Prompting:** Providing a text description of the code you want AI to generate. Refer to the "Crafting Effective Prompts" section for more.

>> **Automating:** Getting AI to handle the creation of boilerplate code and to perform routine tasks.

>> **Explaining:** Asking AI to teach you how a piece of code works, clarify the concepts used by some code, or suggest use cases.

>> **Debugging:** Leveraging AI to figure out why a piece of code generates an error or doesn't work the way it's supposed to.

Learning What AI Can and Can't Do

AI coding assistants have been trained on billions of lines of public code, which is the main reason why they're so good at generating code. That vast training data means that AI tools are exceptionally good at the following:

>> Generating boilerplate code and repetitive patterns with high accuracy

>> Explaining existing code and breaking down complex logic into understandable chunks

>> Converting code between different programming languages

>> Debugging syntax errors and providing quick fixes

>> Suggesting improvements based on coding best practices

Pretty good! But today's AI code assistants also have some critical limitations, meaning there are a few things they're just not good at:

- » Comprehending complex business logic

- » Making architectural decisions that require deep know-how of the current system

- » Debugging issues across multiple, interconnected systems

- » Optimizing for performance, especially with highly specialized code or with code that uses cutting-edge technologies

- » Guaranteeing that generated code is secure

Therefore, it's probably best to think of AI assistants as the equivalent of intelligent junior developers: They write solid code but need guidance on design decisions and business context.

Crafting Effective Prompts

It's not even remotely a stretch to say the quality of your AI code output depends entirely on the quality of your input prompts. Effective prompting is a skill that dramatically improves AI tool usefulness.

The context-first approach works best:

- » **Example of a poor prompt:** "Write a function to sort data."

- » **Example of a good prompt:** "I'm working on an e-commerce web app using JavaScript. I need a function to sort product objects by price, name, or rating. The product interface has the following fields: id, name, price, rating, and category. Please follow camelCase convention, use only vanilla JavaScript (no frameworks), and comment the code liberally."

Here are some proven prompting techniques for code:

- » **Specify requirements clearly.** Always include error handling, documentation needs, and edge case considerations in your request.

- » **Use iterative refinement.** Start with just the basic functionality and then build complexity through follow-up prompts rather than trying to get everything perfect in one request.

- » **Apply constraint-driven prompts.** Specify limitations such as "use only vanilla JavaScript" or "keep under 50 lines" to get more focused code.

>> **Try the documentation-first pattern.** Write detailed comments describing what you want, and then ask AI to generate code based on those specifications. This enables you to specify lots of detail about what you want AI to implement.

Learning to Code Using AI

First, the good news: AI can actually *accelerate* learning to code when you use it thoughtfully (as I describe next). Research shows that AI-assisted programming increases student motivation and reduces programming anxiety. Now, the bad news: If you use AI as a crutch to always handle the parts of the code you don't know or don't understand, you end up with gaping holes in your knowledge. And over the long term, if you become dependent on AI, your ability to solve problems independently atrophies to the point of non-existence. Not good!

You can and should use AI to help you learn to code, but that learning will serve you best if you approach it in phases:

>> **Fundamentals phase (no AI assistance):** Master the basic syntax of your programming language of choice, hone your logic skills, and solve problems, all without AI assistance. This builds the foundation that you're going to need to effectively direct AI tools down the road.

>> **Skill building phase (moderate AI assistance):** Use AI for specific tasks such as generating boilerplate code, brainstorming ideas, generating test cases, or explaining complex concepts. However, *you* still maintain all responsibility for your app's core logic and algorithms.

>> **Advanced integration phase (full-bore AI assistance):** Leverage the full capabilities and tools of your AI assistant to help you with complex projects. However, you still need to keep your eye on the big picture by controlling the overall architecture of the project and by critically evaluating all code generated by AI.

Avoiding AI Dependency

I mention in the preceding section that long-term use of AI as a crutch to handle difficult coding tasks can create an unhealthy dependency that erodes rather than enhances your skill as a coder. To avoid that fate, here are some practical strategies aimed at promoting a balanced use of AI:

» Treat AI as a smart but occasionally careless assistant that requires your supervision and direction.

» Schedule regular AI detox periods where you do without any AI assistance. This approach will help revitalize your coding skills and knowledge.

» For all but the most basic boilerplate, avoid the temptation to copy-and-paste AI-generated code. Type the code yourself to transform passive answers into active learning.

» If you're not sure what AI-generated code is doing, always ask AI to explain it line-by-line.

» Practice debugging coding problems independently to keep your trouble-shooting skills sharp. If you're still stumped after giving a problem an honest shot, you can ask AI to tackle it.

Reviewing the Major AI Coding Tools

The AI coding landscape is always changing and pretty much the only thing you can count on is that the tools will become more powerful, more useful, and more reliable with each release. From the perspective of a beginning coder, you probably can't go wrong with whatever tool you use because, at this point in the evolution of AI coding, all the major models are mature and powerful. That said, understanding the current options and how they can assist beginning coders might help you choose an AI assistant:

» **GitHub Copilot:** Probably the most popular AI coding tool with over 15 million active users, more than 1.3 million of which are paying customers. GitHub Copilot is a great choice for beginners because it offers a powerful free tier, it integrates seamlessly into VS Code and other editors, and it offers an autocomplete feature that suggests code as you type. There's also a chat feature for explaining code and debugging problems.

» **ChatGPT (OpenAI):** Probably the most versatile general-purpose coding assistant because you can build everything from simple functions to full-fledged apps with simple text prompts. ChatGPT is a popular choice for coding beginners because even the free tier gives you access to powerful OpenAI models and it offers excellent code explanations for learning. Subscribing to Plus gives you access to the Codex AI model, which enables you to run code right from a chat.

» **Claude (Anthropic):** Probably offers the highest code quality of the major AI coding assistants. Claude can turn plain-language project ideas into working code. Claude is a great beginner's choice because even the free version can build app prototypes quickly from simple, natural -language prompts.

» **Gemini (Google):** Probably the easiest tool to use if you're already using other Google tools and you want to stay within the Google ecosystem. Gemini is a conversational AI with code writing, debugging, and web-search capabilities. A free subscription is available.

If you're still not sure, give GitHub Copilot a whirl. It's free (with limitations). it integrates directly into VS Code, and it gives you a choice of which AI model to use, including OpenAI's GPT (the model behind ChatGPT), Anthropic's Claude, and Google's Gemini.

Vibe Coding Is Fun

Vibe coding refers to describing the app or web page you want to build in natural language, letting AI generate the code, and then repeating these two steps to gradually refine the result, all without examining the code itself. Essentially, you're just talking to AI and describing what you want; you're not coding at all.

Vibe coding is great fun when you just need a simple app or a prototype for a larger app, but it's not a great technique to rely on over time or for larger projects. First, you don't learn anything about building apps or scripts or pages if you let your AI lackey do all the work. Second, it's distressingly common for AI-generated code to include security vulnerabilities and subtle errors that could cause huge problems down the road.

Best Practices for Integrating AI

Successfully integrating AI into your coding workflow is mostly a matter of treating AI as a powerful collaborator rather than a replacement for human judgment. Some tips to make this work for you:

» **Start small.** Begin with basic autocompletion and syntax help, and then gradually expand to more complex tasks as you build confidence and understanding.

» **Establish context.** Always provide comprehensive background information, including project structure, business requirements, coding standards, and technical constraints.

- » **Be the boss.** Position yourself as the senior developer directing an AI assistant, never the other way around.

- » **Keep your focus on long-term skill development.** Focus on building durable skills that complement AI tools, including system design, debugging methods, and big-picture thinking.

Avoiding Common Mistakes

New programmers often fall into predictable traps when using AI tools:

- » **The 70 percent trap:** AI tools can help beginners get apps up to 70 percent functionality without breaking a sweat, but that last 30 percent (which includes crucial components such as error handling and edge cases) is the difference between a polished product and a mere working prototype. Avoid bypassing that final 30 percent just because it's difficult and unglamorous.

- » **The let-AI-do-it trap:** Becoming over-reliant on AI-generated code causes your programming skills to atrophy. Maintain some balance by regularly coding without AI and focusing on understanding the code rather than just pasting it.

- » **The over-sharing trap:** AI tools can leak confidential information. Never share proprietary, sensitive, or confidential code with AI tools that train on user data.

- » **The knowledge gap trap:** Skipping core computer science concepts in favor of AI-generated code creates knowledge gaps that compound over time. Build strong programming foundations first before relying heavily on AI assistance.

Understanding Code Before Using It

The biggest mistake beginners make is copying-and-pasting AI code without comprehension. This creates technical debt (not understanding the code now can cause problems later), security vulnerabilities, and missed learning opportunities that compound over time. Before you copy any AI-generated code, run through the following checklist:

- » **Understand how the code flows.** Figure out exactly how the code executes step by step.

>> **Validate input and output.** Know what data goes in and what comes out.

>> **Check error handling.** Identify how the code behaves when things go wrong.

>> **Vet third-party tools.** Verify all external libraries suggested by AI to ensure that they're legit and that you have the right to use them.

>> **Check for edge cases.** Recognize scenarios where the code might fail.

» The top ten HTML tags of all time

» Ten CSS properties for all your styling needs

» Bonus: Ten ridiculously useful CSS selectors

Chapter **17**

Ten Vital HTML Tags and CSS Properties

HTML elements enable Web-page designers to mark up a document's structure, but beyond trust and hope, you don't have any control over your text's appearance. CSS changes that. CSS puts the designer in the driver's seat.
—HÅKON WIUM LIE

TML and CSS aren't programming languages, but you can't get very far with browser-based JavaScript if you don't know how to build a web page around your code. Building a web page requires HTML for the overall structure of the page and CSS to make that structure look good (or a reasonable facsimile of good, depending on your design skills).

So, even though this is a book about coding, I'd feel remiss if I didn't offer you at least a taste of what HTML and CSS have to offer. (After this appetizer, if you want the full HTML and CSS meal, please check out my book *HTML, CSS, & JavaScript All-in-One For Dummies*.) In this chapter, you learn the ten most useful HTML tags and CSS properties. As a bonus, I also take you through ten particularly useful CSS selectors. Bon appétit!

Ten HTML Tags You Need to Know

A web page is really just an undifferentiated sea of text unless you structure that text in some way. This structure comes via the HTML tags that you insert strategically into your file.

The basic HTML template

All your web projects need a strong beginning, and the following template does just that (refer to chapter17/example01.html in this book's example files):

```
<!DOCTYPE html>
<html lang="en">
    <head>
        <meta charset="UTF-8">
        <meta name="viewport" content="width=device-width, initial-scale=1.0">
        <title></title>
        <style>
            /* Your styles go here */
        </style>
    </head>
    <body>
        <!-- Your page text and tags go here -->
        <script>
            // Your JavaScript code goes here
        </script>
    </body>
</html>
```

Here are a few things to bear in mind when using this template:

>> Put your page title (that is, what you want to appear in the browser tab when someone surfs to your page) between the `<title>` and `</title>` tags.

>> If you want to specify CSS style rules for just this page, plop them between the `<style>` and `</style>` tags. If, instead, you want your styles to apply to multiple pages, add the rules to a separate file — called, say, `styles.css` — and then in each page replace the `<style>` and `</style>` tags with a reference to that file (including the path to the file subdirectory, if needed):

```
<link href="styles.css" rel="stylesheet">
```

» All your text and HTML tags go between the `<body>` and `</body>` tags but above the `<script>` tag.

» If you want to use some JavaScript for just this page, insert the code between the `<script>` and `</script>` tags. If, instead, you want to use your code on multiple pages, add the code to a separate file — called, say, `code.js` — and then in each page replace the `<script>` and `</script>` tags with a reference to that file (including the path to the file subdirectory, if needed):

```
<script src="code.js"></script>
```

The top ten tags

Okay, with your HTML template saved as a `.html` file, you're ready to populate the `body` element with your text and tags. HTML has something like a hundred tags, but the following ten categories contain the workhorse tags you'll use most often:

» **Structure:** HTML defines seven tags that you use to form the overall structure of your page:

- `<header>`: Holds the introductory content of the page, such as the main title (almost always an h1 element), a subtitle, and a logo.

- `<nav>`: Holds the navigational content of the page, particularly links to other site pages.

- `<main>`: Holds the main content of the page which, in practice, means one or more `<article>`, `<section>`, and `<aside>` tags.

- `<article>`: Holds a self-contained composition, such as a post, a blog entry, or an article.

- `<section>`: Holds a standalone portion of the page content. For example, if a page article has one or more logical sections, each with its own heading, each of those sections should be surrounded by `<section>` and `</section>` tags.

- `<aside>`: Holds content that is indirectly related to the current `<article>` or `<section>` content.

- `<footer>`: Holds the closing content of the page, such as a copyright notice, author information, or links to other site pages.

» **Headings:** HTML defines six heading tags, from `<h1>` to `<h6>`, with `<h1>` representing the highest level and `<h6>` representing the lowest. Pages should have just one `<h1>` tag.

» **Paragraphs:** The `<p>` tag holds the content of a single paragraph.

- **Divisions:** The `<div>` tag represents a separate container for page content. Use this tag when structural tags such as `<article>`, `<section>`, and `<aside>` aren't appropriate for the content.

- **Line breaks:** The `<br>` tag creates a line break, where the text immediately following the `<br>` tag appears at the beginning of the next line.

- **Spans:** The `<span>` tag surrounds a run of text, which can be as short as a single character or as long as a multiword phrase. You almost always span text in this way to apply some CSS styling to it.

- **Links:** The `<a>` tag turns the specified page text into a clickable link to another page or site. Here's the basic syntax, where *url* is the address of the page or site and *text* is the page text that you want the user to click:

  ```
  <a href="url">text</a>
  ```

- **Images:** The `<img>` tag inserts an image into the page. Here's the basic syntax, where *image* is the path to the image file and *text* is alternative text that describes the image:

  ```
  <img src="image" alt="text">
  ```

- **Lists:** The `<ul>` (unordered list), `<ol>` (ordered list), and `<li>` (list) tags create lists. Use `<ul>` to create a bulleted list, where each bullet item is surrounded by `<li>` and `</li>` tags. Use `<ol>` to create a numbered list, where each numbered item is surrounded by `<li>` and `</li>` tags.

- **Buttons:** The `<button>` tag creates a clickable button. You need to add a JavaScript event listener that listens for clicks on the button and then performs some action. Check out project 2 in Chapter 15 for an example.

REMEMBER

With the exception of the `<br>` and `<img>` tags, all the tags just mentioned have a corresponding closing tag (the same tag, but with a / shoehorned inside it). For example, you mark the start of a paragraph with the `<p>` tag, and then you mark the end of the paragraph with the closing `</p>` tag.

Ten CSS Properties to Memorize

While HTML tags define the structure of the web page, the look of the page is the domain of CSS. Unfortunately, CSS is *huge*, with several hundred properties to play with. Happily, though, when you're just getting started with web design, you'll spend almost all your time working with just ten properties. For a specified element or selector (refer to the next section, "Ten CSS Selectors to Swoon Over"), here's what these ten properties do:

≫ background-color: Sets the background color. To set a color in CSS, you have four main ways to go:

- *Color keyword:* Such as red, green, or magenta. Check out www.w3.org/TR/css-color-4/#named-colors for the full list.

- *RGB code:* A code of the form #rrggbb, where rr specifies the red portion with a hexadecimal value between 00 and ff; gg specifies the green portion with a hexadecimal value between 00 and ff; and bb specifies the blue portion with a hexadecimal value between 00 and ff.

- rgb(*red green blue*) *function:* Replace each of the *red*, *green*, and *blue* values with a number between 0 and 255.

- hsl(*hue saturation lightness*) *function:* Replace *hue* with a number between 0 and 359; replace *saturation* with a percentage value between 0% and 100%; and replace *lightness* with a percentage value between 0% and 100%.

≫ border: Sets the width, style, and color of the surrounding border using the following syntax (where you replace *width* with a CSS length value; *style* with a border style keyword, such as solid, double, or dashed; and *color* with any valid CSS color value):

```
border: width style color;
```

≫ color: Sets the text color. Use any of the color techniques specified previously in the background-color item.

≫ display: Sets the layout to use for the element's content, such as grid (for CSS Grid) or flex (for CSS Flexbox). You can also use none to hide the element.

≫ font: Sets various font properties:

- font-family: Sets the typeface, such as font-family: "Comic Sans", sans-serif;.

- font-size: Sets the type size, such as font-size: 1.5rem;.

- font-style: Sets the type style, such as font-style: italic;.

- font-weight: Sets the font weight, such as font-weight: bold;.

≫ height: Sets the height. Use a value with any valid CSS length unit, such as px, em, rem, vh, or %.

≫ margin: Sets the size of the margin that lies outside the border. Use a value with any valid CSS length unit, such as px, em, rem, or %.

>> `padding`: Sets the size of the space between the content and the border (which is called the *padding*). Use a value with any valid CSS length unit, such as `px`, `em`, `rem`, or `%`.

>> `text`: Sets various text-related properties:

- `text-align`: Sets the text alignment using a keyword, such as `left`, `center`, `right`, or `justify`.

- `text-decoration`: Sets the appearance of decorative lines on text. This property is most often used to remove underlines from links:

```
a {
        text-decoration: none;
}
```

- `text-indent`: Sets the size of the indent of the first line of the text. Use a value with any valid CSS length unit, such as `px`, `em`, `rem`, or `%`.

>> `width`: Sets the width. Use a value with any valid CSS length unit, such as `px`, `em`, `rem`, `vw`, or `%`.

Ten CSS Selectors to Swoon Over

When you add a CSS rule to an internal or external style sheet, you assemble your declarations into a declaration block (that is, you surround them with the { and } thingies, known in the trade as *braces*) and then assign that block to the page item (or items) you want to style. For example, consider the following rule:

```
h2 {
    font-size: 1.5rem;
    font-family: Verdana;
    text-align: center;
}
```

The h2 that appears before the opening brace ({) tells the browser that the property declarations that follow are to be applied to the page's <h2> tags. The text that specifies which elements are to be styled (such as h2 in the preceding example) is called the *selector*.

The selector you assign to the declaration block doesn't have to be an HTML tag name. In fact, CSS has a huge number of ways to specify a selector to define what parts of the page you want to style. Lucky for you, the ten that I take you through in the following list should cover most of your web development needs:

» **Type selector:** An HTML element name, such as p, header, or h2. The browser applies the style declarations to every instance of that element on the page.

» **Class selector (.):** The name of a class, preceded by a period. The browser applies the style declarations to every element on the page that includes the class name as an attribute. For example, if you have one or more elements with the class caption — such as <div class="caption"> — then you can style every such element as follows:

```
.caption {
    font-size: .75rem;
    font-style: italic;
}
```

» **ID selector (#):** The id of an element, preceded by the hashtag symbol (#). The browser applies the style declarations to the element that has the specified id attribute value. For example, if your page has the tag <h2 id="subtitle">, you can style that element as follows:

```
#subtitle {
    color: gray;
    font-size: 1.75rem;
    font-style: italic;
}
```

» **Universal selector (*):** The browser applies the style declarations to every element on the page. You normally use the universal selector to apply what's known in CSS as a *reset*, where you remove some of the browser's defaults. Here's a simple reset:

```
* {
    margin: 0;
    padding: 0;
    box-sizing: border-box;
}
```

» **Attribute selector:** An element name, followed by an attribute name in square brackets ([and]). The browser applies the style declarations to every page element that includes the attribute. For more specific styling, you can set the attribute equal to a particular value. For example, to match every ‹input› tag where the type attribute equals text, you'd do the following:

```
input[type="text"] {
    border: 2px dashed blue;
    font-size: 1.25rem;
    margin: 0.5rem;
}
```

» **Child combinator (›):** Two selectors, separated by a greater-than sign (selectorA › selectorB). The browser applies the style declarations to every instance on the page where selectorB is a child element of selectorA (that is, selectorB is contained in selectorA). For example, if you have an ol element (a numbered list), it will contain two or more li elements. Those li elements are the children of the ol, so you can style the li elements as follows:

```
ol › li {
    color: darkgray;
    font-family: 'Times New Roman', serif;
    font-style: italic;
}
```

» **Descendant combinator (space):** Two selectors, separated by a space (selector1 selector2). The browser applies the style declarations to every instance on the page where selector2 is a descendant element of selector1 (that is, selector2 is the child, or the child of a child, and so on, of selector1). For example, suppose you have an article element that contains multiple section and aside elements, each of which contains one or more p elements. Those p elements are the descendants of the article element, so you can style the p elements as follows:

```
article p {
    font-size: 1.1rem;
    padding: 1rem;
    text-indent: 0.5rem;
}
```

» **:hover pseudo-class:** The text `:hover` preceded by a selector. The browser applies the style declarations to an instance of the selector when the user hovers the mouse pointer over a page element represented by the selector. For example, the following rule temporarily changes the background color of a button element when the user hovers the mouse pointer over that button:

```
button:hover {
    background-color: red;
}
```

» **:first-child pseudo-class:** The text `:first-child` preceded by a selector. The browser applies the style declarations to every child element that is the first of a parent element's children. For example, the following rule targets every p element that's the first child of a parent:

```
p:first-child {
    text-indent: 0;
}
```

In case you're wondering, yep, there's a `:last-child` pseudo-class that targets every child element that is the last of a parent element's children.

» **:nth-child(*n*) pseudo-class:** The text `:nth-child(*n*)` preceded by a selector. The browser applies the style declarations to one or more elements based on their position in a parent element's collection of siblings. The parameter *n* is a number, an expression, or a keyword that specifies the position or positions of the child elements you want to match. You can specify *n* in five main ways:

- *A* (an integer): Selects the child element in the *A*th position. For example, `p:nth-child(2)` selects any p element that's the second child of a parent.

- *An* (an integer multiple): Selects every *A*th child element. For example, `p:nth-child(3n)` selects any p element that's in the third, sixth, ninth, and so on, position of a parent's child elements.

- *An+B* (an integer multiple plus an integer offset): Selects every child element that is in the *A*th position, plus *B*. For example, `p:nth-child(3n+2)` selects any p element that's in the second (n=0), fifth (n=1), eighth (n=2), and so on, position of a parent's child elements.

- even (keyword): Selects all the sibling elements that are in even-numbered positions (2, 4, 6, and so on). For example, `p:nth-child(even)` selects any p element that is in an even-numbered position within a parent's child elements. This is equivalent to `p:nth-child(2n)`.

- odd (keyword): Selects all the sibling elements that are in odd-numbered positions (1, 3, 5, and so on). For example, `p:nth-child(odd)` selects any p element that is in an odd-numbered position within a parent's child elements. This is equivalent to `p:nth-child(2n+1)`.

For example, here's a selector that targets just the even elements that use the product class:

```
.product:nth-child(even) {
    background-color: lightgray;
}
```

Index

artificial intelligence (AI) *(continued)*
  coding tools, 299–300
  dependency, avoiding, 298–299
  prompting, 297–298
  strengths and limitations of coding
    assistants, 296–297
  understanding code generated
    by, 301–302
  vibe coding, 300
ASCII *see* American Standard Code for
    Information Interchange
assembler, 52
assembly language, 50–53
assignment operators, 29, 90
`async` function, JavaScript, 288
asynchronous operations, 288–289
attribute selector, 310
automation, 20, 54, 65, 296
`await` operator, JavaScript, 289, 290

B
back end, 21, 55, 56, 61, 65, 288
backtick, 233–234
`before()` method, JavaScript, 262
big data, 3
bit, 12
block scope, JavaScript, 228
block syntax, 34, 35
blockchain, 66
`bool()` function, Python, 93
Boolean
  literals, 29
  Python, 90, 91, 92, 115, 121
Booth, Kathleen, 51
bootloader, 8

break mode, 45, 46, 275, 276
  breakpoint, 276–277
  exiting, 278
  using debugger statement for
    entering, 277
  viewing a variable value in, 278
  see also stepping (debugging)
`break` statement
  JavaScript, 223–224
  Python, 122, 151, 185
breakpoint, 45
  removing, 277
  setting, 276, 277, 280
buffer overflow, 58
byte, 12

C
C, 11, 12, 58–59
C++, 59–60
C#, 60–61
callback function, 245, 246, 268,
    269, 270, 285
camelCase, 25
Cascading Style Sheets (CSS), 55,
    209, 211, 303
  modification of, 264–267
  properties, 306–308
  selectors, 255, 308–312
  see also Hypertext Markup
    Language (HTML)
central processing unit (CPU), 51, 52
`charAt()` method, JavaScript, 236
`charCodeAt()` method, JavaScript, 236
ChatGPT (OpenAI), 299
child combinator (>), 310

conditionals, 33–34

  if. . .else statements, 35–36

  Python, 116–119

  true/false decisions, 34–35

Console window in web browsers, 215,
    216–217, 273

  debugging with, 273–275

  displaying, 274

  executing code in, 274–275

  logging data into, 217, 218, 274

console.log() method, JavaScript, 217,
    227, 228, 229, 230, 246, 247, 274

const keyword, JavaScript, 220, 228

content management systems (CMS), 65

continue statement

  JavaScript, 224

  Python, 122–123, 197

count() method, Python, 100

CPU *see* central processing unit

createElement() method, JavaScript, 261

creativity, and coding, 16–17

cross-platform apps, 63

CSS *see* Cascading Style Sheets

csv.DictReader() method, 181–182

cybersecurity, 66

D

data science, 20, 54, 64

data types, 27

  Boolean literals, 29

  conversion, in Python, 92–93

  mixing, in Python, 91–92

  numerical literals, 27–28, 90

  Python, 91–93, 176

  string literals, 28, 90, 91, 232–234

date and time, JavaScript, 236–237

  arguments, 237

  current, 238

  extracting information about, 238, 239

  setting, 239–240

  specific, 238

date class, Python, 139–140

Date() function, JavaScript, 238

datetime module, Python, 135, 139–140

debugger statement, JavaScript, 277

debugging

  Python code, 174–176

  strategies, 46–47

  techniques, 45–46

  tools, in web browsers, 214, 215, 272, 273

  use of AI for, 296

  and variable scope, 132

debugging, JavaScript, 271

  with Console window, 273–275

  pausing the code, 275–279

  stepping, 279–281

  tools, 272–273

decrement operator, 31

descendant combinator (space), 310

DevOps, 61

dictionary, Python, 113–114, 168, 181–182

distributed systems, 61

Django, 20, 55

do. . .while loop, JavaScript, 222–223

Document Object Model (DOM), 252–253

  getting data about event, 269–270

  listening for event, 269, 270

  manipulation of elements, 260–263

  modification of CSS, 264–267

filter, in Python list comprehensions, 156–157

`find()` method, Python, 100

Firefox, 215, 272, 274

firmware, 8

`:first-child` pseudo-class, 311

Flask, 20, 55

`float()` function, Python, 93

`float` keyword, JavaScript, 25

floating-point numbers, 25, 27–28, 240, 241–242

`for. . .of` loop, JavaScript, 247, 256

for loop
  JavaScript, 221–222
  Python, 112, 119–121, 128, 147, 198

`forEach()` method, JavaScript, 245–247

f-string (formatted string), 99, 128

full-stack developers, 64

function scope, JavaScript, 229

functions, 38–40
  Python, 128–134
  and stepping, 45–46, 280–281

functions, JavaScript, 224–225
  calling, after page is loaded, 226–227
  calling, when `<script>` tag is parsed, 225–226

G

game development, 21, 54, 57, 58, 59, 63, 66
  see also anagram guessing game (Python project)

Gemini (Google), 300

`get()` method, Python, 167

`getDate()` method, JavaScript, 239

`getDay()` method, JavaScript, 239

`getElementById()` method, JavaScript, 254

`getElementsByClassName()` method, JavaScript, 254, 255

`getElementsByTagName()` method, JavaScript, 254, 255–257

`getFullYear()` method, JavaScript, 239

`getHours()` method, JavaScript, 239

`getMilliseconds()` method, JavaScript, 239

`getMinutes()` method, JavaScript, 239

`getMonth()` method, JavaScript, 239

`getSeconds()` method, JavaScript, 239

`getTime()` method, JavaScript, 239

GitHub Copilot, 299, 300

global scope
  JavaScript, 230
  Python, 132

Go, 25, 61–62

Golang *see* Go

Google Chrome, 214, 272, 274
  break mode, 276
  Console window in, 217, 218
  HTML viewer in, 216, 273

graphics, 59

H

hardware control, 55

high-level languages, 11, 51, 60

high-performance applications, 58, 59, 61

histograms, 202

`:hover` pseudo-class, 311

JavaScript *(continued)*
  loops, 221–224
  math object, 240–244
  nesting quotation marks in, 28
  objects, 42, 231–249
  photo gallery project, 284–285
  real-world uses of, 20–21
  strings, 231–235
  TypeScript, 67–68
  variable scope, 228–230
  variables in, 25, 220–221
  see also Document Object Model (DOM)
JavaScript Object Notation (JSON),
    168, 290–291
`join( )` method
  JavaScript, 249
  Python, 102, 183
JSON *see* JavaScript Object Notation
`json( )` method
  JavaScript, 290
  Python, 168
JVM *see* Java Virtual Machine

K
key (Python dictionary), 113–114
key-value pairs (Python
    dictionary), 113–114
keywords, definition of, 10
Kotlin, 63–64

L
`lambda` keyword, Python, 198
`lastElementChild` property,
    JavaScript, 259
`lastIndexOf( )` method, JavaScript, 235

`len( )` function, Python, 98, 106, 112, 156
length
  of arrays, JavaScript, 248, 256
  sentence, analyzing, 200–202
  of strings, JavaScript, 234
`let` keyword, JavaScript, 220, 228
lexicon-based sentiment analysis, 203
libraries, Python, 54, 141–142, 193–194
  importing and using, 143–144
  installation of, 142–143
  for interacting with APIs, 166–167
list comprehensions, Python,
    183–184, 186, 200
  adding filter, 156–157
  setting up, 155–156
lists, 26
lists, Python, 105–106
  adding items, 108–109
  changing an item in, 108
  constructing, 106
  getting an item from, 107–108
  looping through, 120
  from range of numbers, 106–107
  removing items, 109–110
  searching in, 110
literals
  array, 244
  Boolean, 29
  definition of, 27
  numerical, 27–28, 90
  string, 28, 90, 91, 232–234
local scope
  JavaScript, 229
  Python, 133–134

Python *(continued)*

strings, 97–104

survey bot (example), 123–215

text analyzer project, 193–206

tuples, 111–112

variable scope, 131–134

variables in, 24, 90, 99

version number of, 75, 82

see also libraries, Python

Python, APIs in, 165–166

connection, 166–167

handling errors, 173–174

repositories, 169–170

working with API data, 167–169

Python, installation of, 75

checking installation status, 76–77

on macOS, 79–80

on Windows, 77–79

Python, OOP in, 158–159

building class, 161–162

class, 159–161

creating objects, 163–164

using objects in code, 164–165

Python launcher (Windows), 82

Python Package Index (PyPI), 142

Python Software Foundation (PSF), 135

Q

`querySelector()` method, JavaScript, 255

`querySelectorAll()` method, JavaScript, 255

quotation marks, in string literals, 28, 90, 232, 233

R

`raise_for_status()` method, Python, 174

`random` module, Python, 135, 151, 186

random quotation from API (JavaScript project), 286–287

asynchronous operations, 288–289

await operator, 289

`fetch()` method, 289–290

handling errors, 291–292

handling JSON data returned by the server, 290–291

interface, 286

`range()` function, Python, 106–107, 121

RapidAPI, 170

`read()` method, Python, 146

`readlines()` method, Python, 147

`remove()` method

JavaScript DOMTokenList, 264, 266

Python, 109–110

REPL (read, evaluate, print, loop), 72, 81, 85, 92, 93

`replace()` method, Python, 100

requests library, Python, 142–144, 166–167

reserved words, 10

`reverse()` method, JavaScript, 249

`reversed()` function, Python, 107

runtime errors, 45, 46

Rust, 65–66

S

Safari, 215, 272, 274

sandbox, 52

strip() method, Python, 147, 185

style property of HTML elements, 264

substr() method, JavaScript, 236

substring() method, JavaScript, 236

substrings, JavaScript, 235, 236

Swift, 66–67

synchronous operations, 288

syntax

  block, 34, 35

  definition of, 10, 34

  single-line, 34

syntax errors, 44

sys.exit() function, Python, 181, 195

systems programming, 66

T

template literals, 233–234

TensorFlow, 20

Terminal

  launching on macOS, 74

  launching on Windows, 73

  shortcuts, 74–75

text analyzer (Python project), 193

  analyzing sentence length, 200–202

  analyzing text sentiment, 202–204

  cleaning the text, 195–196

  finding longest words, 199

  finding most common words, 196–199

  full code of, 204–206

  library installation for, 193–194

  opening and reading text file, 195

textContent property, JavaScript, 262–263

thinking skills, and coding, 16

time see date and time, JavaScript

TIOBE Index, 50

title() method, Python, 100

toggle() method, JavaScript, 267

traceback messages, Python, 170–171

transistors, 11–12

true/false decisions, 34–35

try block, Python, 171–174, 195

try/catch structure, JavaScript, 291

tuples, Python, 111–112

type() function, Python, 176

type selector, 309

Typescript, 67–68

U

universal selector (*), 309

unpacking, tuple, 112

unshift() method, JavaScript, 249

upper() method, Python, 100

V

VADER (Valence Aware Dictionary and sEntiment Reasoner), 203

var keyword

  Go, 25

  JavaScript, 220

variable interpolation, 233

variable scope, 227

  JavaScript, 228–230

  Python, 131–134

About the Author

Paul McFedries is the president of Logophilia Limited, a technical writing company, and has worked with computers large and small since 1975. While now primarily a writer, Paul has worked as a programmer, consultant, database developer, and website developer. He has written more than 100 books that have sold over four million copies worldwide. Paul invites everyone to drop by his personal website at `https://paulmcfedries.com`, or to follow him on X (@paulmcf) or Facebook (`www.facebook.com/PaulMcFedries/`).

Dedication

To Karen and Chase, of course.

Author's Acknowledgments

If we're ever at the same cocktail party and you overhear me saying something like "I wrote a book," I hereby give you permission to wag your finger at me and say "Tsk, tsk." Why the scolding? Because although I did write this book's text and take its screenshots, those represent only a part of what constitutes a "book." The rest of it is brought to you by the dedication and professionalism of Wiley's editing, graphics, and production teams, who toiled long and hard to turn my text and images into an actual book.

I offer my heartfelt thanks to everyone at Wiley who made this book possible, but I'd like to extend some special thank-you's to the folks I worked with directly: executive editor Steve Hayes, project editor and copy editor Susan Pink, and technical editor Guy-Hart Davis.

Publisher's Acknowledgments

Executive Editor: Steve Hayes

Managing Editor: Sofia Malik

Project and Copy Editor: Susan Pink

Production Editor: Magesh Elangovan

Technical Editor: Guy Hart-Davis

Proofreader: Debbye Butler

Cover Images: © Luis Alvarez/Getty Images,
Screen capture courtesy of Paul McFedries